D0393731

Gettysburg

Gettysburg

A MEDITATION ON

WAR AND VALUES

Kent Gramm

INDIANA UNIVERSITY PRESS   BLOOMINGTON · INDIANAPOLIS

The paper used in this publication meets the minimum requirements of
American National Standard for Information Sciences—Permanence of
Paper for Printed Library Materials, ANSI Z39.48-1984.

Manufactured in the United States of America

Library of Congress Cataloging-in-Publication Data
Gramm, Kent.
    Gettysburg : a meditation on war and values / Kent Gramm.
      p.   cm.
    Includes bibliographical references and index.
    ISBN 0-253-32621-4
    1. Gettysburg (Pa.), Battle of, 1863.   I. Title.
E475.53G73 1994
973.7'349—dc20   93-19551

1 2 3 4 5   99 98 97 96 95 94

for Signe

. . . it is the province of the historian

to find out,

not what was,

but what is.

—Thoreau

Contents

1. Economy 1

2. Where They Fought, and What They Fought For 18

3. Reading 38

4. Sounds 46

5. Visitors 56

6. McPherson's Woods 62

7. The Seminary 81

8. The Town 96

9. Higher Laws 105

10. The Peach Orchard 115

11. The Round Tops 135

12. The Rose Farm 142

13. The Wheatfield 149

14. Walking 157

15. Culp's Hill 177

16. Pickett's Charge 186

17. Dorsey Pender 210

18. Conclusion 238

Note on Sources 261
Index 264

Gettysburg

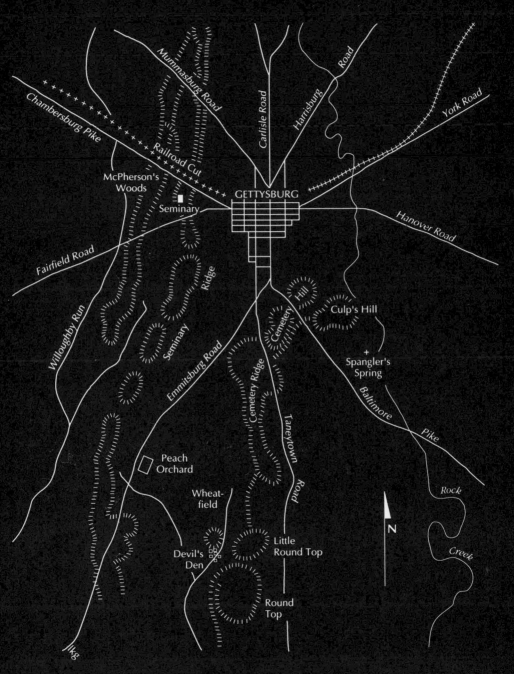

1 Economy

When I wrote the following pages I had spent ten years regularly visiting a place in Adams County, Pennsylvania. I tramped its fields; I walked in its woods; I climbed its hills. It is the most beautiful place on earth. But death is everywhere—in every meadow, along every Virginia rail fence, all over those quiet, rocky hills at sunset. Some say they have seen ghosts.

I would not obtrude my Adams County life upon readers except that particular questions were directed at me this year. On a clear, moonless, starry night about 10:30 or 11:00 o'clock, I was walking the grounds of the Seminary at Gettysburg, for which of course Seminary Ridge is named. I am especially interested in that part of the field because that is where the men of the Iron Brigade made their final stand on the First Day of the battle. I happened to be looking at Old Dorm, the original Seminary building, which was there at the time of the battle—a pale orange brick building which looks pleasant enough now but on the afternoon of July 1, 1863, it must have looked like the Gate of Hell—in the high heat, behind the Iron Brigade's line of flashing rifle-muskets, the slope already covered with gray and butternut bodies. If you were General Pender, for instance, or one of those people in the 26th Regiment, North Carolina Infantry, you saw that building in a harsh light—the light of the fact that in an instant your life and your soul could be laid bare. A tall, commanding young woman stepped out from behind a corner of the building and demanded of me: "Who are you and what are you doing here?"

She was Campus Security; I sensed that she knew more martial arts than the Army of the Potomac. She expected an answer. I told her I was nobody in particular and, well, sometimes I didn't really know what I was doing there—or that was something of how my stammered answer sounded from where I stood. I elaborated in circles and wondered how a night in the Gettysburg jail, one of the few parts of town I hadn't yet seen, might feel and how it might be explained to posterity. But evidently something in my answer gave her the impression I was just some poor shlemiel with a love for Gettysburg. I have tried to answer her question in these pages.

She told me there had been a break-in on campus that week, and people were on the alert. A break-in? At a seminary? Yes, indeed; someone had got into the bookstore. One might spend a dispassionate moment thinking about that. A seminary bookstore is full of basically nothing but theological books. What sort of psychological profile would the fellow have who breaks into a place like that? With what hopes? Or more pertinently, With what prospects? I'd like to meet the poor slob.

But his expedition was not so different from mine. To mistake me for him, or her, was not entirely a mistake. My ghostly Viking ancestors, for whom the pillaging of churches was a calling, finally might have recognized me as one of their own. I had come, however, to pillage the whole battlefield, and to carry the better part of it away.

But the fellow who had broken in had been interested in money after all, and this raises its own questions. Gettysburg receives on the average 3,018,123 visitors per year, who spend $81,077,687. I have made these figures up, but they will do. You would think everyone in this beautiful place would be rich. Evidently they are not. (Nor is everything beautiful, of course—but in due time.) This is a baffling phenomenon, and it makes a little discussion of economics necessary.

This misguided burglar confused needs with material desires; I do not think he needed money to survive. In fact, it is my profound conviction that he desired the money for the purpose of buying a ticket to the National Tower. But regardless, the fact is that he wanted money.

In the Union forces during the Civil War 360,828 men died (I am not making up any more figures; these are from Livermore), 110,010 of battle and 249,458 from disease or by accident. In the Confederate forces the figure was probably similar, but by estimating 10 percent fewer, we get approximately 700,000 deaths in the American Civil War. At Gettysburg about 8,000 of the roughly 50,000 casualties were killed outright or died within two days. In the Gulf Campaign (1991) the United States lost 125 soldiers, and the Parade, ostensibly in honor of the soldiers in the operation, cost $12,000,000, or about $120,000 per fatality. For the Civil War the corresponding figure would be $84 billion, total—enough to buy Kuwait, rebuild New York City, or educate a Republican Vice President.

The point is that there are some wrong economics in this country. This requires some explaining.

The beginning of the Battle of Gettysburg could be traced back to Adam, if not farther, but the immediate economics of that battle began at Brawner Farm on August 28, 1862, the summer before Gettysburg. It happened something like this.

General Lee had repelled McClellan's peninsular advance on Richmond. Lee had lost much more heavily than McClellan, both proportionately and in plain numbers, but the Union army was retreating, departing by ship back up around to Washington. Meanwhile, another, smaller Union army was coming down via Manassas. Lee sent Stonewall Jackson's Second Corps toward Manassas; Lee would follow with the rest of his Army of Northern Virginia once he was satisfied that McClellan was really gone.

Stonewall Jackson and his corps marched rapidly, burned the Union army depot at Manassas, and then disappeared. The Federal Army of Virginia, under General John Pope, tried to find and attack Jackson before the rest of Lee's army, the First Corps under Longstreet, could come up and reinforce him. Pope's army was spread out looking. During the afternoon of August 28 it seemed to Stonewall that he had done his job too well; Pope's army might not find him. Before long, McClellan's troops would be added to Pope's, and the total would be too large to deal with conveniently.

In the early evening Jackson's wish appeared to come true. His corps was lying in a wooded railroad embankment two miles long, a half-mile from a road leading to the old First Manassas (Bull Run) battlefield. Four brigades of Union infantry—constituting the division of Rufus King—had appeared from the South, marching toward Manassas. Jackson himself went out near the road on horseback to observe them. He let the first brigade go past. He would concentrate on the second one—throw the whole Stonewall Division at it and slaughter it. Then, tomorrow, all of Pope's army would be there; Jackson would entertain it while Longstreet would come up and deliver a devastating right hook. Except for that evening, it would indeed turn out as Jackson envisioned it. But it is that evening we are interested in.

Jackson didn't know what Union troops were marching unsuspectingly up that road, but his choice would seem to have been a perfect one. It was Gibbon's Brigade; except for one regiment it had not been in battle. It had never fought as a brigade. Its four regiments—the 2nd, 6th, and 7th Wisconsin and the 19th Indiana—formed the only "Western" brigade in Pope's or McClellan's armies. Its general was a new man in the infantry himself; he had been captain of Battery B, 4th United States Artillery, before being made a brigadier general of volunteers. John Gibbon had decided to take advantage of the brigade's difference, and turned it into a distinction by issuing Regular Army frock coats instead of the customary short jackets, and, most noticeable: instead of the standard kepis, or short-visored caps, Gibbon issued tall black hats. The hats were to be worn with one side fastened up; there was a brass insignia on the front, and a braid around the crown. The new general had drilled them all winter. Gibbon had a low opinion of volunteers but he noted that these men seemed intelligent. There was a good spirit in the brigade; his own intelligent treatment of them had fostered it.

Stonewall rode his little horse restlessly, back and forth, watching this brigade. The sun was low in the west. Obviously, those men in the untorn blue uniforms thought he was only a Rebel cavalry scout. They were a big new brigade, ripe as a soft peach, walking route step, enjoying the calm Virginia summer evening. A battery of six guns was coming along behind them.

In the woods the whole Stonewall Division waited, watching its officers, who were watching Jackson in the distance. A. P. Hill's Division was on hand too. They had these guys four to one, if Jackson chose to commit everyone. Which he wouldn't. Two or three to one would do it quick enough. Jackson wheeled his horse and galloped back toward the woods. Now, gentlemen. The officers ordered the men up, and, according to one of the Southerners, a hungry, savage growl rose from thousands of throats. ("We hate you, sir," a Confederate prisoner would inform his captor later in the war.)

General Gibbon was riding at the head of his brigade. He passed a farmhouse and buildings up on a low ridge several hundred yards to the left. The lead regiment of the brigade went through a woods straddling the road and emerged where some open fields stretched toward a long line of trees. Gibbon, the old artilleryman, saw some horses emerge from those woods in the distance; when he saw them turn he knew it was not a squad of cavalry but artillery going into battery. As they unlimbered at the edge of the trees one of Gibbon's aides was already galloping down the road through the wondering new troops with orders for old Battery B to come up.

When the first Confederate shell came *whoosh!* over the road, Gibbon's lead regiment was ordered to fall against the roadbank for cover; its own battery came pounding fast toward the head of the column.

Gibbon saw a second Confederate battery emerge and unlimber. Battery B would handle them both. But the *desideratum* was to take or drive off those guns, which Gibbon assumed to be horse artillery with no infantry support. He sent orders for the 2nd Wisconsin, still in the woods, to backtrack and advance up through the farm buildings and threaten one of the Confederate battery's flanks.

The Second advanced, found Confederate infantry skirmishers among the farm buildings—there weren't supposed to be any rebel infantry here—and advanced toward the line of woods just as the Stonewall Division came out. Four or five brigades of Rebels! The Wisconsin boys in the skirmish line ran back, hit the ground as their regiment fired, waited for the Southerners to return fire, then jumped up and hurried to their position on the regiment's right flank.

The rest of Gibbon's Brigade left the road and advanced to the ridge on both sides of the Second. Eventually two regiments from the brigade behind Gibbon joined in, giving him a total of 2,900 men. Attacking them were 6,400 of the most famous troops in the Confederacy. One of the most hideous and amazing events of the Civil War ensued.

Gibbon's new brigade stood its ground, as did Stonewall's infantry, and for two hours both lines of men, shoulder to shoulder without the protection of trenches or breastworks, at a maximum distance of 75 yards, fired incessantly at each other as their friends were shot down around them. After the War, Gibbon said this was the most terrific fire he ever heard, and by then he had been in quite a few battles. If Stonewall ever met a stone wall, this was it.

In the Civil War most infantrymen carried a long single-shot musket with a turned groove, or rifling, inside the barrel. You loaded it from the front. To prepare a rifle-musket for firing took nine distinct steps and about seventeen moves: you bit off the end of a paper cartridge and poured the loose powder down, dropped the bullet—a soft, concave-base, conical .58-caliber slug—rammed it home, replaced the rammer, or in such fierce action as at Brawner Farm stuck it in the ground, took a percussion cap out of its box on your belt and put it on the nipple at the breech—all the while exposed to fire. You stood within elbow touch of the man on each side of you; there was initially a double line of men firing. You advanced slowly and if the enemy gave back under the pressure you went on; at the same time, you had a natural tendency to move back as if you were in a strong wind. This kind of fighting did not change until after Gettysburg.

A good infantryman, *in theory*, could fire three aimed shots per minute. There is a kind of economy of firepower; you would expect Gibbon's men to have been overborne in fifteen minutes. Instead, Confederates reported afterward that *they* had been outnumbered. Gibbon's men had fired faster than troops normally did, and they had not moved back, and they had hit their targets.

Theoretically the range of the Civil War rifled musket had increased the range of a soldier's power to kill from the Revolutionary or Napoleonic smoothbore's 50 yards to 300 yards. But in practice the difference was very small, and the generals, made to look doltish by many Civil War writers, were not unreasonable in keeping to the Napoleonic tactics—solid lines held together in order to break the enemy's line and prevent the enemy from breaking yours. And at Brawner Farm, as at Gettysburg, most of this Black Hat Brigade were not equipped with modern Springfields or Enfields but with heavy, clumsy Austrian rifle-muskets.

Still, they stood. The next summer their comrades returned to the field and found the remains of bodies and battle still there in a line straight as a fence.

Into the sunset battle raged. Smoke clouded the field, light waned, men fired at musket flashes. The losses during these terrible two hours were horrifying. On the far right the 6th Wisconsin lost only 22 killed, wounded, and missing; but the Second lost 298 of 500 men—60 percent. The Nineteenth and the Seventh lost 40 percent. Figuring in the lighter totals of the New York and Pennsylvania regiments which joined Gibbon, the total Union loss was 33 percent, or 912 of 2,900 men.

These losses are unacceptable by World War II standards; a veteran of that war with whom I once spoke thought such a percentage meant the unit was a poor one, not being able to protect itself. But in the Civil War it was the best units which stood the high losses: they didn't fall back readily. Brawner Farm (also called Groveton or Gainesville) was a standup fight, for two hours, with no cover and no movement to speak of—unusual even in the Civil War.

But this Black Hat Brigade, which from August 28, 1862, through its virtual death at Gettysburg ten months later lost more men than any other Union brigade, began here at Brawner Farm its invariable feat of inflicting worse damage, terrible damage, upon those it fought. Jackson lost 2,200 men. Of his 6,400 engaged this was only a bit more than the 33 percent loss in Gibbon's Brigade, but, though outnumbering the Yankees more than two to one, Jackson lost 80 percent of Gibbon's whole force. One typical Virginia company of 17 men reported 6 killed and mortally wounded, 5 severely wounded. Those "dammed black hat fellers" fought with discipline, efficiency, spirit, determination. Within two weeks, at South Mountain, Gibbon's men would be called the Iron Brigade, a name they would confirm at Antietam and Gettysburg. The experienced fighting men of the Army of the Potomac, men who brooked no pretense, who jeered cavalrymen, and who were jealous of their own units' reputations, would remove their caps in silence when the Iron Brigade marched past.

A list of Lee's five units which lost most during the Civil War moves one to a similar silence: four of those five had fought the Iron Brigade. How did these black-hatted men become what they were? Their discipline, ability, and morale were earned. Their victories were not yellow-ribbon affairs over Grenada or Iraq. They paid in hard currency for durable goods.

The Iron Brigade was a factor in an economy of glory which caught up with Lee at Gettysburg. Jackson's losses were at first invisible; the Confederate tide was high, the shimmering pride and euphoria increased at Second Manassas two days after Brawner Farm—they didn't see what was happening to their infrastructure, their command and their manpower. Luther would have called this, like the *theologiae gloriae*, an Economics of Glory. Both lines had stood; Gibbon ordered a withdrawal of several hundred yards after the firing waned, and that night his men marched back toward Manassas Junction. But the Southerners had lost men and officers they could not replace. General Ewell, who was to command Jackson's corps at Gettysburg, lost a leg and did not return to the army until shortly before that battle.

He came back a changed man, no longer the fiery, decisive fighter he had been. Ewell's role in the Confederate loss at Gettysburg cannot be overemphasized; he was first to admit it. When Lee said one reason for his loss was that he hadn't had Jackson, he was saying in part that he lost because he had Ewell instead. (Like Lee, Ewell became a better commander after Gettysburg.)

Sometimes Robert E. Lee could be a bad economist. It was a matter of numbers. Lincoln understood the War's "arithmetic," as he called it—a brutal arithmetic, unnecessary perhaps had the North had the South's military leadership, Robert E. Lee in particular, early in the War. If the Confederates kept winning at this cost, Lincoln saw, then it would be a mere matter of time. In Grant he finally found a man willing to persist in applying the numbers. Lee's instinct for the offensive, which the South couldn't afford, was a kind of economy of glory—in other words, an economy of death. For Lee in 1862 and 1863, as for America in the 1980s, apparent victories sustained an illusion.

Today the National Park Service finally owns the Brawner Farm area, and plans to remove the postwar farmhouse and buildings. The removal is almost a pity, though I generally favor Civil War sites not having modern features. Those buildings are in their way effective. Deserted, gray, brooding, they are an ominous sight, foreboding and fatal.

There is—or was, at my last visit there—also an enormous dump of auto parts on the farm; gas tanks, if I remember correctly. A pile of automobile gas tanks you wouldn't believe could exist in one place.

The woods have expanded. In the spring, the flowering under-growth in the woods of Virginia is heartbreakingly lovely. One thinks, even in the Civil War, of the damage war does to nature, the waste which we have no right to inflict, and which will of course be disaster for us when the glory of our abuse fades.

In the Civil War they used a lot of metal. The former mining town of Platteville in southwestern Wisconsin sits on a honeycomb of aban-doned tunnels—a prophecy of contemporary America, perhaps: hollow catacombs under the surface. These were lead mines, used for bullets for Union armies. Elsewhere iron was gouged from the earth in order to make cannons and projectiles. Artillery ammunition was extremely expensive (though not so much as now); a dozen or so rounds required their own heavy wooden crate. Saltpeter and other ingredients of black powder were dug from the earth. Sulfurous clouds smothered the lovely landscapes of the Civil War. If these things seem trifling it is only because of the unimaginable damage we do today. In war Earth first feels the wound. During my last visit to Gettysburg 150 oil wells were burning, spuming volumes of smoke into the atmosphere, and the waters of the Persian Gulf were a sus-pension of oil. I am told the war was a victory, but I have not been told convincingly for whom.

There was to be a shopping mall built across the highway from Brawner Farm. Protest came from around the country, and for now the developers have retreated back into their lairs. This is the kind of Civil War battle that is seldom won these days; it shows that hope may not be entirely without vocation.

My most recent stay in Gettysburg cost me as follows, figured on a weekly basis:

transportation	$115.00 for gas (or $.26 per mile, the true cost, leaving aside ecology, etc.)
tolls	12.40
room	140.00
total	$267.40 (really more)

I could have lessened the room costs—very cheap by Gettysburg standards—by camping, but my time was limited and I did not want to spend it going to and from the town and battlefield or messing with camping details and paraphernalia, in addition to which it might have caused an encampment chapter. Applied to this, an aspect of Lee's economics is altogether fitting and proper: those with fewer resources have to take the longer risks. Time was at a premium. Furthermore, I mitigated much outlay by cooking for myself, as follows:

3 1/2 gals. milk	$ 7.46
1 loaf bread	.99
2 doz. eggs	1.78
1 can grapefruit juice	1.59
1 can apricot juice	1.89
1 can V-8 juice	1.49
1 1/2 lb. strawberries	1.96
3 boxes cereal	6.87
3 cans soup	1.77
1 lb. turkey franks	.97
2 lbs. apples	1.26
1 lb. pears	.89
2 boxes instant macaroni and cheese	1.58 (a mistake)
1 box graham crackers	1.19
1 box fig bars	1.59
1 box raisins	1.69
1 jar wheat germ	2.29
1 lb. butter	1.59
1 ovenproof bowl	1.99
less for items unused	−6.01
total	$34.83

The following items I will omit from tabulation as being too difficult to put a value on, and embarrassing to divulge: books, a pen, paper, notecards, and miscellaneous. Giving for all reported expenses a total of: $302.23.

To this total I decline to add the unreported items in the paragraph above, which I am still trying to pay off; but interest from that week is still accruing, and I trust will continue to do so after all monetary bills are paid. (I maxed out my card.)

A grant paid for my housing and mileage, and I would have run up a food bill even if I had stayed at home. I thus conclude that one can pass among the dead cheaply, and reach higher stages of happiness and enlightenment at negligible material expense. But most of us lead lives of constant waste.

We seem to labor under the belief, or rather superstition, that the great machine of our material activity is going somewhere and will at some happy day arrive, when in fact the only truth is that it is actually bound somewhere, or we rather are bound, and to it. Its greatest if not only product is friction, and its exhaust is us. In this latter it is an efficient machine indeed, because there is little left of us at the end, and generally not a precious little.

What we live is not life but occupation, for which the sacrifice of blood through our history seems absurd if not evil. The liberty dearly bought is cheaply wasted. Instead of liberty we have mere options, and all of a kind. We are like fundamentalists of capitalism, obeying the letter of its manufactured beliefs and aspirations as if they were dictated by the high power Himself, and as if they were the exclusive formula for salvation. They have been dictated by a great power, perhaps, but it is a power we have assented rather too hastily to serve, and do so at some peril.

The economy of the United States in 1860 was our progenitor, based as it partly was on black slavery. The North, as Lincoln acknowledged, drew substantial profit from the South's peculiar, though perhaps not unique, institution. But the great machine of industry was thriving in the North, and was dooming the South, for modern wars are fought according to the rules of that machine, which tries to make everyone and everything its servants; and not being satisfied with some slavery at the South merely, the machine inexorably moved to rake the nation as a whole into its steel grasp. In life on this earth we usually trade one evil for another.

The United States economy of 1860, artificially divided into two (for there was at that time no genuinely separate South), became two greatly disparate material economies. The North had a railroad advantage over the South in a ratio of 22:1, for example. The South had, for practical purposes, only two iron works, one in Atlanta, and Tredegar in Richmond. Factories were of the ratio 85:15, and bank deposits 80:20, North to South. The South had a white population of about 5.5 million, plus 3.5 million slaves to back up a war effort by their work at home (a fact which Lincoln recognized); the North had about 22 million whites from which to draw soldiers, and eventually blacks in large numbers took on the Union uniform too. Whether inclusive or exclusive of slaves, which the Southern economy defined as capital, the North had a massive preponderance of capital. Its labor pool was much greater than the South's. The North had a navy. And in the long run it had the deeper infrastructure of military officers: the War killed off the South's good generals as it was bringing the North's up to visibility.

In other words, there was a larger economy at work: the economy of time. On the First Day at Gettysburg the clock sounded, quietly. The South needed to win before that clock ran out. On the first morning at Gettysburg, as at Brawner Farm, the Iron Brigade traded the material of this world for an invisible commodity; in that, there was something like real glory. The world, which was running on another kind of glory, did not see it—but the point is that economies participate in each other: what seems to be arithmetic is also time; what seems to be material is also distance.

One thing Lincoln concluded during the Civil War was that an evil in the political or material economy can arouse a reaction in the moral economy—the existence of which he staked his career upon, indeed gave his life for. Slavery was that evil then. One wonders whether our material and political economies now contain potent evil, or are simply a harmless fool's game.

One thinks of the automobile industry. What are the Numbers and Losses of the American "love affair" with chrome, plastic, and speed? During the Vietnam era we lost, in killed, as many on our highways per year as we lost in the whole Southeast Asian war (during the war.) Since then the number killed in transit has equaled the number of Civil War deaths—more than the number killed in all our other wars to date together. Sixty percent of urban pollution is caused by the automobile; how many deaths shall we add for lung cancer, congestive heart failure, and countless other diseases produced or aggravated by the breathing of poison—not to mention the noise from all those damn trucks? Ah, but think of the gains! The gains are that we have more automobiles.

We define "high standard of living" by the things that are produced and consumed; then we produce more of those things and get a higher standard of living. I'm not sure even generals Grant and Lee would have accepted such losses for such gains.

Our situation could have been less blackly absurd. America could have built safer cars, and more efficient cars, and thus reduced the butcher's bill. But—though the unions get the blame for our emphysematous auto industry—the executives made decisions to manufacture big, shoddy, dangerous cars; and they are not in jail or even in discredit, but have reaped the material profits more than anybody else. And, as in 1980 and 1984, the American public supports the deadly farce overwhelmingly. Again the economy is that of a rich man's war and a poor man's fight. For what? Employment? What kind of employment?

(You can get to Gettysburg by train and bus.)

Computers have generated computers. Husbands across the country have bought these things, coming up with childish arguments to convince their wives they ought to have one for the home. Buy a computer and change our lives. They spend two or three months' salaries for one, and it sits. Then new software comes out, better monitors, bigger drives. It is not "Simplify, simplify," but "Upgrade! Upgrade!" Upgrade our stuff and upgrade our lives. Schools demand more money so they can buy computers, and hire consultants to tell them how to develop their hardware and software capabilities, and hire a support staff, upgrade hardware and software to handle all this, and generate laser-printed communications. Students now are advanced in video skills, computer skills, and interpersonal skills, and illiterate as Visigoths.

The so-called information explosion is the best example of this symbiotic parasitism. Communication is proliferating to an extent that would embarrass decent people. So many new things to communicate, with nothing better to say. The quality of our speech seems to move in inverse direction and proportion to its quantity. There is little worth storing and communicating; all that information functions merely to sustain the computer economy. Instead of waterers of horses and oxen we are feeders of hardware and software. We do not manage our information. Was man created for the chip or the chip for man, that we should be up to our nostrils in them, and driving petroleum, the buffalo of Western civilization, to extinction? We need to generate some answers.

But to live without cars, computers, and modern information? Do you want to go back to the nineteenth century? We have gone back much farther than the 1860s.

A recent article in the *Chicago Tribune* contained some information. Executives of companies which sold more than $250 million worth of "goods" last year got paid somewhat over $300,000 in Canada, Germany, and Japan. In the U.S. the figure is over $600,000. The average top executive salary in ratio to the average worker's salary has gone from 50:1 in 1960 to 80:1 today. Truly, Solomon in all his glory was not arrayed like one of these.

There is some immorality here. All ultimate wounds are self-inflicted. That the majority by its actions consents to the devolution of our country is faint comfort, ironically appropriate though it may be. Evil is more easily identifiable in great powers and principalities than in ourselves, but less easy to eradicate. On the other hand, it may be easier to replace one dictator or executive with another than to replace convenience with courage. The closer we come to ourselves, the more we are mocked.

Settlers in the 1870s used to build the schoolhouse before any other public structure; today our states try to fund education with lottos and dog racing. But in other things we make very fine discriminations. In our businesses, whom will we hire; and whom do we build our homes next to and choose to send our children to school with? Inside those homes (*economy* means "household") what quality of children do we manufacture; what shoddy, unsafe, wasteful lives do we produce? But hardest of all, how does each of us spend our time and thought? The savage tribes turned in better bottom lines.

At the turn of the millennium we will have a labor-force crisis, it is predicted. The numbers will be too low: drugs, dropouts, early pregnancies will slice away workers. Three of four new jobs will require some postsecondary education (no surprise, considering what secondary education is today), but the skills will not be available. We might find out that dollars depend on learning, on justice, on morals, on character. "People talk about a leadership crisis," General Norman Schwartzkopf has said. "It's never a competence problem. It's an ethical, moral crisis. It's a problem of character." We refuse to believe that America must change or die.

Nearby, as I stop on the Seminary campus to write some notes, two tragically obese young people sit comfortably in the sun. Poor souls, they have gorged themselves on guns; downed millions of video calories; swallowed enough high cholesterol from Madison Avenue, the White House, Congress, and the Pentagon to kill people with less mysterious traditions. As it is, they are dying of their own weight, their own willed ignorance. Every few seconds their bulk collides with hearts made for a different body. Perhaps only God can save them. There must come—there already is, an *economica crucis*—an economics of the cross. Unfortunately, much of our religion is not theology but ergonomics.

In America we have enshrined not confession but confection; we have built for our spirits a cathedral of glass. But the economy of spirit—though concentric with the material economy—does not come out of a pocket any more than it can fit into a book. Life's transactions are more refined than we think.

The First Day of the Battle of Gettysburg is seen as a lucky one for the Confederate army. This is wrong. It was horrendously unlucky. The worst thing possible happened. The Southerners needed either to win early in the day, or to be repulsed all day. Neither occurred: they won sometime past midafternoon.

What they won was nothing, worse than nothing. Two brigades got slaughtered forcing the Iron Brigade out of McPherson's Woods and off Seminary Ridge; Heth's, Pender's, and Rodes's divisions took terrific losses in driving two divisions of the Union First Corps from the high ground west and north of the Seminary. The worst of it was, their generals thought they had won. But it was the Iron Brigade and the First Corps, finally retreating through town, that had won.

Federal artillery and General Hancock were on Cemetery Hill behind Gettysburg when the First and the Eleventh corps came streaming up there. General John Reynolds, dead six hours now, had won
the day—his troops, his decision to fight west of town. Early that
morning he had written a hasty message: I will try to hold them west
of town, but I fear they will be able to occupy the heights behind the
town before I can. The "heights" were Cemetery Hill and Cemetery
Ridge. The Confederates did not get there before the rest of the Union
army, marching hard to the sound of Reynolds's guns. Colonel Freemantle said General Lee drove Meade into a strong position, and
Meade had the sense to stay there; but it was Reynolds who had chosen it.

So Lee lost twice that day. First, when Heth's Division didn't drive
back the Iron Brigade and Cutler's Brigade. Second, when they
thought they had won enough and Lee, Ewell, and Early didn't try to
move heaven and earth in a desperate attack on Cemetery Hill as the
Union position was still solidifying. They hadn't won a damn thing.
The battle west of town was really a battle for the heights behind, east
of town, and they didn't know it. Reynolds had known it all along.

"We made the battle," Longstreet said later. John Reynolds made the
battle.

The question is, what *should* have happened for the Confederates,
short of winning in the morning—as opposed to what they thought
should happen? The coincidences and results of the First Day have all
the irony and ambiguity of a Delphic oracle.

They thought it was providential that Ewell's Corps arrived on the
north end of the field just in time to drive the Union Eleventh Corps
and outflank the splendid First Corps. But it was a disaster. Lee's army
needed to maintain contact west of town, not lose it, making it more
likely that the First and the Eleventh would have been reinforced
where they were. All effort should have been made to prevent, rather
than compel, withdrawal to the Cemetery Ridge line. This was the
only substantial opportunity at Gettysburg, once the morning and
early afternoon had been lost. There was a larger economy than the
perceived one at work.

But of course the Southern generals did not know that a position
like Cemetery Hill lay behind the First and the Eleventh corps. They

had no observation balloons, no reconnaissance overflights—they had insufficient distance. Thus the nature of the great human problem.

Gettysburg is a glimpse into another world. Through the fog of war the ghostly face of General Lee stares back, angry and baffled. We are more like him than anyone else: *iustus et peccator simul* in a loose sense—"at the same time justified and a sinner"; trapped in his own insolvent household, victorious he thought, but the complicit victim of an economy he could not or would not see. That larger economy becomes, in unexpected oblique moments, almost visible. His is our face; what we can see around him we can sense around ourselves, concentrating against us as we grope forward within our own illusionary version of the world.

Surely a vast and intent divine gaze sees all this senselessness and slaughter. Theodicy is a kind of physics, a study of the nature of distance; and time is but a hill we stand a-looking from.

2 Where They Fought, and What They Fought For

Our whole life is startlingly moral. There never is an instant's truce between virtue and vice. Goodness is the only investment that never fails.

—Thoreau

Gettysburg is in south central Pennsylvania. The chief topological feature of the Gettysburg battlefield is the so-called inverted fishhook, its eye at the south, and the bend up at the town curving to the east. The barb is Culp's Hill; the curve is Cemetery Hill just overlooking the town, the shank is Cemetery Ridge, the south end of the shank is Little Round Top, and the eye is Round Top. On the Second and Third days of the battle, the Union Army of the Potomac occupied this whole fishhook, and Lee's Army of Northern Virginia made a larger fishhook west and north, resting chiefly on Seminary Ridge, parallel to Cemetery Ridge and about three-quarters of a mile west of it. Lee's line went through the town itself and extended around the barb, which was the Union far right. In front of the Union left center ran the Emmitsburg Road, coming up into Gettysburg from the town in Maryland only a dozen or so miles away. Out in front of the Union line, touching that road, was (and is) a peach orchard; in back of that, closer to the Union line, was a field ripe with wheat. A little southeast of the Wheatfield, just in front of the Round Tops, is a strange little hill with huge jumbled rocks the size of rooms, as if a solid stone house had been emptied out of a giant's pocket: this was called Devil's Den. On the Second Day of the battle, before the Union army completely filled the fishhook, Lee's main attack was against the Federal left, sweeping across the Emmitsburg Road to Devil's Den, the Round Tops, the Peach Orchard, and the Wheat-field. On the Third Day the famous Pickett's Charge was a frontal attack against the shank of the Union line.

The battle of the First Day, July 1, 1863, did not take place around the fishhook but west and north of town. This was due to the oddity of the Southern army's arriving from the west and north, and the Northern army's coming up from the south. In May Lee had won a great victory at Chancellorsville in Virginia. Tired of fighting battles in the South after which the Yankees simply retreated, changed commanders, pulled themselves together, and came down at them again, Lee invaded the North to try to force a decisive issue. After Stonewall Jackson's death Lee divided his army into three corps: the First still under Longstreet, the Second now under Ewell, and the new Third under A. P. Hill. (Each corps contained three divisions, the divisions contained several brigades each, and a brigade was made up of regiments. Regiments varied in size from 150 to 800 men, though a regiment's ten companies were supposed to contain 100 each—but after two years of war the average Union regiment was about 230 and the Confederate about 250. The Confederacy sent new recruits into old regiments, while most Union states used new recruits to form new regiments, creating more officers and therefore making more political friends.) Lee's three corps had gone north through Maryland behind the cover of the Appalachian mountains, then had come out east through the pass near Chambersburg, Pennsylvania. They had fanned into the rich farmland of south central Pennsylvania, collecting food and horses, the Second Corps going as far east as York. Philadelphia, Baltimore, Harrisburg, and Washington itself were all threatened by the invading army. On June 30, however, having learned that the Union army was following him more closely than he had planned on, General Lee ordered his corps to concentrate at Gettysburg, where nine roads came together.

Roads were important during the American Civil War, even though there was no motorized transport to use them. Artillery and the miles-long wagon trains needed them, cavalry moved faster on them, and crossing fields, fences, woods, and streams would have made marching long distances nearly impossible for infantry. As it was, marching was usually misery, the men caked with sweat and dust, inhaling the thick cloud raised by thousands of tramping feet. Or they slogged through mud when it rained—a welcome relief from heat and suffocation, however. It was an important and difficult task for commanding generals and their staffs to plan marches so that their divisions would not jam together, get in each other's way, impede each other with their supply trains, and render poor roads unserviceable. Most roads were packed dirt, but some roads to Gettysburg were macadamized.

By seizing the initiative, Lee intended to use the difficulty of marching against the Union army. It would have to remain south of him, staying between him and Washington in order to protect the Capital, and it would have to stay very spread out, the Federals not knowing where Lee was heading. Therefore Lee could concentrate when, where, and how fast he wanted to, but once he did so the Federals would have to scramble, arriving on the battlefield exhausted from forced marches. While this happened to some extent, one of Lee's brigades, Law's, had to make a terrible forced march—and then immediately fight a crucial action upon which the whole battle depended.

General Hooker, who commanded the Army of the Potomac as Lee's invasion began, distributed his corps well and came north from his lines in Virginia more rapidly than Lee had anticipated. General Meade, who took over in place of Hooker just before Gettysburg, continued the deliberate speed of the Union advance, and when his cavalry reported large bodies of Confederate infantry in the vicinity of Gettysburg he moved fast, sending a third of his army there and moving the rest within reach but keeping them back far enough to fight elsewhere if necessary. Neither general knew what the other was doing, or where the enemy's main force was.

Robert E. Lee, already perceived as one of the greatest generals in history, had been winning victories for a year against superior numbers, stunning the enemy and the public with brilliant, fast, bold tactics. His veterans were supremely confident of themselves and their commander, and contemptuous of the Yankees they had beaten—with what should have been ominous exceptions at Antietam, Malvern Hill, Brawner Farm—time after time. The character of the Army of Northern Virginia foot soldier was a marvel; they were "a lean and hungry set of wolves," a Northern observer said, with "more dash than our boys," and they would march carrying little except their well-cleaned rifles, constantly banter and shout, and, as Lee said, do anything he asked of them. Two of the corps commanders were new at commanding more than divisions, but Lee's "War Horse," James Longstreet, could not be bettered; several of the division commanders were excellent: Hood, McLaws, Pender. Most of the brigades were superbly led.

Though the Army of the Potomac was larger (unknown to the Northerners), individual Union units were smaller than their Confederate counterparts. A Union brigade was made up of one or two fewer regiments, and in some cases, smaller ones; a Union division contained as few as two brigades, though usually three, whereas a Confederate division often had five brigades. Therefore a Union corps was only as strong numerically as a Confederate division. The Army of the Potomac had superior artillery, and many outstanding corps and division commanders. The character of its volunteer soldiers, fighting losing battles time and again but never losing faith in themselves or losing belief in their cause, would be displayed at this decisive battle. And finally there was no commanding general to mask the quality of his officers and troops by his own bumbling or failure of character. George Gordon Meade, while known hardly at all to the army as a whole, had been an efficient and aggressive brigade, division, and corps commander. Lee, who knew his Union generals well, was grim when he heard of Meade's appointment: "He will make no mistake on my front."

As A. P. Hill's Third Corps marched toward Gettysburg from the west on the morning of July 1, Union cavalry was waiting on a ridge west of town, and the best corps in the Union army, Reynolds's First Corps, was stepping into column on the Emmitsburg Road a few miles to the south. Soon the rest of both armies would be hurrying, having heard the report: *Heavy fighting at Gettysburg.*

It is too simple to say that the War came from a moral issue—too simple for comfort. There was the tariff, the constitutional disagreement over states' rights, the problem of sectional power, but "all knew" that negro slavery was the cause. Not slavery itself, but the moral issue of it.

A Quaker lady came to Lincoln one day with what she considered to be a divine message concerning what the President should do about slavery. Lincoln's sardonic and more or less disrespectful reply is well known. It was his idea that he himself—the person most directly involved, as he saw it, at the center of the war effort—would be the one, if *anyone* would be, whom God would deliver messages to—and not to a Friend or a delegation of ministers. His thinking on this was that of a lawyer rather than that of an Old Testament scholar or a reader of Greek plays; it is the point of view of a person in power rather than that of a critic or private citizen. "Is there any word from the Lord?" was once the question of kings as much as of anyone else.

Nevertheless, Lincoln's understanding of the War has not been surpassed. Lincoln's mature explanation, his final theory, was given in the Second Inaugural Address. The everyday world is a visible part of the moral universe, out of whose depths retribution comes.

The difference between Mr. Lincoln's moral conclusion and the moral arguments usually made during wartime is that his did not identify the enemy alone as evil: "If . . . He gives to both North and South, this terrible war, as the woe due to those by whom the offence came. . . ." The North owned ships that were used to transport slaves; it owned factories that made cloth from Southern cotton; the whole nation was complicit. The moral universe has the curvature of earth. Doing evil sets something in motion.

Lincoln's assumptions are not modern. To him, the universe is not random, is not morally neutral, is not masterless; and humankind has to answer for its actions in a cosmos that is not only physical but moral. The difference between good and evil can sometimes be known. There are such things as duty and responsibility toward others. We are not the ultimate judges. And, as in the Old Testament, *nations* are held accountable as if they were individuals.

All this has changed now, in people's minds. Since World War I the idea of a moral universe has looked absurd, bitterly ironic, or at least questionable. Nations are not responsible to other nations; individuals likewise are responsible only to themselves, if that. Good and evil are problematic categories, and the language with which we talk about them may be a power matrix rather than a transparent medium. The past, the present, the physical universe are extensions of ourselves.

Wouldn't it be awkward now if the only thing that hasn't changed is the validity of Lincoln's conclusion? " 'The judgements of the Lord are true and righteous altogether.' "

Each historian, each philosopher, each Civil War buff would like to think through to the real issue of the war. But perhaps it is wisdom to accept the conclusions of the man at the center: the man who dreamed of his own death ("Who is dead in the White House?"); who saw a ship sail into mysterious waters before decisive events of the war, including the assassination; who had a vision of his two terms, one healthy and the other like a wraith; who delivered the unforgettable word at the central place of the War; who saw it through to the end, dying at the finish; one of the strongest, most intelligent, uncanny, able, human, and humane figures in history.

According to Lincoln, there is no vacuum out there, but an electric plasma of a living will, a clean judgment, a mysterious but perfect power. Upon this tensile ocean each of us sails in the small cup of our lives, upon it the United States has sailed thus far and still drifts its uncertain way, upon it Lee's veterans moved, and the men of the Army of the Potomac. If Lincoln was right, "a terrible beauty is born." The soldiers marched to a distant drummer.

America is having a megaparade for its Gulf Campaign returnees as I write these pages. It is really fitting and proper to praise these soldiers, because there is virtually no one fighting our real enemies. Once again, the war for this country's fundamental survival is civil. Once again, the war really is a moral one, with certain groups of people the tragic victims, whose fates will decree the fate of the country.

Today a young black man in an urban ghetto is worse off than his father or grandfather was. If you are poor, young, and black you have as little hope as a slave had, but you are demoniacally taunted with the advertisements of material enjoyment and power. Your chances of dying violently are greater than your father's, your chances of contracting disease are greater, your chances of becoming a victim one way or another of addiction are greater—and your chances of getting educated, and getting a job, are worse. America is dying in the streets.

Meanwhile, the emunctory suburbs expand, with their malls and effluvia of plastic, carbon monoxide, and yellow ribbons. The poor, blacks, Hispanics, the sick, the old—the ones who show us what we are and who will assign our fate if there is some truth behind the visible world—they lie perishing outside the gate.

"As I would not be a slave," Lincoln said, "so I would not be a master." If there really is some underlying moral, spiritual reality, then in the long run it is not the poor who suffer, but their oppressors; it is the rich who will beg for a drop of cold water from across a great, fixed gulf.

Our activities are distractions. Oppression is an evasion of ourselves. We are the war.

The megaparade is a dishonor to the soldiers who went to the Middle East in the belief they were putting their lives at risk. It's a satire, heavy-handed and unintentional of course. The size and length of this ceremonial yellow ribbon is a more telling index of what's going on in America.

The designation for cavalry was a yellow stripe down the trousers, and yellow braid for officers—an unfortunate choice, in view of the infantryman's question: "Have you ever seen a *dead* cavalryman?" The cavalry had the reputation of riding out for glory and staying out of fights.

Stuart's absence is one of the reasons given for Lee's failure at Gettysburg; without the eyes and ears of his cavalry, the supremely alert and efficient Stuart at their head, Lee walked into Gettysburg blind, and didn't learn Union strength and dispositions for two days. Like all reasons given for Lee's failure, this one assumes the outcome would have been different otherwise, which of course overlooks the fighting and generalship put up by the Army of the Potomac at Gettysburg. (Years afterward General Pickett was asked why the Confederates lost the battle. Maybe the Union army had something to do with it, he said.) The battle would have been different, but would the outcome have been?

Nevertheless, the string of mistakes and misfortunes certainly suggests to many the possibility that perhaps there was a Plan, that the stars in their courses fought against the South; retrospect gives the sensation of height. Gettysburg's unexpected events can seem somehow cogent when arranged together, divinely elusive in import and too weighty to have resulted from human activity alone. Does our sense of the battle's odd incompleteness yet perfection result from trying to read another dimension from this one, or simply from our regret over the battle's achingly contingent moments? In the latter respect the memory feels like tragedy, aesthetically crafted and rounded, embodying the great themes, but the players are horribly unable to get up during the applause.

The case of Stuart is at least interesting to consider. His and Lee's attitudes are, each in its own way, an example of false glory. Lee's fault was more in the way of pride, while Stuart's was vanity, but both were based on the illusion that they or their troops were superior to human beings.

It is thought that Stuart's ill-resulting ride around the Union army, a trick that always used to work, was conceived when the Southern cavalry was surprised and almost defeated at Brandy Station (Fleetwood), in the midst of a splashy, vain review, appropriately enough, right before the Gettysburg campaign. So one of the lessons of history here is that vanity often leads to humiliation (though we have "The Emperor's New Clothes" fable to tell us this without the blood 'n guts): at Gettysburg Stuart was so mortified by the rebuff Lee gave him that nobody ever was willing to write about what really transpired. Quite possibly Lee blew his cork, and Stuart cried. Stuart, of course, was very tired.

The ride of the cavalry was a nightmare. Finding the Union army more trailed out than he had expected, therefore necessitating a longer ride (or a decision early to turn back, which would have been the right course), Stuart and his troopers spent days and nights in the saddle, men dropping off their horses in a stupor of fatigue—and then, after a week of harrowing exhaustion, hearing faintly, with a chill, the distant guns. Heavy fighting at Gettysburg. When Stuart rode up late the second day and reported with the usual bravura the capture of 125 wagons, the response of General Lee must have been a phenomenon.

The outstanding cavalryman at Gettysburg was General John Buford, First Division United States Cavalry, whose efficiency and fighting qualities were matched by his courage and modesty. In a profession full of wide receivers he was lost to view, and his death that

December of exposure and overexertion exempted him from postwar notoriety in the West. (There is, perhaps, some reward for hard work.) Buford's men felt out the initial advance of Hill's Corps, and held them at bay for two hours, until Reynolds's First Corps arrived. A common misconception is that Buford's men had Spencer repeaters, could "load on Sunday and fire all week," possessing man-for-man firepower three or four times greater than Heth's infantrymen. They had Spencer breechloaders, not repeaters. This did increase their firepower, but not enough for two brigades of cavalry stretched on a mile-long front to have even odds against a division of veteran infantry. Afterward, when Buford could have been scouting the Confederate right flank on day two, cavalry chief Pleasanton sent him south and off the battlefield.

Had Stuart been present on July 1 and 2, all the Yankee cavalry would have been right there with him. Just before Gettysburg the Union mounted service had come of age. Initially they could be ridden circles around, but no more. They were tough and well-mounted, well-equipped and well-led. Not only did they have soldiers of the quality of Buford and Farnsworth, they had that incredible jerk Kilpatrick and that vainglorious travesty George Armstrong Custer— both, unfortunately, highly effective young generals, waiting for a commander like Sheridan to come along smacking his fist into his palm saying, "Smash 'em up! Smash 'em up!" Though Stuart's men were tired, the fact remains that they lost their battle against the Yankee horse on the third day.

And Lee did have a brigade of cavalry on hand from the beginning, but it was not gainfully employed. The surprise he suffered in learning that the Army of the Potomac was already up in Maryland was as much the result of Lee's glorying miscalculation as of Stuart's absence; Lee hadn't dreamed that the Yankees could be clever enough or able to move as fast and well as they did.

When Heth's infantry walked toward Gettysburg to get shoes, they ran into Buford. Buford hadn't the brilliant moves of Stuart, nor any of the nonsense either. He wouldn't lose the big one. Buford didn't have the charisma of Turner Ashby, Stuart, or Wade Hampton; he had none of the brilliant instinct for victory and mayhem of Bedford Forrest; he hadn't the incredible bravery of Judson Kilpatrick, a hair-brained jackass even Sherman called a "damned fool"—but whom he of course wanted for his campaign of vandalism in Georgia. A member of Meade's staff said he couldn't look at "Kill-cavalry" without wanting to laugh. (After Pickett's Charge, Kilpatrick sent his gallant, capable subordinate, Elon Farnsworth, on a useless and stupid splash into Confederate infantry, for which Farnsworth and others had to pay with their lives. Criminal behavior.)

But Buford strikes you as being one of those rare individuals in warfare who seems to have dropped in from another world or from the future—someone who knows what he's doing, someone who is, incredibly, not in the fog of war nor in the fog of his own time's conceptions. Buford recognized the importance of Gettysburg, and knew it was vital to hold McPherson's Ridge. It was he who gave Reynolds the option of holding Seminary Ridge; Reynolds seized it, and there was a battle at Gettysburg. If you wanted a man to save your life, day in day out, and to tell you what to do and it would be right; if you wanted a man to save your country—it would be John Buford. Some glory belongs to him.

A different case is George Armstrong Custer, who dressed and acted for what he thought was glory. "A circus rider gone mad" he was called because of his wardrobe—tight, fancy velvet pants, wide-brimmed decorated hat, flashy jacket; and his blond ringlets. He was an excellent cavalry general, though only twenty-four at Gettysburg—bold, alert, brave. His brigade had the highest total loss of any Union cavalry brigade through the War: 525 killed in action or dead of wounds. (More on this later.) He had eleven horses shot under him. (An inhumane practice, Mark Twain said; they should be shot *over* the troops.) He reminds you of a present-day entrepreneur or consultant. At Appomattox he eyed Longstreet's mount and said, "I want that horse." He was informed by the tall Georgian that the horse was offered neither for sale nor for theft. Some of these fellows were at heart criminals, as Custer proved by his subhuman work on the Indians. Glory, in the long run, is withheld from would-be soldiers who are uniformed murderers.

But the East Cavalry Field at Gettysburg does have a certain glory. I had not gone to see it in all the years I have been coming to Gettysburg, until this past spring; it had been an omission.

The fields are quite plain, bounded by woods, and the area is large. There is a farm in the middle. As you move along the modern road past the Confederate and the Union lines, forming an acute angle, you see actually there on battlefield markers the names so glorious in books, and in the imaginations of people then: "Stuart's Cavalry," "Hampton's Brigade," "Fitzhugh Lee's Brigade," "Custer's Brigade." You look across the field and imagine the pounding, thunderous initial charge, the jingling clash and the shouts, rearing horses screaming—then, out of the woods, sabres lifted, a long gray line with pennons, Virginians on their trim horses riding as loose and easy and fast as Saracens; a few shots, then the whole line gathers and streaks forward; from the field on the left a heavy Union line picks up its advance from a walk to a trot—an officer with yellow ringlets gallops out front, a trooper with pennon just behind him, he waves his hat, orders are shouted, and the horses canter into a dusty, crowding thunder—and then the *charge!*—the shock of meeting, the melee with sabres raised and brought down, pistols pointed and fired, horses wheeling and squads swirling around each other in breathtaking tumult. Meanwhile Pickett's men are walking toward a fight that really meant something.

The 525 killed in Custer's Brigade were lost over the course of the whole War. In the Gettysburg campaign it lost 13.3 percent, including 32 killed. In Pickett's Charge, Kemper's infantry brigade lost 43 percent (121 killed); Armistead's Brigade, 63.7 percent (187 killed); Garnett, 65 percent (231 killed). On the cavalry field, the 7th Michigan of Custer's Brigade lost 26 percent, a much higher rate than that of any other cavalry, the closest being 17 percent and most being well within 10 percent. Fifty-four Union infantry regiments lost more than 50 percent at Gettysburg.

When I visited the East Cavalry Field there was a tornado watch in Adams County, and from the horizon heavy gray clouds climbed in an uncertain line. But the sky was clear everywhere else, light streaming from a high heaven, a washed cerulean blue, with bright, clean, white cumulus here and there sailing smooth and fast and unspeakably grand. The fields were fresh and the spring woods filagreed with pale green, here and there a glimpse of white or pink, and near the barn spread the effusive waste of lavender wisteria. The farmhouse itself, in that vast, calm field, surrounded by woods at a distance—what an absolute peace in the lap of quietude; the fields in warm beneficent repose, those fields of memory, soft and deep. In and around that house what stillness, if one had the content for it.

Here as I sit by the shore of a busy lake, powerboats buzz back and forth in front of me, jet-skiers sluice up wilting monuments of spray at fantastic speeds, yelling like rebels; only the ducks sit still as cannons in their ghost-eyed sleep; behind me trucks roar and mutter and grind, motorcycles like thousand-dollar mosquitoes charge through stopped traffic, and spewing, air-conditioned cars honk and squeal and accelerate with little yellow ribbons like pennons on their antennae. How I long for the glory of that other field!

U. S. Grant thought the Civil War was caused by the Mexican War. One might agree with him not only because of the political consequences of the Mexican War. One might agree if one thinks there are laws in the universe—like physical laws, which govern more than physics, but whose results are as visible as granite, as visible as the headstones in the National Cemetery at Gettysburg. The Greek playwrights believed that human action calls down responses, predictable responses, from somewhere. Shakespeare, in a bleaker mode, states the possibility of self-induced retribution: "Mankind will perforce prey upon itself, like monsters of the deep."

A political consequence of the Mexican War was that all the new territory helped fuel sectional conflict: Will the new States be slave or nonslave, and will its congressmen vote therefore with them or with us? (The idea that voting is nonviolent is wistful; the physical violence is merely at one or two removes.)

But political conflicts can be solved. Another consequence of the Mexican War was self-flagellation. America knows when it does right or wrong. The fact that it does wrong much of the time unites it with all people of all ages and places—but like an individual with a trained conscience (healthy or unhealthy), America gets sick or well, violent or irenic, according to the state of that conscience. And the Mexican War was wrong. From somewhere, from some realm of collective conscience or from some corner of the moral law of action and reaction, came a righteous sentence of fire.

The Old Testament treats nations personally. A nation does evil, it is burned. Its rulers or a handful of its people can corrupt it. There is such a *thing* as a *nation*, and it is so intimate with the individual that no man, woman, or child is too far removed, too insignificant, too uninvolved, to suffer. There may be no real political democracy on earth, but in the moral world, each person is fully responsible and there are no excuses, no escapes. A nation, like an individual, has a conscience; it has a fate, a story, a mind, a heart.

Lewis Thomas thinks one of the great mysteries of the world is bees: together, they form a mind. Is a nation any less a wonder, any less a mind, than a hive of bees?

The United States took half of Mexico's land, on the slimmest sham pretense, and we've kept it. But the U.S. considered itself moral; its individuals had been raised with an idea of decency, Christian virtues, and the notion that violent theft was wrong. Wrong is not a mere verbal judgment, an observation: it is a dynamic force, an action, and actions set in motion other actions and reactions.

Fifty-nine thousand Americans died during the Vietnam War; as of 1990, 159,000 veterans had killed themselves. (The figure includes only death by such obvious weapons as gun and knife; all the others—overdoses, automobile crashes, and so on—were uncounted.) A recent survey of Vietnam vets showed that 25 percent of them were or are suicidal. These are big facts; not an information explosion but explosion information. We're ignoring an elephant behind us in the dark. Our distractions aren't working.

These men felt what they did was wrong. Others may smile at American naive moralism, and rightly despise American hypocrisy; but Americans are stuck with their moral structure, and without it there is nothing here but California. Like it or not, we are a nation of principle. Too many combat soldiers readily or perforce did things blatantly and grossly inimical to their picture of what they and all Americans should be; the guilty American public did not reassure them when they returned; there have been explosions. And implosions.

However, the Mexican War did not affect only the soldiers who fought at Buena Vista and Chepaultapec. It affected the whole country (us included), just as the Vietnam War affected not only the grunts but everyone. The explosion is an oxidizing despair. America seems helpless today. The Civil War generation "saw the elephant"; we try to ignore it. But it doesn't go away.

It's a matter of economy. A human body has circulation. We have been expending everything, and putting nothing of a moral nature back in. Drugs, entertainment, private religion—none of these are nutrients. Out goes the children's education, out go the poor, the homeless, the Hispanics and blacks, out go the old people, out goes Nature itself; out go 159,000 vets and 300,000 Iraqis: the elephant is standing on our chest. Our blood is draining. In come the Japanese. They at least value our real estate.

What is our Real Estate?

Millions of acres were taken from Mexico; millions more simply cleared of Indian people. This is no different from any other place on earth, most of which is stolen land. But we know better.

In Gregory Coco's *Wasted Valor: The Confederate Dead at Gettysburg*, it is mentioned that on the Lutheran Seminary grounds seven Confederate dead bodies were crudely buried "within arms reach" of Dr. Krauth's rear door. Nearly fifty-six bodies were buried, with no names marked, in a shallow trench. The garden of the Schmucker house—like Krauth's, still standing on the Seminary campus—was the grave of more Southern dead.

It is not new for bodies to be laid at the doorstep of religion.

The mainline denominations were never the main line of American Protestant religion. With quite restricted local exceptions, such as the Unitarianism, Congregationalism, and Presbyterianism found in some places in New England, the religious program has belonged to American fundamentalism and American "evangelicalism." These groups are similar to the extent that they may be characterized by biblical literalism. Much of Methodism has been an exception, not believing in biblical inerrancy; and of course the Lutherans at the Gettysburg seminary would have been exceptions too.

But the Confederate young men lying in the soil at the Seminary would not have been evangelicals in the European, Lutheran sense; if they had been believing Christians, they likely would have been literalists. There were revivals in Lee's army, the greatest occurring in 1863. They produced a wide mixture of comfort, inspiration, illusion, discarded pipes and playing cards, resolutions to treat their "servants" better, and Bible reading. One always wonders of the literalist subculture whether it has as profound effects upon spirits as it has had upon politics and public opinion. One hopes not, of course.

It seems, in fact, that the chief product of the literalist, shall we say "fundagelical," engine is more fundagelicals. It is another self-contained economy. And, of course, its chief fault is that it is a *theologiae gloriae*, an economy of glory. Its idea is that by right believing and right behavior (especially as regards trivia, such as accepting biblical inerrancy and not dancing or smoking), you can replace sin with saintliness, damnation with salvation. You change your own human nature this way. The sinner is regenerated, becoming a member of the glorious kingdom preached by Jesus of Nazareth—right now. Many of the soldiers shooting at each other on July 1 believed this.

A fundamental of human nature is selective vision. A literalist need not be smarmy or brutal to be in error, any more than a Nazi needed to be a concentration camp guard. Many of both have been honest, decent, friendly, and sincere people, loving birds and taking good care of their cars. Nevertheless, an economics of glory is an economics of death in the long run. Call it allegiance to the father of lies or immersion in *Maya*, illusion; it is the same tyrannical principle: Whatever I desire is your law; I am your authority.

Presumably the Lutheran professors at the Seminary understood not only the futility but also the evil of such labor—and they would have understood, with Luther, who that work's real employer is. All that those "Dutchmen" *(Krauth? Schmucker!)* could do was look at the graves on their quiet hill, and perhaps wonder what these Americans meant. Luther's well-known phrase "the priesthood of all believers" did not mean that we are each our own priests, but that we are all each other's priests.

It would be tempting to give the world's fundamentalists some simple utensils (so as not to draw everyone else into an apocalypse) and let them fight it out. A dozen years ago, in a neighboring county, an old couple were found dead in their kitchen, blood smeared and splattered everywhere: they had killed each other with fork and spoon. What a slow, implacable ballet of hate, choreographed by the resentment and unfulfilled hopes of decades! So husbands and wives do the deadly work today, if not with fork and spoon, then with morning and evening, with money and sex; a long, twilight struggle, with no pity when the other collapses—with your last strength you crawl as close as if in bed and apply the last enervated strike; and so the religious battle.

All quarrels are domestic, especially religious ones—cruel perversions of the nearest kind of intimacy possible on earth, and the most deadly. So it is not true that fundagelicals produce only fundagelicals; they have made and will make corpses to jam the graveyards of the globe.

Neither North nor South could have sustained or inflicted the protracted butchery of the Civil War without their religion, which not only told them they were right but also comforted them and sustained them when the long lists began coming in. Heroism, self-sacrifice, and mayhem—all inextricably together. Human nature remains what it is.

But the paradox of that nature is that, in spite of all this, humankind is essentially spiritual, and its need is religious. We have set up a prodigious, ferocious economy—a glorious supermarket with nothing that will keep us alive for long, while down the dusty road a shabby man with nowhere to rest his head is trying to give away the one thing we need.

The men under the Seminary sod had no doubt been destitute. Confederates carried virtually nothing except a toothbrush stuck in a buttonhole. In their rolled blanket there was just as likely nothing as something. In their haversacks some sugar, flour, a little pork perhaps, some corn, maybe local bread or apples—and somewhere a Testament, deck of cards, pipe, tobacco, needle, extra pair of socks. They were the poor of the earth, "Lee's Miserables"; no two were dressed alike. Their canteens were usually made of wood instead of Yankee tin; their buttons likewise, instead of brass or bone. If they wore jackets, they were perhaps dyed with butternut juice. Southerners wore either homespun cotton or wool in the heat that started in the low 80s on July 1 and got to the upper 80s on July 3. Their undergarments were linen or cotton in summer, and they wore a set until it was bad enough to throw away and there was a replacement available. Their wealth may have been a few Confederate notes, but chiefly a photograph of their wife and small children.

They didn't own a slave, most of them, nor had much use for the class that did, except that they respected them, and had no liking for blacks. They almost all had a hat, and their muskets they kept terribly clean and shiny. They were observed to march in less order but with more spring and spirit than their Northern counterparts; the Northerners marched, unless it rained, in a kind of endurant, almost sullen, silence—but the Rebels talked and joked constantly, and were "incredibly profane."

All they had was the Stars and Bars, each other, Marse Robert, and those memories: wisteria along the fences in the lush, sweet spring, and the dogwood; stillness beside quiet waters in the absolute deep summer; "My Shepherd Shall Supply My Need," sung in the white clapboard church; and the faces and gentle voices at home. For these we will fight, for these we will die rather than let you threaten them; for this is our honor, and this is our glory; this is all we have.

Who shall say, then, that they were poor?

So they lay in their rags on the dirt behind Krauth's house, despised now more than feared, loathed or pitied perhaps, but, I am convinced, never understood. Not for religion they died, not for politics or slavery or money, but for honor, the one word that fixed for them the ineffable dearness of their time and place and people: *honor*, the measureless word of love for their ancient home and acceptance of their chosen fate. The myth of the Old South is not fraudulent—its cypress and molasses, young folks in the quiet summer noons, corn cakes on the stove, afternoons with a cane pole by the river, the dark eyes of the only one who sees your soul—it is the redolence of their undying love.

The Seminary, with its buried thoughts and flesh, reposes with them. Its quiet, leafy trees are clean of time, silent in their uniform of vigilance, ready now to die again with hands outspread, green above the cannons on the glinting sunset lawns, coloring the very lucency of air. There is a photograph of three captured Southerners, taken perhaps some hundred fifty feet from that back door where their bloated comrades lay. They are jaunty and resistant, impermeable and individual: spirit made flesh. Those three may have been stragglers, they may have been survivors. Who among us knows them? The light pale blue of chicory is their heaven's color. These men are mysteries a seminary can't contain, can't keep under ground or in the books; like figures on a fragile bowl, the soldiers in their photographs and graves inscribe a poetry of faith. Silent lawns and old buildings:

> Thou, still-unravished bride of quietness,
>   Thou foster-child of Silence and slow Time,
> Sylvan historian, who canst thus express
>   A flowery tale more sweetly than our rhyme:
> What leaf-fringed legend haunts about thy shape
>   Of deities or mortals, or of both . . . ?

Walt Whitman knew the nature of the War better than anyone else, with the possible exception of Lincoln. It is generally forgotten that this was so, but the man we think of now as a literary man only, said that the War was the center and circumference of his whole life. A great war had its great singer, prophet, and sufferer. Whitman in his forties spent most of the War visiting hospitals—the Washington ones mainly, but also some in the field. He knew soldiers better than anyone—and that is why most of us study war, to know the people.

He also had been an observer of the national scene for years prior to the War. His analysis of the origin of the War is so different, so startling, so simple, and so disturbing, that it has been ignored. But it should not be ignored, because with Lincoln, Whitman speaks of the War not as the scribes and pharisees, but as one with authority. That his statement of the War's origin seems to come out of a different dimension should be no mean recommendation for it. He does acknowledge the central role of slavery. But he also affirms the essential unity of the American character, North and South, the shared beliefs, hopes, and values of each side, the identity of virtues and the agreement on liberty's essential place.

The War did not have to happen. (Lincoln's transcendent cause analysis let us leave aside for the moment.) All the traditionally assigned causes—slavery, tariff, states' rights, abolitionism—existed before the War, and could have been dealt with also during the 1850s and in 1860.

The material cause of the War, according to Whitman, was the saturation of venality and incompetence throughout American political leadership. His list of the types at a political convention is memorable:

> The members who composed it were, seven eighths of them, the meanest kind of bawling and blowing officeholders, office seekers, pimps, malignants, conspirators, murderers, fancy-men, custom-house clerks, contractors, kept editors, spaniels well trained to carry and fetch, jobbers, infidels, disunionists, terrorists, mail-riflers, slave-catchers, pushers of slavery, creatures of the president, creatures of would-be presidents, spies, bribers, compromisers, lobbyers, sponges, ruined sports . . . crawling, serpentine men—the lousy combings and born freedom-sellers of the earth.

He says these people were elected all across the country, to state houses, city councils, judgeships, commissions; they occupied governor's chairs and the White House. They were out for self-interest, and they were unqualified. Leadership and character, both. Whitman was America's most enthusiastic patriot and its harshest critic.

Webster, Clay, and Calhoun were passing from the scene in the 1850s. Figures like Corwin and Lincoln are highly exceptional; Douglas was exceptional too but charged with questions and uncertainties. Behind these was a mass of midgets. This seems clear when one reads of the decades before the War; the contrast to the first generation of the Republic is stark.

Still, Whitman's answer has not been accepted. Why? Because he was not a political analyst or historian—yet he was. Because his answer is too hard to deal with, surely. Slavery can be dismissed today in a literal sense. It can also be explained. But how do you explain the influx of inferior political material? And more to the immediate point, How do you dismiss them? The ones waiting behind them are as bad.

Whitman's analysis must be traced to the American people themselves. Here we arrive at a baffling contradiction of the War. Whitman recorded an American character sterling in its profoundest qualities:

> One night in the gloomiest period of the war . . . as I stood by the bedside of a Pennsylvania soldier who lay, conscious of quick approaching death, yet perfectly calm and with noble, spiritual manner, the veteran surgeon, turning aside, said to me that though he had witnessed many, many deaths of

soldiers and had been a worker at Bull Run, Antietam, Fredericksburg, etc., he had not seen yet the first case of a man or boy that met the approach of dissolution with cowardly qualms or terror. My own observation fully bears out these remarks.

But at the same time there was a sordidness, shallowness, a seediness about the American scene and body politic. *Simul iustus et peccator*. The Civil War is our image of human nature, our local self-portrait. Somehow two currents within a personality were married, supporting each other yet fundamentally and implacably at war.

The facts are in our hands, but as always meaning is not down at the realm of facts. Because the energy, colors, grand forces, distances, logic-breaking particles, and thought of the universe are ultimately unexplainable and beautiful, the supreme analyses are made by prophets and poets. The great war must have its Homer; its heroes in blue and gray deserve no less, and we must learn or die.

> . . . the land entire saturated, perfumed with their impalpable ashes' exhalation in Nature's chemistry distilled—and shall be so forever—in every future grain of wheat and ear of corn and every flower that grows and every breath we draw.

> The origin and conditions out of which it [the War] arose are full of lessons, full of warnings yet to the Republic, and always will be.

3 Reading

That error breeds error is obvious, at least in the written record of humankind. History is an economy of error, in which the principle of error compounds. Comforts, pleasures, safeties, and abilities have increased; we have inherited these like a mask passed down from generation to generation. But what we see is less than what we get, for evil seldom plays unmasked. Its essence is deception, and it succeeds only through illusion. Good is always fighting on another plane, increasingly invisible as we enter further the world of shows and shadows. If in this late time grace the more abounds, it is only to cover a bulkier multitude of sins. If history has one true face, it also has a thousand hands, each passing a different mask in front of the face.

A few trivial examples from Civil War literature. The simplest is the well-known Gettysburg photograph of dead bodies lying in front of a woods, which for years had been labeled "Dead of the 24th Michigan." William Frassanito has shown that the uniforms are Confederate, not Iron Brigade, and the woods are not McPherson's but Rose's. The photograph was mislabeled years ago, and has been reproduced uncritically ever since. Likewise the photo of a dead supposed sharpshooter in Devil's Den, rifle standing neatly at the little wall he had built, was accepted even to the extent of being displayed by the Park Service on a plaque before the actual, still remaining wall—until Frassanito showed that the photographers had dragged the body from elsewhere and put the rifle there themselves. But such cases are obvious only when someone points them out; until then blindness is impenetrable, though contrary evidence is there to see. We see what we expect or want. Only that fact dawns to which we are awake. The prophet's eyes, more than his mouth, anger king and country.

More influential are attitudes toward rifled muskets, the effectiveness of artillery, and the value of the bayonet. After the Civil War many assumed that the reason for those horrible losses was the invention of the rifled musket. The thinking, which is echoed in writing about the War down to the present, is that the increase in effective range was from 60 yards (Napoleonic) to 300 yards. The change was due to a groove milled into the smooth rifle barrel to make one spiral from breech to muzzle, giving the bullet a spin, enabling a flatter trajectory and a straighter flight. (Actually it was not the barrel but the bullet that enabled the change. The rifled barrel had been around for some time; the Minié ball—called "minnie"—was invented only in the 1850s. The concave base of the soft lead slug would fill and expand with the powder's explosion, making the lead conform to the barrel and groove. Previous bullets or balls either more or less rolled out the barrel upon firing or, if large enough to take the grooving, got stuck.)

It might be observed that the more modern the reader, the more distorted the idea of what "flatter trajectory" meant in 1863. An M-16 shoots a trajectory flat as a pond surface compared to the Springfield rifle-musket. We get the idea from our modern weapons that a Civil War soldier could shoot 100 yards virtually point blank, but this was not the case. The Civil War rifle fired an arc; the bullet went up and came down. This is why officers, even at close range, told their troops to fire at the knees of the enemy. At longer range the effect was increased. The weapon had a sight that had to be adjusted for different ranges, and soldiers had to be reminded to use it.

It is not commonly realized that Civil War soldiers did not get target practice. This is extremely significant. So is the fact that rural men who had done some hunting did not necessarily have an advantage over factory or office workers. To shoot at deer and squirrels is one thing; to shoot at men, *while they are shooting at you*, is another entirely. Winston Churchill said that being shot at "wonderfully concentrates the mind"—but not upon the complicated seventeen-step process of loading a Civil War musket. A battle is virtually nothing but distraction—being shot at, primarily, but also noise, confusing orders, smoke, smell, heat, crowded loading conditions, unfamiliar territory, men getting hit, and your own emotions. Battle creates euphoria, terror, rage, the feeling of invincibility, fatigue, and any number of unpredictable things. You are not your known self. Sometimes you don't really know what you're doing. Some people lose themselves entirely to berserk rage or the unfazeable shock of fear. Thousands of rifles were picked up on the Gettysburg battlefield improperly loaded: two or more loads, a few right up to the muzzle; bullets in first, powder afterward; cartridges rammed in whole; ramrods in the barrel. *Thousands*.

Soldiers were drilled in the "load in nine counts." If they would often fail to do it properly under the pressure and distraction of battle, how can one expect that they would have done properly something they *hadn't* been trained to do—aim and fire? Under the circumstances, they did well: the Confederate ratio of bullets fired to enemies hit, in the high density of Gettysburg, was about 100:1. For the Northerners, who fired much more freely, it was about twice that. (One Yankee praised the Southerners for firing, as he said surely with exaggeration, only once to their 300.)

How rapid was the fire? Again, it is assumed without critical reflection that the drill rate of three loads and fires per minute for a well-trained infantryman applied also to the battlefield. And the more modern we are, the less accurate picture we have when Civil War diarists record what to them were terrific rates of fire. Writers have faithfully repeated this three-shots-per-minute figure from book to book. (It is now, of course, an entirely literary war, with the partial exception of reenactors and, of course, the battlefields; nearly all we have is in books.) But I have fired a Civil War rifle. Now, I am not in the shape of a Civil War veteran (Meade's men might carry up to sixty and more pounds; even Lee's men carried those heavy rifles), nor am I drilled. So we'll leave aside the heaviness of the weapon as a factor, though it must have become more and more a factor the longer a battle went on. The main factor is that the rifle's discharge kicks hell out of you. It's like being hit in the shoulder by Muhammed Ali. Once every time you fire: *Pow!* Soldiers wrote of firing an unusually large number of rounds and becoming black with bruise from the chest all the way to the hand. Meanwhile you are inhaling sulfurous smoke, it's hot and you're wearing wool, *and you're not used to this*. The last time you fired a few shots was seven months ago at Fredericksburg. Three shots a minute? You fired fifteen to twenty-five per half-hour.

How many shots did a man fire during battle? In heavy actions, such as Brawner Farm, unusually efficient infantrymen ran out of the standard forty rounds. But not in fifteen or twenty minutes. Sometimes before an engagement the soldier was given an extra ten or twenty cartridges, which he would have to carry in his pockets. The 20th Maine on Little Round Top ran low on ammunition, even with resupplying themselves from fallen friends. Replenishments were sometimes brought forward to the firing line from the rear. But most soldiers at Gettysburg probably did not run through their forty rounds each day in close action.

The main thing, however, is *how close* the soldiers fought. As far as I know (and I am an illustration of the problem here), until Paddy Griffith, no one really investigated the claim handed down from book to book: Napoleonic close-order tactics continued to be used even after the rifled musket made them suicidal. Civil War generals were lummoxes.

The Napoleonic smoothbore was used by lines of shoulder-to-shoulder men, making a regiment in effect a shotgun. The idea was to break the enemy's line with a solid mass of men; a broken formation resulted in loss of firing effectiveness and command cohesion. You advanced at a walk, shoulder to shoulder, two or three double lines deep: short-range muskets allowed this possibility—but, the tradition says, the new rifles killed soldiers effectively beginning at 300 or even 500 yards, and frontal assaults in the Napoleonic manner were plain butchery. Assume, say, five thousand men able to fire three aimed shots per minute beginning at 300 yards—leaving aside the controversial cannon fire: how did *any* of Pickett's men get to the stone wall?

Griffith finds that the test range of the rifled musket was not the same as its range when used in battle. Civil War soldiers usually fought at Napoleonic distances: 60 yards, often less. In the West, and in the trees along the Chickahominy and Rapidan, and at many locations on most other eastern battlefields, terrain was not open and fields of fire had to be short, even down to 20 yards. The 69th Pennsylvania, positioned in front of the Clump of Trees during Pickett's Charge, were ordered to hold fire until—as in the first battle of the Revolutionary War—they saw "the whites of their eyes." (Each man had a half-dozen or more muskets next to him, loaded with buckshot.)

It seems that the rifle could have made Napoleonic tactics obsolete, but because of the way it was used, it did not.

At Gettysburg Cutler's Brigade engaged in long-range rifle fire against Rodes's attacks on Paul's Brigade, and Pickett's men trying to climb the fence on the Emmitsburg Road found that the rifle could be accurate at 200 yards, but generally the effective fire was delivered very close. Good units tended to hold their fire, and volley at nearly point-blank range, as at the Sunken Road at Antietam; this was extremely effective. Settling down to relatively long-range at-will firefights decreased casualties, as soldiers later in the war learned; and the psychological impact of close fire was eliminated.

At Brawner Farm they stood and fired for two hours at 75 yards. The casualties were so high not because of anybody's rifles (the Wisconsin men had poor weapons anyway) but because of the two hours. Death in the Civil War was related more to courage or bravery than to technology.

Another idea passed on from book to book is that cannons and bayonets were nearly irrelevant weapons. Someone looked up how many soldiers were treated for bayonet wounds and found almost none. Ergo, the weapons were virtually extraneous, romantic pieces of fluff—what an impressive surprise to the average person! The conclusion seems hard-nosed and realistic, but common sense and Griffith contradict. The measure of success in Civil War battle is not how many enemies you kill or disable. Lee took the heavier casualties during the Seven Days, and had nearly the same number killed and wounded as Hooker at Chancellorsville. The idea is to destroy the enemy's cohesion—take his position—disperse his army. The bayonet charge succeeded not by killing but by shocking, as at Little Round Top—a decisive use of the bayonet if there ever was one. (It alone would have justified the presence of the bayonet in the Union army.) And a bayonet might not leave a wound any doctor would be able to treat.

Cannon fire accounted in injuries for roughly its proportion of men, that is, 10 percent of Confederate wounds, 10 percent of the Army of the Potomac serving artillery—very roughly. But its effectiveness was much greater than this. Wounds are only part of the facts. How many atomic-bomb wounds were treated in downtown Hiroshima? Many of the "missing" in battles simply could not be physically found. The great killing power of the Napoleon (favored over the less reliable and less versatile Parrots and 3-inch Rifles) was in the use of canister at close range. If you were in an attacking line and heard the command "Double canister! Load!" you had not long to live. Holes were blown through human lines by shotgun-like blasts of iron spheres the size of golf balls.

Psychological effects should not be overlooked. Artillery sections sometimes fired solid shot at close range simply because of the effect of that load's terrific flash and crack. The associations with solid shot were the worst; its wounds were the most fearsome. And the presence of friendly artillery returning the enemy's punishment was fortifying to infantry, as Hancock knew perhaps too well July 3.

These errors handed down have made the War still more different from itself—which is to say that we know less about how and why those people felt and thought and acted as they did than we think we do, leaving us even more ignorant of ourselves than we know. The sins of the fathers are visited upon the third and fourth generations.

Serious historical work is an effort of the imagination, ultimately to tell, in the words of Thoreau, "not what was, but what is." The imagination is a mill dependent upon its grist; and we are what we think.

Around the time of the Civil War, Nathaniel Hawthorne complained about the "damned lot of scribbling women" selling hundreds of thousands of copies of artless, sentimental novels true to neither circumstance nor imagination. Those popular books appear innocuous enough compared with our novels, certainly compared with our films and videos. But this is to judge by rather superficial moral terms. The fault in the two eras is probably roughly the same: lies of one kind or another. Visions must be true to be good—true to the eye and the heart. It is true and essentially human not to sink too much lower than the angels, or the insects—just as it is true not to try to place oneself too high in relation to them, as the sentimentalist does. Some-how, I think, both errors lead to fighting, and fighting means killing.

Reading is the antidote to reading. Looking at the weapons and the battlefields is a tiny part of how we learn about the War. Griffith's books correct false notions on weapons and tactics; the books of Alan Nolan, Alan Gaff, and Lance Herdegen and William Beaudot tell the story of the Iron Brigade, along with the memoirs of its soldiers and the *Official Records of the War of Rebellion*. Books are the fires with which to consume books.

The volumes of the *Official Records* fill ten shelves. That is nothing to the number of books on the Civil War, fifty thousand when counted some years ago. By now we might have seen that for every book in our library, there is another library full of books—as it was discovered that for every star in our galaxy there is a whole galaxy; and now the scientists, our mythmakers, are thinking there might be other universes. The father of a friend of mine bought out a hospital library—and found a trove of Civil War books, including the *OR* itself. Books are being exhumed like shrapnel and soldiers. Soon we might be trading them like comic books or baseball cards. But for all this we don't know the one thing we want to know: What was it to be a soldier in the Civil War? For that, all we can hope is that the reincarnationists are right, and look into our memories.

Regardless of the value of that theory, are we not in the same position as to the fundamental questions: What is life? Who are we? Where are we? Who and where is God? Deny it though we might, we bring with us into each pleasure, crime, and joy our essential human nature, sick and spiritual. Even if the Bible had a thousand books in it, and commentaries were stacked in the streets, we wouldn't know what we were made to know. Holy books may be inspired, but any inspiration in them is worked in the human heart by the mysterious spirit that moves where it wills. Inspiration would work only hit-and-miss in the mind, which like the holy books themselves is made of time and changes, part of that vast shifting world of illusion. Let the texts bury the texts.

Where then do we turn? What principle do we use to sift the true from false, the good from bad? As a citizen of my world today I should believe that the observer makes the verses jump through this hole or through that. I am uncomfortably aware that someone next year may discover facts to show that cannons were not useful and that the rifled musket changed tactics early in the War. Today *John* is said to have been written in 60 A.D.; yesterday it was written in 110; tomorrow maybe Matthew wrote it. The battlefield itself is like a holy book, motionless yet always moving, palpable but always new. Similarly all the world: infused, shot through, with mystery, terror, and beauty, changeless but changing as we are changing. Neither world nor holy books can be rested in. They baffle us, they tease us out of thought; illusion is suffered to destroy itself; we are born to be reborn.

Today we are aware of the changeability and subjectivity of intellectual truth: this is a philosophic version of the View of Death such as is seen when ages are about to pass, when civilizations fail, and new armies march to Bethlehem for birth. Our books—historical, scientific, literary—are like the cadaverous statuary of fifteenth-century Europe: a *danse macabre,* a waning of the age.

Books are mirrors. Do we read the facts and numbers, read the meteorology, but not the signs of the times?

4 Sounds

Many an irksome noise,

go a long way off,

is heard as music,

a proud sweet satire

on the meanness

of our lives.

—Thoreau

They sang songs they would die to. "Sweet Evelina," "Aura Lea," "The Battle Cry of Freedom," "Dixie." Their songs reached into the heart. We call them sentimental.

This is a great paradox of the Civil War. The most terrible four years in our history were part of what is known as "The Great Sentimental Age":

> The years creep slowly by, Lorena,
> The snow is on the grass again,
> The sun's low down the sky, Lorena,
> The frost gleams where the flow'rs have been.
>
> But the heart throbs on as warmly now,
> As when the summer days were nigh;
> Oh, the sun can never dip so low,
> A-down affection's cloudless sky.

The sentimentality was unabashed, sounding beautifully innocent to us:

> A hundred months have passed, Lorena,
> Since last I held that hand in mine,
> And oh, our hearts beat fast, Lorena,
> Though mine beat faster far than thine.

It is the connection of death with this ready feeling that puzzles and embarrasses us—yet it is a natural connection.

Death and love, with one more element we seem to have lost:

> There is a future, O thank God,
> Of life this is so small a part,
> 'Tis dust to dust beneath the sod;
> But there, up there, 'tis heart to heart.

One of the two or three most popular songs of the war and associated particularly with Southern troops, "Lorena" was written by a
Wisconsin minister. A married man, he had fallen in love with
someone else. He bit the bullet; he did not leave his marriage but
lived the long, low, dull hope of his faith. Soldiers sick for home and
love sang his song through the war. Now such a song would be
discouraged by the authorities as being demoralizing, perhaps. But
Civil War soldiers were strangely honest; they sang about death and
home and grief:

> Sometimes I feel like a motherless child,
> Sometimes I feel like a motherless child,
> Sometimes I feel like a motherless child,
> A long ways from home.

I wonder what that most "sentimental" of writers would have
thought had he seen the yellow ribbons all over Elkhorn, Wisconsin,
this spring during the "Gulf War." There is some kind of lie, somewhere, in actual sentimentality, which substitutes a programmed
response for a real experience. "Lorena" and the soldiers' feelings
were real, however. Perhaps some of those sensations around the
pianos in the evening parlors were easy, but the War visited so many
families. One cannot without self-contempt compare at length the
feelings of America during the Civil War and the pathetic yellow-
ribbon stuff of 1980 and 1991. This year's sentimentality came
cheap to the country taken as a whole—hardly an American family
was stabbed by that campaign. But the cheaper the sentimentality
the more murderous, because actual sentimentality *covers* real experience: 100,000 Iraqis dead for what? And the number still rising;
and this doesn't count the blind or the maimed. Not that in war you
ever pity the enemy, but our government learned a lesson—the
wrong one—from Vietnam and applied it with a thoroughness that
would have left Joseph Goebbels breathless with admiration: don't
let the people know what's happening. No pictures of wounded or
dead people—ours or theirs. We kicked their butts all right. Carpet
bombing, blood in the air like drizzle, pieces of humans—brains,
hair, teeth. Butts.

This is how one of their songs, back then, viewed someone who got his butt kicked:

> Into the ward of the clean white-wash'd halls,
> Where the dead slept and the dying lay
> Wounded by bayonets, sabres, and balls,
> Somebody's darling was borne one day.
> Somebody's darling, so young and so brave,
> Wearing still on his sweet, yet pale face—
> Soon to be hid in the dust of the grave—
> The lingering light of his boyhood's grace.
> Somebody's darling, somebody's pride.
> Who'll tell his mother where her boy died?

Both sides during the Civil War took as much as they inflicted. Would we have taken 100,000 dead in four weeks this year? (Or one million, which is proportionally closer to the United States' population.) Our sentimentality is much more vicious than theirs was; and sentimentality is vicious. But theirs was more than sentimentality, it was sentiment, and they were larger than we are: they took it all, they looked at Brady's and Sullivan's photographs of the dead, they saw their boys come home in boxes by the tens of thousands, they wept, they cheered, they endured, they wondered, they rioted, they believed, they sang.

> Sometimes I feel like I'm almos' gone,
> Way up in de heav'nly lan'.

After the end they were too weak to let memories stand, and the war took on the real sentimentality: it became romance instead of tragedy; the *theologiae crucis* of Lincoln was replaced by a popular *theologiae gloriae* some of the veterans themselves helped to invent. What you can stand when it happens you cannot stand in retrospect; what you have learned about yourself you cannot leave alone. The Civil War is really a problem of *exegesis*, of reading out from, but of course, like all history, it has become *isegesis*, reading into.

That is the nature of history, especially in this age of quantum physics, when we have either realized or decided that all observed phenomena are affected by the observer. There is no naked eyeball, in Emerson's sense, but only manipulation by those with something at stake.

And what we have made of the Civil War! Our mythic history of the War exposes a wistful racism: we have made of the prewar South the Antebellum South, white-columned, redolent with magnolia (not verbena); a fine, high civilization, characterized by honor and reserve, apotheosized by Robert E. Lee. The North has become in Bruce Catton a prototype of the egalitarian, free-opportunity republic we think we are. Both inventions in their own way ignore the black man and woman—and *that* is characteristic of us.

I've always thought Bruce Catton got the *sound* of the War wrong. He translated it into mid-twentieth-century tones, but as Frost says, "poetry is that which is lost in translation." It was an age of poetry, and only poetry in the original language preserves the sound of the times, the feelings of its people, their authentic thoughts and spirits. One must read Walt Whitman to hear what he called "the real war" that will never get into our books. They were another people, those Northerners and Southerners, and it was a different time. The boys, men, women in blue and butternut and gray did not fight, think, talk, feel, or believe like GIs.

Most of all it was their songs that tell us what they were like, what it was like—not only the words but the melodies. Perhaps there is no such thing as Thoreau's "simply seeing," and it may be likewise impossible now to simply listen:

Just before the battle, Mother,
I am thinking most of you,
While upon the field we're watching,
With the enemy in view.
Comrades brave are round me lying,
Filled with thoughts of home and God;
For well they know that on the morrow,
Some will sleep beneath the sod.

. . .
Hear the "Battle Cry of Freedom,"
How it swells upon the air;
Oh, yes, we'll rally round the standard,
Or we'll perish nobly there.

Civil War songs span the range and variety of human nature. "Oh, I'm a Good Old Rebel" is as vicious a song as you'd care for, and "The Invalid Corps" as funny and unkind. Each side had its pointed ones:

Jeffdavise rides a white horse,
Lincoln rides a mule,
Jeffdavise is a gentleman,
And Lincoln is a fule.

But the fact itself is nearly beyond comprehension: the soldiers sang. They had bands, though their numbers diminished as the War went on and the world became modern. For the Civil War was its own anti-dote: as illusion became disillusionment, sentiment became sentimentality, blood became roses, romance became what is erroneously called realism.

The real soldiers, when they finished singing around the campfires, fell silent as the bands (sometimes on both sides of the picket lines) took up "Home Sweet Home." Eyes misted; the soldiers began to sing. For this was the favorite of all Civil War songs. They wanted, like all veteran soldiers in all times and places, to go home.

Why did they do it all, then? I think there was something more than the causes of the War that caused the War. The songs tell us; the volunteers of the first two years of the War fought out of the fullness of their hearts. There is a certain madness that compels a soldier, not only in battle, but before battle. It may be crowd psychology, but even that has a foundation; there is a necessity no one understands.

The War's mystery might bear a tragic interpretation. It was a fate few deserved, a fate easily avoidable by rational human beings normally, or by those who could *see*. Each side expected "a result less fundamental and astounding." Southerners fought for their homes, their freedom, their beliefs; so did Northerners. There was only one

American culture, one American tradition, no irreducible Sections, a tiny minority of fire-eaters and incompetents—"and the war came." What was this irresistible fullness in their hearts?

On US Route 30, the Chambersburg Pike, you hear the heavy trucks, the rushing servile swish of cars, and if you're out tramping from the Railroad Cut to McPherson's Woods it's a menacing string of inconvenience through which you venture your keester at undignified speed. No orderly advance like Cutler's men, no defiant slow withdrawal like the Black Hat Brigade—just pick your spot and run like hell. This, at a glimpse, is the difference between their era and ours, but we are kidding ourselves if we don't admit that *they* gave us this.

Gettysburg is interesting because it's right on the cusp—the cusp of just about everything, including the interval between the volunteers of '61 and '62 and the draftees of late '63 and following. After Gettysburg, the veterans had enough of gallantry for gallantry's sake. Unless ordered otherwise, you kept your head down and your tail low. You learned that the Shermans and the Sheridans were taking over, and it was men like them who would win wars and probably always had. Let the French have their *élan;* we'll take German artillery. In Patton's ungentlemanly and ungallant phrasing, the idea is to make the *other* poor bastard die for *his* country.

I would object to the Chambersburg highway except it's the road I usually arrive on. When we visit the past, we get there in a Toyota. We see with what we are.

There is a mean ugliness about what we are. This applies foremost to our common human nature, of course, but I intend the more superficial manifestation—our daily lives. It's hard to believe that the American Way of Life was arrived at any other way than on purpose. How could randomness produce Toys R Us? A sharp intelligence is at work here. You leave your suburban split-level in a rattling big General Motors sedan (a startling visual and conceptual phenomenon in itself), stop at Burger World on a fast-food strip for some fries and a Coke, spend a couple hours in Sudbury Towers Mall grabbing a snack at Snacktown while the kids play among big plastic, go home through the Eighth Circle of suburban Chicago traffic, arrive in time to catch

"America's Funniest Home Videos," plug in a video of Metalcop VI afterward, watch the local "news," and go to perdition.

The reason I go to Gettysburg is that it's the most beautiful place on earth: the weathered fences across green pastures, the familiar barns and always strange monuments amidst silent standing cannon; still, slow time, and ever-returning time; a vast mystic garden of vegetable gold, a strange perplexing peace deeper than memory. It was not always so.

Gettysburg produced the greatest ugliness in North America. Even the buzzards left after the cannonade and attack of July 3. The place was shot apart. Trees were blasted to splinters or filled with poisonous bullets. Compute the gallons and pounds of urine and turds from 50,000 horses and mules and 150,000 toxic human beings. The humans wore wool clothing, and that smell, with the sulfurous blackpowder smoke, must have been like a Nixon press conference. But I don't refer to these items; what I'm thinking of is human limbs everywhere, brains dashed against the rocks at Devil's Den, sun-blackened, swollen corpses, and the smell that on July 5 made veterans vomit. You can't approach this kind of thing even with a K-Mart, of which there are 514 on US Route 30 between Atlantic City and the Pacific Coast.

You see I bought this pen and paper, not at a K-Mart perhaps, but at a place very much like, just as I get my notions about what's going on from radio and television. My information on such items as what really happened in "high"-level discussions pertaining to Iran-Contra comes from press conferences conducted by Mr. Bush himself. My Vice President is Dan Quayle.

So I can hardly complain; I just have this feeling that all is not as it ought to be. Yet the beauty of Gettysburg, after "what they did there," gives a profound and sustaining hope. To such I return, with ever-returning spring.

When I have been in Gettysburg with a car I have listened to rock music, loud, going from one site to another—the dependency of a degenerate addict to music. Perhaps I do this to make up for the unaccustomed silence—no radio, no classical discs, no television, little conversation aside from the silly things I say to myself. Perhaps I do this to make sense of what I see.

We are beings of several senses rather than a single one, and we become disoriented when all our signals are not the same. Isn't it the same world out there, one sense or another—one thought or another? A blue lake and powerboats? A man saying one thing when we know the truth is another? A powerful, omniscient, good God—and Gettysburg? We live perilously when sight and sound do not match, when words and music deny each other; the unconsidered life is a dangerous disharmony, unheard by the conscious mind but known in the stomach.

Will music harmonize our inarticulate memories with what we see now? I would have thought that the music lingering over McPherson's Woods would be the Third Movement of Schubert's *Ninth Symphony.* But one spring ten years ago as I walked toward those woods I heard the droned grinding of an approaching tractor, and above that, sudden clear and loud music. The man working the field had a huge radio mounted on the tractor, and as he plowed the field which the Iron Brigade crossed, up came the words of a song. I walked toward the woods and still heard it, and even now, within the irresistible heroism of the *Ninth*'s "Trio," I hear it still: those who are afraid to die will never learn to live.

Why can we never forget what they did there? What is our involvement with those hundred-fifty thousand now? What was our involvement then, dearer than life and deeper than memory? Do their songs sound familiar? Is this the wheel of birth and death?

What is not reconcilable in thought is harmonized in song. O powerful western fallen star—solitary singer—sprig of lilac on the black-draped past . . .

The rifle-muskets on display are terrible. We think of Civil War rifles as quaint and old, rusty perhaps; not things you'd fire. But in the glass cases they gleam, heavy and dutiful. At the displays in that inauthentic place, the National Military Park Visitor Center, the war becomes more real, because there you can see that its weapons were real.

Their sound was only a cracking pop, but when heard from a distance, after the thump of artillery, their sound was terrible. The infantry volleys and sustained fire meant serious killing, real battle. Such noise was compared to the tearing of canvas; the tearing of souls from bodies, of eternity from time.

The bullets from those rifles didn't leave much to repair where they struck. You get sick of the war when you see the weapons in their cases. To kill a human body is the most evil thing there is, the greatest usurpation. To pound or chop or shoot a creation meant to mate here with a soul, meant to think and sing and walk—for what purpose and by what right? With what justification may it be done?

Along with rifle fire, the worst sound—even worse—was the order given by an artillery officer for a double or triple charge of canister. That and then perhaps the metallic clang of the brass Napoleon—the last sounds you heard.

A howitzer made a hollow *whump*. Three-inch rifled cannon fired a vicious report with a rush of air. Its grooved shells were heavy iron.

Solid shot, while not being as deadly as spherical case (round shot with a charge inside) or shells, was the most hideous, the most frightening. Texas boys approaching Devil's Den on the Second Day saw the lead man in their column decapitated by a solid shot.

All these tools are on display. Only the sounds of them, and the effects of them, remain for the imagination. One would not want to know the old sounds connected to the present-day sights on display; it is enough, too much, that they are suggested. The voluminous growl that battle sounded like, the curses around Devil's Den after both sides were licked July 2, the demoniacal howls after the shocking battle in McPherson's Woods, the screams and moans of the wounded and dying, the squeaking of gasses from bloated bodies, the command *"Fi—"*

Why do we go back? We are sick of war. General Lee's nonsensical statement tells part of it: "It is well that war is so terrible, else we should grow fond of it." *That* is part of it, its terrible beauty. But he meant the beauty of serried ranks, the terrible beauty of an army with banners. Lee was a war lover, but we are not, nor do we see the Army of the Potomac approaching over sloping fields, bright flags in the clear air. What interests us now, after all these years, after the last lone veteran is gone, his statue only gazing where the Virginians and North Carolinians came in gray lines over the wide July field to scream and die before the Yankee iron and brass?

It is a new beauty, an aspect of beauty ageless, reconciliation of agony and honor in silent glory, a still mystery. Who can touch it? Have we bought it with our lives, this beauty? It was not too high a price. It is heaven won by sacrifice, by the last full measure of devotion, winning not mere political freedom but complete freedom: Beauty. The ineffable answer to the questions.

> "All quiet along the Potomac tonight,"
> Where the soldiers lie peacefully dreaming.
> . . .
> While the stars up above, with their glittering eyes,
> Keep guard over the army while sleeping.

5 Visitors

In dealing with truth we
are immortal.

—Thoreau

On the Confederate side many black men served as teamsters, orderlies, and servants. They were in a sense visitors. Drovers, washwomen, merchants, and many others traveled behind the Union army; after the battle doctors, nurses male and female, undertakers came to Gettysburg, and relatives searching for their dead and wounded. Likewise correspondents and later photographers, historians, politicians, and tourists have come as noncombatants; and the battle, after the combatants left, has become theirs—or rather ours. It was in fact ours all along. The soldiers did not fight it for themselves, but for causes which gave the battle its existence and, finally, meaning. Gettysburg is a place of visitors.

An acquaintance whom I consider reliable in most respects has said that as he sat in a library about six weeks after his father's death, he became aware of his father's presence. It lasted for a short while—perhaps only an instant in physical time—but during the quarter-hour or so the effect remained he was for the only time in his life absolutely fearless, and said he would have faced a firing squad with entire indifference. He knew it was his father more reliably than he had ever known anything; the experience was more reliable than any skeptical arguments or evidence, and the fruits of the experience were benign and of a high order.

Similarly, visionaries report that the visitations they receive impart a certitude somehow firmer than knowledge or conviction, and generally not as intolerant. Mystics *know* in a sense the rest of us do not; and if the fruits of their experiences are peacefulness, love, and courage, we should be embarrassed to quibble.

But our resistance to such experiences and visitations is strong, even though it may be at least as bizarre as the events themselves. (That a useful meaning has not been established for the word "authentic" as applied to such experiences leaves quibblers undaunted.) I heard a Protestant fundamentalist assert positively that the reported experiences at Medjugorje are not authentic because, of all things, adoration of the Virgin Mary is "not biblical." The visions, messages, and healings, in his view, therefore are either psychological in origin or, more likely, are demonic. (It is amazing the lengths to which the devil will go to fool the rest of us, not being able to get around these clever fundamentalists.) Tell that to the blind who see and the lame who walk; tell it to someone who has seen a field filled with angels.

Perhaps all these miracles, sightings, visions, transports are mere hysteria brought on by a sense in the Western world of impending doom. Carl Jung noted ten years before the Second World War that something dark was moving in the Germanic unconscious. Death has overwhelmed us; the very denial of it is as much a symptom as anything. As the nuclear threat eases temporarily, we become more conscious that the humanly inhabitable world is suffocating in a poison we can't seem to swear off. Economic disaster waits around some corner, and death by crime or accident proliferates like artillery shells. This has been the century of death unequaled, and all of it seems now mere prelude, overshadowed by what waits. This would be a time for visions, dreams, escapes.

But none of them is new. It is only that now, under this pressure, we acknowledge once again the odd encounterings in human life, the meetings so different yet so exactly right. Perception changes more than things, as facts shift with attention. This century has shown the limits of the rational, so once again we listen for these visitors.

"Courage!" they often say. They should not have to tell us this, assuming they do; it is within our field of memory, if not our field of view.

The real grip of Gettysburg on most people who are affected by it is its uncanniness. Visitors drive and walk among the rows of strangely tense monuments and fields where it seems the echo has just this instant died, and are surprised the place feels as "interesting" as it does. The battle itself presents a study of what-ifs and nearlys, and one is always on the edge of wondering about divine intervention. What glimmers in the still heat? And someone once has seen here the charioteer with the mild, clear eyes. "There is something about the place that gets you," people have said.

Sometimes I find myself as interested in the visitors to the field as I am in the battle. One told me that the first time he walked onto the Rose Farm he involuntarily said aloud, "I died on this farm." He had dreamt twenty years before that he had been shot in a field where a high hill—which he now identifies as Round Top—stood off to the right, and a stone house—the Rose house—was in front on his left. He now looks for the low stone wall he lay behind, but in several trips to the farm he has not found it, and I doubt he will. But I now look for it myself.

A stranger talks more freely than the closest relative at times; he does not have to live with a skeptic, or with someone who nurses in her heart the quiet conviction that he is a fool. A noble gentleman from Virginia once told me that he had lost his thirty-year-old son just recently; he seemed like a father who might have quietly walked the fields and hospitals looking, in the summer of 1863.

I always wonder whether some meetings are arranged.

I like the tourists at Gettysburg; I suppose I had better. Anyone who comes to Gettysburg must have something of the original image in them. They keep me company. These are lonely fields, with only the past in them, and death, and heroism. The place is a vast cemetery, but it is not this at all; it is the beauty of the place that begs company. At times the sky opens, and then you need someone else to see it too; millions per year are not too many.

The soldiers themselves were visitors, of course.

Wesley Culp was part visitor, part returnee. He died on his uncle's hill, not having been able in the flesh to deliver that message to Jenny Wade, the only civilian killed in the battle. What extraordinary lengths are gone to sometimes, to deliver messages.

Ornithologists think that the buzzards living now on Round Top are descendants of those which were attracted to Gettysburg after the battle, wheeling intently from as far away as New England. There must be something still to feed on. In walking the summit of Round Top one feels in spite of oneself a bit uneasy, vaguely penitent.

I usually meet Germans when I visit Gettysburg. I want to ask one day whether the place is uncanny to them also, or whether it works only upon us who have the mental categories and whose memories lie sleeping on these fields. The Germans are inheritors of evil too, like all of us, but more obviously so, and they raise a question here. What Bergen-Belsen, Dachau, Buchenwald have we in our back-yards, whose chimneys tinge our skies, whose administrators drink in our restaurants and hire us to do their laundry or deliver their goods, whose work we profit from and maintain our intimate igno-rance of? But it couldn't happen here we say, walking the fields of Gettysburg.

I wonder if I meet them on schedule, exact as that of the *Bundesbahn*.

Angels, or messengers, are sometimes sent in prophet's clothing:

> An end! The end has come
>   upon the four corners of the land.
> I will punish you for your ways,
>   while your abominations are among you.

Such visitors are usually unwelcome, except by the wise. Prophets are essentially witnesses, who at a touch from somewhere become minis-ters of fire. What they see of heaven and of earth strikes the tinder of their tongues.

Germany during Hitler's years had a large state church, a popular religion, though obviously it was a secular country. The small inde-pendent Confessing Church, wanting to save Germans from them-selves, criticized and pulled the reins of Christianity back from the zyklon chariot of the state. Outsiders these pastors and people were, rounded up for concentration camps; they spread like ashes in the darkening sky.

Hitler was elected, by a minority, and then supported because he promised and delivered new pride in the nation, brought jobs and relief from depression, though of course it was at a certain hidden cost, and enabled the people to cherish their prejudices; one difference from 1980 here is that Hitler didn't sell off Germany's future.

The old generation in Germany has never confessed its guilt, but as in the Jewish cemetery whose broken-down headstones waited up the hillside from where I lived for a couple of years, the past lies waking somewhere. It will make its demands. The more it is ignored, the stronger it will have to become to slip in.

For years afterward families came to Gettysburg to find bodies and send them home. Compared with their interest, how academic ours must seem! They carried the richest elements of the field away, but Gettysburg, like the precincts of heaven, accrues rather than diminishes by such deductions from the soil. It is more fertile now than ever.

Thousands of Southerners were left on the field after the battle, under falling echoes of the solid vigor of Union cheers. Some nights you can see them in the Milky Way, in ranks and rows behind the rising faces of the newly dead: exchanged, transformed, and recovered from the steamy sacred pain of battle death.

Of all the visitors to Gettysburg, President Lincoln was the strangest. Nobody knew him. His face alone was incomprehensible; Whitman said there was no accurate portrait; a penetrating eye and another ghostly one still more penetrating, the mouth meaning "I'll break your arm if I have to and I can"; no malice there, and no nonsense. He was the kind of man who could have embarrassed Mark Twain just by looking at him, and entertained him; the kind of man who could have shaken hands with Henry Thoreau. They've tried since his day to make a simple rail-splitter of him—a man whose law practice earned him more money than the governor of Illinois was paid; whom everyone called "Mr. Lincoln" and nobody "Abe" more than once: they've tried to erase him but there's a residue that can't be handled or masked. That's a particle of the real man. Is he really gone, and not heard from since?

His speech at Gettysburg was war propaganda but it was also an early stage in his trying to explain the War to himself. What he said is less penetrating than how he said it. Where did he get those sounds?

What was he listening to? Did he hear some Urania who intincted his ear with cadences to justify the ways of God to man?

Afterward his Second Inaugural Address and death seemed true and righteous altogether, striking at last the mystic chords of memory that no appeal, no reason, no interest could reach before; and the better angels of our nature wait.

I'm sure I have entertained angels unaware at Gettysburg. This spring the field Kershaw advanced across was plowed in high ripples of chunky, crumbly soil, and I chose to march over it, in reverse of his direction, a baked bookster in the sun, hat aslant, pen and notecards spilling with the sunglasses, boots and workman's outfit: Yo, Land Surfer! in a tube of history, plunging with each infant step; self-appointed inspector of battles, diddling with the sacred. I can almost hear the laughter. "You don't have it right—and you'll *never* get it right!" Surely such absurdity is not in vain, and the six-winged cherubim are kind. Maybe?

On Cemetery Ridge one clear night I stood near the Clump of Trees. I saw no angels, or spirits either; it was difficult enough to picture the brave, dying men at Cushing's guns. I thought it would be my last visit for a while, so I tried again to pierce the historian's quietude. As if in comment a nearby carillon began playing "I'm a Yankee Doodle Dandy." The stars up above, silent ministers of fire, were amused no doubt, if they happened to notice, and thought their own thoughts, high above.

> *Sylvan historian . . .*
> *What leaf-fringed legend haunts about thy shape*
>   *Of deities or mortals, or of both . . . ?*

6 McPherson's Woods

The greatest gains and
values are farthest from
being appreciated.
We easily come
to doubt if they
exist.

—Thoreau

Just who began the infantry battle is in dispute. It was probably Cutler's Brigade, rather than the Iron Brigade, but some Wisconsin veterans who wrote about the battle were convinced their charge took place before Cutler's New Yorkers and Pennsylvanians were fired on by Davis's Mississippians. On the other side, an officer claiming the first volley for the 56th Pennsylvania added that they also had the distinction of "running like sheep" immediately afterward. The midwesterners and easterners probably didn't see each other arrive, fixed as their attention was upon the Confederates directly in front of them in each case; the disagreement is no doubt an honest one. But it was sharpened by the distrust midwesterners feel for the East and by the attitude of superiority common among easterners; someone in the 14th Brooklyn's trying to steal a flag captured by the 6th Wisconsin didn't help any. The dispute over who began the infantry firing is indicative of how confusing battle is and suggests that, as Heinrich Böll says, the most problematic part of memory is sequence.

The first weapon was fired early in the morning by a cavalryman from Wheaton, Illinois, taking a potshot at distant Confederate skirmishers and then skedaddling. Some time after that—about 8:00 A.M. that warm, humid Wednesday, July 1—General Buford established his cavalry line on Herr Ridge, and though falling back to McPherson's Ridge, held off the Southern infantry for two hours. General John Reynolds arrived on the field during the cavalry fight, studied the situation, ordered Buford to try to hold on, and galloped back to hurry up his first division. He had decided to make the fight right here.

Meade, Reynolds's old friend, had been in command of the Army of the Potomac only four days. He dealt well with the calamity of being put in command (a command which Reynolds had declined early in June, not wanting the interference from Washington that came with it). Hooker, his otherwise able predecessor whose tenuous character had collapsed at Chancellorsville, had done a good job of getting the Army on the move northward, judiciously keeping himself between Lee and Washington without committing all his corps to one place yet not fanning too much—and moving a whole lot faster than Robert E. Lee was willing to believe an army of Yankees could move. Now Meade was having to decide how aggressive to be: advance into Pennsylvania, or wait on a good defensive line in Maryland? He did both.

Meade ordered Reynolds, thought by many to be the Union's best general, to take command of the left wing of the Army—Buford's cavalry, Reynolds's own First Corps (now commanded by Abner Doubleday, the noninventor of baseball), Sickles's Third Corps, and Howard's Eleventh. This was one-third of the Army; it was ordered to advance to Gettysburg.

Not that anyone planned to fight exactly there. But it was, as Rhett Butler termed it, a "crossroads town"—a hub, a web, or perhaps a net in the Aeschylean sense—and you couldn't get there from here without going through *that*. There was a curious blindness and necessity about the two powerful armies' movement there.

Lee's army had spread out to collect supplies. This was done partly to take the war out of Virginia for a change, and allow its farmers to gather in their crops. It was also done to grab as much as was more or less decently possible. The famous restraint ordered by Lee as pertains to foraging requires, and probably bears, some scrutiny. It is well known that Lee issued orders restraining his troops from wanton destruction and theft of civilian property. The motivation for and nature of General Orders No. 73 are interesting.

> . . . the duties exacted of us by civilization and Christianity are not less obligatory in the country of the enemy than in our own.

The commanding general considers that no greater disgrace could befall the army, and through it our whole people, than the perpetration of the barbarous outrages upon the unarmed and defenseless and the wanton destruction of private property that have marked the course of the enemy in our own country.

Such proceedings not only degrade the perpetrators and all connected with them, but are subversive of the discipline and efficiency of the army, and destructive of the ends of our present movement.

It must be remembered that we make war only upon armed men, and that we cannot take vengeance for the wrongs our people have suffered without lowering ourselves in the eyes of all whose abhorrence has been excited by the atrocities of our enemies, and offending against Him to whom vengeance belongeth, without whose favor and support our efforts must all prove in vain.

There are two sides to the matter. One is that the order *was* meant to restrain the kind of vandalism perpetrated by Federal troops in the Shenandoah Valley. It was not a modern order; it did not sanction wholesale devastation of a civilian population. This is the chief point. We are, by comparison, barbarians.

On the other hand the orders (Nos. 72 and 73), while decent, were not angelic. "Requisitioned" (No. 72) goods were to be paid for in Confederate money—worth as much in the North as legal tender then as it would be now—and civilians had no option of refusing. It was organized, euphemized theft. But why not simply cut a smoking swath through Pennsylvania, as Sherman was to do next year in Georgia? The reasons, in ascending order of importance, are self-serving entirely, rather than saintly—though they existed within a context of decency more or less:

3. Pillaging would alienate the population and potential foreign friends.
2. Pillaging would cause the morale of Lee's army to deteriorate.
1. Lee believed that God would not prosper, in the long run, an army which violated the laws of decency and Christian conduct.

The religious reason was foremost in Lee's mind. I wonder whether it was part of his mistake during July 2 and 3; I wonder whether it was an element of what appears to be fatal pride behind the defeat. His attitude was not one of complete arrogance in going to battle. Lee is said to have expressed great anxiety as to Stuart's whereabouts, as he rode toward the sounds of A. P. Hill's guns at Gettysburg on July 1, remarking that the ravines and gorges they were passing could be retreated back through and would "shelter us from disaster." The account of these unexpected remarks sounds so much like Lee's language that it has to be credited. But the first day appeared to be such a success, and so Providential in timing, that Lee might well have thought that God was on the side of the decent battalions—the Southern ones.

Educated, articulate Southerners were in general eminently decent, and compare favorably to their Northern counterparts. *The Children of Pride* (edited by Robert Manson Meyers), for example—an immense collection of letters written among a Southern family—shows religious, sensitive, Christian people upset and alarmed by Northerners, who seem crass, dissolute, and hypocritical by comparison. They are eminently fine people. On the basis of their thoughts, one could hardly believe that a just God would allow them to be defeated by an avaricious, immoral, destructive society, the forerunner of our own. The American idea of God's favor is crudely material and worldly, as if the New Testament had never been written. If the Master of the Universe came to us mounted on a bicycle we would flatly refuse to believe our eyes. And we Americans have always felt ourselves to be specially favored by God. Perhaps it's our capitalism that He especially admires. Or it could be freedom; though the connection between American freedoms and the freedom proclaimed in the four Gospels has not been established. The problem of the moral life is that it is conducted in a fog like the fog of war. The more vast and fundamental the crime, the less perceived by its perpetrators. The recent megacelebrations on our otherwise tragic streets did not seem to embarrass the American public. Human nature did not change with the Declaration of Independence. What is our counterpart to antebellum slavery?

Anyway, Lee did not think he and his men could lose to Yankees. (Even at Appomattox, they had not lost; they had been "compelled to yield to overwhelming numbers and resources.") We generally see not what is there but what we are looking for. But where we twentieth-century Westerners expect to see evidence of randomness and subjectivity, Lee expected to see an orderly unfolding of God's favor toward the relatively righteous South. He saw, not what happened, but what ought to have happened, on the first day at Gettysburg. He trusted in God's justice, which is as usual a way of saying his own idea of justice.

Henry Heth, whose division initiated the action, is an exaggerated, rather pathetic, example of this—almost comic, in fact. Heth is a lower-order character, however, because his motives were blatantly personal. (After Gettysburg, at Falling Waters, Heth tried to cover up his failures and his casualties again.)

Heth went in, with the carelessly confident approval of A. P. Hill—who knew of Lee's directions not to "bring on a general engagement"—in order to get shoes for his troops. This would have been a stupid reason, because Early's Division had passed through Gettysburg only four days ago, and could have been expected to have cleaned the place out. (Leaving Confederate money.) John Mosby later speculated that Hill and Heth wanted to scoop up some Yankees to present to Lee: glory.

So one of Heth's brigadiers became the first of Lee's generals to be captured by "those people," and a humiliating number of his people were captured with General Archer; officers were down, Archer's Brigade lost nearly 60 percent killed, wounded, missing, and Davis's Brigade 45 percent with missing grossly underreported; Pettigrew's Brigade lost heavily also but all these figures are hard to separate from the division's loss during Pickett's Charge two days later.

That's one of the problems here. Heth didn't give an honest account of his division's being mauled, so the division, under Pettigrew, was used alongside Pickett's on the third day. Not that it would have made much difference except to offer more targets, but Lee would have liked to have known. Heth himself wasn't on hand because a bullet had hit his hatband and with his headache and dismaying losses July 1, he wasn't able to function on the field. Somewhere he had requisitioned too big a hat, and had stuffed a wad of newspaper inside to make things fit, and the bullet's impact was cushioned by the newsprint. The moral is that it's good to steal hats. (That wasn't the first or last time the impact of reality was muffled rather than clarified by newspapers. What Heth had in his hatband was an edition of *CSA*

Today. The descendants of those who wrote for that paper in 1863 were the journalists who covered the Reagan Presidency.)

Henry Heth—one of the few generals Lee called by the first name (Harry)—wrote an amusing report after the battle. Its purpose was not the entertainment of posterity, however, but the justification of himself. He stated that his objective in going toward Gettysburg was actually reconnaissance, to "feel the enemy." His virtually miraculous clause at the conclusion of the report—after mentioning his battle with Reynolds's First Corps and its Iron Brigade, after getting shot to rags, that is—was that "the enemy had now been felt."

His words regarding the disaster to Davis's Brigade at the Railroad Cut were: "The enemy concentrated on his front and flanks an overwhelming force." Assuming Heth meant by "overwhelming force" *numbers*, it is sheer lie or sheer fantasy or sheer confusion—probably some of all three. But more on the Railroad Cut shortly.

At the beginning of the battle, at about 8:00 A.M., John Buford had his two brigades of cavalry on a long front, using their single-shot breechloaders to hold back Heth's infantry division. Badly outnumbered, the cavalry put up a bold front, fighting dismounted, one man holding four horses in the rear—and Heth was not sure about what was facing him. Reliable officers had told Hill and Lee the day before, when these troopers had been encountered by Pettigrew's Brigade of Heth's Division, that the Yankees acted like disciplined, veteran troops—like the Army of the Potomac, in fact. But nobody believed. Heth's Division, without making a serious charge, pressed the cavalry, pushing them back off Herr Ridge to McPherson's Ridge sometime before 10 o'clock. Now Heth ordered an all-out attack to wipe away this "militia" or "detachment" and see what he could catch.

As he had ridden up to Gettysburg earlier that morning, General Reynolds had noted the commanding heights to the east of the Emmitsburg Road: Round Top, Little Round Top, and near town, Cemetery Ridge and Hill. Perhaps he was familiar with these features, having grown up in Lancaster, thirty miles away. At any rate, he realized their importance. A force on them could interdict anything moving south or southeast to Baltimore and Washington. (Meade said that day if Lee got control of Gettysburg—meaning command of the road intersection and that higher ground—all would be lost.) General Reynolds made up his mind that he must try to keep those hills out of Lee's grasp.

He knew he couldn't do it with the First Corps alone. Last night the alert and efficient Buford had sent Reynolds an accurate, terrible message. A. P. Hill's Corps was moving from Cashtown, west of Chambersburg, toward Gettysburg; just behind them was Longstreet's Corps; moving from York and Carlisle, Ewell's Corps. In a small house near Emmitsburg, Reynolds had wrapped himself in a blanket and lain first on some chairs and then on the floor to get four hours' sleep, the best he had had in several nights. This morning he was calm and, according to some, he displayed good spirits. But others thought he was unusually quiet, careworn, sad, even depressed. As he rode into Gettysburg he knew that his First Corps, and perhaps the Eleventh Corps farther back, was all he had to protect those vital hills—and the entire Army of Northern Virginia was converging on the town.

Meade had been a bit too cautious. The other corps of the Army of the Potomac had not been ordered to Buford's forward position at Gettysburg—only Reynolds's left wing. The rest of the Army was still positioned to move toward a defensive position along Pipe Creek, near the Pennsylvania-Maryland line. Reynolds would concede Gettysburg nor Pennsylvania to Lee; he would try to hang on, and his going forward to meet Lee would bring the rest of the Union army to the sound of his guns. But he knew he was overwhelmingly outnumbered, in desperate trouble. If he occupied the heights immediately, Lee would advance to them and push him off. The only chance was a defense in depth: occupy ground to the *west* of town, where Buford already was, so as to be able to fall back slowly, fighting in the streets if necessary, giving time for the rest of the Army to fill in along the heights. Reynolds had confidence in his incomparable First Corps. Howard's Eleventh was on the road behind; they had been shellacked at Chancellorsville, but Howard was, if you could trust him, a pretty good officer. The Third Corps was within a day's march; though Reynolds might have had doubts about the abilities of political generals, he knew Sickles was a fighter, and he had some fine troops and general officers. Hancock's superb Second Corps could arrive that day if ordered forward. The Twelfth and Fifth could come in during the night and next day. Only Sedgewick's Sixth Corps had more than a long day's march—about thirty miles. Reynolds confirmed his intentions a bit later by ordering Lieutenant Rosengarten of his staff to get some citizens together and spread the word to leave town or at least stay off the streets.

The citizens, a mixture of Germans and descendants of the Anglo-Saxon stock who had settled the town with Gettys in the previous century, did not care to be told what to do any more then than they would now, and Rosengarten rode away irritated.

He found his general conferring with Buford. There is, as usual, disagreement as to the actual scene before Rosengarten arrived. Reynolds may have gone directly to the cupola of the Seminary, which obviously afforded a view of the whole area. From there you can see the series of ridges fading off to the west, and you can look several miles down the road toward Cashtown—filled that morning into the distance with gray and butternut columns wider than the road, and dust behind them. Buford was on his way down; a calm voice, Reynolds's, said from the bottom, "What's the matter, John?" "There's the devil to pay," Buford answered grimly. Or perhaps not. At any rate, Reynolds and Buford rode from the Seminary's ridge several hundred yards, through the cavalry division's line of held horses, to McPherson's Ridge.

Reynolds noted the Chambersburg road, fenced on both sides, to his right. Just beyond that was an unfinished railroad cutting through the ridge: it would make a troublesome alley for the rebels to come through. Straight ahead was McPherson's barn, the white structure which still stands, unmistakable and gleaming when the sun strikes it from the east or west; and just to the left of that, a woodlot.

McPherson's Woods was different then. Now it is full of small trees and underbrush; then it was clean of second growth, consisting of spaced, tall trees. Reynolds wanted those woods because in its cover outnumbered troops could be magnified, and could fire on both the Chambersburg Pike and the Fairfield Road a half-mile to the south if the Confederates tried to advance along them. But he saw that Confederate infantry was deploying for an attack from Herr Ridge, which would bring them to McPherson's Ridge and the Woods.

He told Buford to hold on as long as he could, wheeled his big black horse, and galloped back through Gettysburg, turning south from the square down the Emmitsburg Road. Known as a superb horseman, Reynolds, and his staff galloping behind him, must have inspired the townspeople—with courage and with fear, too; they seemed to be in an awful hurry. He had his staff stop along the road below town to tear down fences.

Probably about two miles south of town, down around Little Round Top, Reynolds came upon General Wadsworth at the head of the First Division. Its Second Brigade was first in line, and Reynolds had it ordered forward on the double-quick. It was Cutler's Brigade, a very solid outfit. Lysander Cutler was an unusual commander in that he was in his fifties. Born in Maine, he had moved to Milwaukee, Wisconsin, where he had become a journalist. When the 6th Wisconsin was formed, Cutler was elected colonel. The men liked and respected this wolfish-looking man with the rough white hair and beard; his discipline was strict, but he took good care of them, and he was a real fighter. He had left Gibbon's, now Meredith's, Iron Brigade upon being given his own brigade.

Following Cutler on the road, with their frock coats and black hats, was the First Brigade, First Division, First Corps: the Iron Brigade. Behind them, its brass Napoleons gleaming: Battery B, Fourth United States Artillery. Reynolds rode to the column and gave instructions to Long Sol Meredith, wheeled his horse, and galloped across the fields, followed by the Iron Brigade on the double-quick.

The Brigade crossed the fields now famous for Pickett's Charge, cutting northwest toward the Seminary, which they could see on the higher ground west of town.

Buford, on McPherson's Ridge, watched two Confederate brigades come toward him, "three deep and booming." He knew what the devil's charges were. Slowly at first, the three lines of Davis's Brigade came toward him north of the Chambersburg Pike. He knew that when they charged, his thin single line of troopers would be overwhelmed. Tense-jawed, he watched Cutler's men in column coming up behind him.

Reynolds arrived and directed Hall's Second Maine Battery in position between the Pike and the railroad cut. The cavalry mounted up and went off to guard the flanks. Buford had bought two hours of incalculable value. But that Maine battery was in a dangerous position, still waiting for its infantry support. It began pounding a Confederate battery, forcing two of its guns behind cover. But Reynolds was anxious.

As Cutler's men came onto the ridge—which is merely a long elevation, only about forty feet high at its crest—Reynolds watched Davis's Confederates just a couple of hundred yards away. A corps commander shouldn't have been on the front line. Even Wadsworth, no coward, a division commander, would establish his headquarters back at the Seminary. But Reynolds was a frontline man in a war in which soldiers—volunteers still—liked to be led, not driven, and they admired most the bravest generals who shared their danger with them. And Reynolds knew everything depended upon holding this position. Reynolds personally directed the regiments toward their positions, and then Davis's men hit them.

But Reynolds was already galloping toward McPherson's Woods. Archer's Confederate brigade had entered them.

Those woods look like a patch of level ground on a map, but they are part of McPherson's Ridge, and there is a steep slope up from the west edge, where Willoughby Run flows north and south, up a quarter-mile to a level with McPherson's barn, then more gradually up toward the east edge. On the McPherson property the ridge has two crests; the woods lies across them both. Archer's men were wading the narrow run; they spread to a quarter-mile front or more, wide across as the woods.

The Iron Brigade came jogging up the east slope, *en echelon*, like stair steps, loading as they ran: the 2nd Wisconsin in the lead and farthest forward, the 7th Wisconsin, the 19th Indiana, then the large new 24th Michigan. The 6th Wisconsin and one hundred men drawn from the other four regiments stayed behind in the swale between Seminary and McPherson's ridges, in reserve. Reynolds shouted to the Second, "Forward, men, forward for God's sake and drive those fellows out of those woods!"

It was a little over ten months ago now that this brigade had fought its twilight battle at Brawner Farm in Virginia. Two days later it was conspicuous at Second Manassas, and it formed the rear guard during the ensuing retreat of the army toward Washington. After that victory, Lee had turned his thinned regiments of ragged veterans north to invade Maryland.

As he would do in Pennsylvania, Lee had divided his army, assuming the Federals would not move fast or decisively. But a copy of Lee's orders was found by Union soldiers, and the commander of the Army of the Potomac knew where Lee's elements were. "If I can't whip Bobby Lee with this," said George McClellan, waving the copy of Lee's orders—but the rest of the story is well known. (It should be remembered in McClellan's defense that his *military intelligence*—again an oxymoron—had him convinced he was heavily outnumbered, which accounts to a degree for his general overcaution and his failure to commit his reserves at Antietam.)

McClellan, after an inexplicable day's delay, advanced the Army of the Potomac toward the nearest of Lee's widespread divisions, but to get at it he had to pass through several gaps in the South Mountain chain—and they were being held by such troops as Lee could rush to them. The Iron Brigade fought another twilight battle, at Turner's Gap, an impossibly steep, narrow, rough gorge. Watching from a distance, McClellan and Hooker could hardly believe what they saw. They must be made of iron; it is an iron brigade, they said, watching the four black hat regiments storm up the rocky slope with the Southerners blasting down into their faces.

A couple of days later the Iron Brigade, now "the shock troops of the Army of the Potomac," spearheaded the attack on the Confederate left at Antietam, charging through the Cornfield. As they would at Gettysburg, they fought two battles on the same field—though on that September morning there was no respite between them—heavily outnumbered. Lawton's, Trimble's, Law's, Jones's brigades all engaged the Iron Brigade, as did the famous Stonewall Brigade again and Hood's Texans. By the time the Black Hats retired through the Cornfield the place was, according to General Hooker, cut down entirely by the shooting, as close to the ground as if each stalk had been pared with a knife. The Cornfield at Antietam is one of the most horrifying mute monuments of the Civil War; it is small enough to make one wonder how so many could have fought there so long, and anyone at all survived. Losing 42 percent, the Iron Brigade had inflicted much worse.

Seeing their corps commander on his horse as bullets clipped through the branches, the men of the 2nd Wisconsin rushed into the woods shouting. Their furious downhill charge stunned Archer's veterans; then the 7th Wisconsin hit them. All of Archer's Brigade recoiled. *It's them damned black hat fellers again! That ain't no militia; it's the Army of the Potomac!* As the two lines poured fire at each other the 24th Michigan and the 19th Indiana came down on the Confederate right, swinging into them like a gate.

The Iron Brigade charged like Confederates, not with deliberate, stalwart determination, but with a savage rush. Archer and perhaps two hundred to three hundred of his men were captured. In that war of gentlemen—as it appears to us—Archer was treated with respect as he was brought to the Union rear. "General Archer! How happy I am to see you," exclaimed his old acquaintance General Doubleday. "Well I'm not happy to see you by a damned sight!" retorted the mortified general, still stunned and enraged by the shocking decimation and capture of much of his brigade. The survivors were fleeing back toward Herr Ridge, with the Iron Brigade splashing across Willoughby Run and halfway to the ridge in pursuit. McPherson's Woods was lost to the Southerners for now, and the Union line south of the Chambersburg Pike was stabilized.

But up at the east edge of the Woods, General Reynolds lay dead. One of his aides sat on the ground cradling his head, pierced behind the ear by a sniper's shot perhaps, or, more probably, by a stray bullet. He had just been turning in his saddle toward the last Iron Brigade unit . . .

His aide, Charles Veil, found and removed the medallion which the thirty-eight-year-old General had never let anyone see. It was a Catholic medal, on a chain which also held a gold ring in the shape of two clasped hands. Engraved inside the ring were the words "Dear Kate." His own West Point ring was not on his hand.

Two days later his body lay in his sister's house in Baltimore. His family had not known of the lady General Reynolds loved. That morning there was ringing at the door, and a note given to be carried in to the family, stating a desire to see the remains. "Is she Kate?" asked Ellen Reynolds. She was. The lady was welcomed by the family, who recognized extraordinary qualities in her.

Four years previously the two had met as John Reynolds returned from his assignment on the West Coast. And now, they had been planning to meet only five days from this day in Philadelphia, whence he would bring her to meet his family. Katherine Hewitt came from a wealthy family, and the two had planned to go to Europe after their marriage, and after the War ended.

On July 12 she applied to enter St. Joseph's convent, Sisters of Charity, in Emmitsburg, Maryland, a dozen or so miles from where her General fell.

Katherine, "Dear Kate," was lost to view five years later. She did not stay at St. Joseph's but returned to New York State, where she had been born, living several years at a school also called St. Joseph's. In September 1868 she left, without taking vows.

Where did she go? Why did she leave? Did she enter another convent, perhaps in Europe? Did she marry eventually? No further record of her was found by Reynolds's biographer, Edward Nichols. She does not seek our company; to us she is forever alone with her thoughts.

This is no kind of historical knowledge, but one hundred twenty-six years after the battle I visited again the marker which stands on the mound made at the place where General John Reynolds was killed. Looking at the small blue and white flowers growing nearby, in the shady grass, I thought of John and Kate. I picked a few of the flowers but, not wanting to be seen for a sentimentalist, I carried them around to the back of the small monument, where nobody sees, to leave them there. On the grass at its base on that side there already lay a small bouquet, gathered and put there just that day.

The 6th Wisconsin and brigade guard were ordered forward to the Chambersburg Pike, because north of it Davis's Brigade had broken through Cutler's and was pursuing three retreating regiments. This outflanked the rest of the Iron Brigade in the woods south of the road. As the men went forward in the flat swale between ridges they saw staff officers carrying a body wrapped in a blanket. They were not told who it was. Doubleday was now commanding the corps.

Davis's men were at right angles to Colonel Dawes and his Wisconsin men; a volley from the Sixth stopped them, tearing through them unexpectedly from across the road. Seeing the railroad cut between them and the road, Davis's men wheeled into it, combining with other Confederates already using the cover of the cut to advance through. From there they opened a murdering fire on Dawes's men standing in line out in the open at the fence along the south side of the Pike. "Kowardly sons of bitches," one Wisconsin soldier wrote.

It was a post-and-rail fence at the Pike, and such fences were made well by those Gettysburg farmers—as Pickett's men would discover, also under fire, two days hence. It could not be pushed down like a worm fence. So the men went up and over. Climbing and pushing down the second fence and covering the next 175 yards to the cut, Dawes lost 160 men. But the regiment got there—joined two or three minutes later by the 95th New York of Cutler's Brigade—and before the surprised Confederates realized they heavily outnumbered these surviving black hat fellows, Dawes and his men, bayonets fixed, were shouting "Surrender! Surrender! Throw down your muskets!" There was a deadly struggle for a Rebel flag. Some of Dawes's men got into the cut where its sides came down to field level: they and the men at the top could have poured a butchering fusillade into the crowd of Southerners jammed in the cut. (Herdegen says about half the men's rifles would have been loaded.) That they shouted for surrender instead is a marvel, and to the imperishable credit of those men.

Why, how, could the Iron Brigade have done what they did? Morale is the answer. Discipline, belief in themselves and the justice of their cause, skill, self-sacrifice, a faith in larger things, courage, and trustworthy leadership created high morale. It cannot be artificially sustained; one volley of real bullets tests its mettle.

The American national character, though prone to plunges and black holes, has always tried to be decent. We have been simultaneously just and sinning, as Luther might put it, freeing the slaves while overrunning the West, and the like—but we have believed in the decent side, and this has been a source of American morale—not victories over puny powers, or cynical parades.

The morale of the United States eroded during Vietnam because we did what we knew was wrong. Thousands of men and women trained on the decent values of not shooting women and children, and so on, have not been able to live with what we did there, and the effects have rippled out to the country as a whole whether we know it or not. And there were lies at the center, in the White House. America has had barbaric enemies, and has competed with countries that believe in *Realpolitik*, but when we fight on their terms we may gain the whole world temporarily but lose our souls.

> . . . no greater disgrace could befall . . . the whole people, than the perpe-
> tration of the barbarous outrages . . . that have marked the course of the
> enemy. . . .
>   Such proceedings not only degrade the perpetrators and all connected
> with them, but are subversive . . . and destructive. . . .

We have lost the whole world too, not to mention

> offending against Him to whom vengeance belongeth, without whose favor
> and support our efforts must all prove in vain.

We have now a society increasingly uncivilized and more pervasively without conscience, and everyone else knows it.

However, Vietnam was not the worst thing for American morale. The *acquiescence* in illusion, the *choice* of illusion, may have become still more corrosive. During Vietnam there was idealism, both in fighting the war and in fighting against the war, even as the napalm fell; but in 1980 all America became an actor, playing a part to deceive ourselves. Like locusts, like an undisciplined and demoralized army invading our own soil, we said, To hell with everything and everybody including our children, let's get some money. And hey. Everything's O.K.

All during the Reagan years I went to Gettysburg. I stood in the shadows of the Iron Brigade's monuments, and traced the letters in their granite. I have walked in the Railroad Cut, followed the slope of the Woods down to Willoughby Run; I have tried to picture the steady lines advancing toward the Seminary, and tried to imagine how the last Wisconsin, Indiana, and Michigan men felt as the attacks came on again; I have stood by their dead up on Cemetery Hill; and the doom grows upon us still.

For a time there was quiet on the fields, except for the moaning and screaming wounded. The Confederates had drawn back to reform;

Davis's Brigade—he was the Confederate President's nephew—was judged unfit for further action, and Archer's was in shards. The other Union corps were several hours closer. (But of course Pender and all three of Ewell's divisions were about on hand.) Reynolds and his First Corps had chosen and staked out their field of battle, drawn the army to it, and defended the crucial heights. Had they not held, there would have been no further battle at Gettysburg—would have been no "fish-hook" position, no batteries on Little Round Top and Cemetery Hill. Of all the factors contributing to the Union victory, surely position was the chief. "Physiology is fate." Surely no action in the War was more decisive than this one fought by the Iron Brigade, and its subsequent delaying and crippling of the great Confederate advance that afternoon. There were many such decisive actions at Gettysburg—maybe all the actions were decisive; but none at such odds, at such cost, and fought so well. Heroism. Glory goes to the First Day losers; in the larger economy of the battle they were victorious.

Pettigrew's and Brockenbrough's brigades of Heth's Division were still on Herr Ridge waiting; behind them Pender's whole division came off the Pike, deployed into long, long lines, and waited for the word to advance.

Up to the north, across the Pike, another of the three First Corps divisions had arrived, extending the line toward Oak Hill, where Seminary and McPherson's ridges come together. They were attacked by Rodes's Division of Ewell's Corps from the north, but they too held against the numbers, partly through good work of their own and partly, as in the case of Archer and Davis, through poor troop handling by overconfident Confederate officers, Iverson and Rodes especially.

The Eleventh Corps began arriving and, Buford's constant vigilance again felt, extended the Union line, not north-south to meet Hill's Corps, but at right angles to the First Corps, across the north roads into Gettysburg, to meet Ewell coming down.

For hours the Iron Brigade waited. Hall's Maine Battery had left for Cemetery Hill, and in its place, defiant across the Chambersburg Pike, was old Battery B, Fourth United States. The 2nd and the 7th Wisconsin rested in position—on a short line, the survivors, about 150 yards for both regiments—at the crest of the elevation in the woods. Next to them the 24th Michigan, the center of the line that would face the very worst; next to them the 19th Indiana. They tried to clean their rifles, tried to be still and not sweat so much, talked quietly, tried to help their wounded friends, ignored more or less the dead bodies in gray and butternut. They knew what was coming.

Next to them, straddling the Pike, Cutler's regiments lined up at their original positions. The Second Division battled, then firing there died down. It was warm, low 80s and humid. Hands slipped a little on the musket barrels.

Most of Lee's Second and Third corps had arrived. Their numerical preponderance was very heavy, both overall and in front of McPherson's Woods. The 6th Wisconsin had about 344 men at the beginning of the day, the 19th Indiana 308, 2nd Wisconsin 302, the 7th Wisconsin 364. The 24th Michigan, having joined the Brigade after Antietam, was 496 strong. This was well, for the Wolverines were about to be hit by the 26th North Carolina, a regiment of 843 men.

Arms seemed to matter less than men at Gettysburg. It is generally assumed that the average Yankee had a better weapon than the Confederate, but that is not true. The variation in shoulder arms carried by the Northerners is dismaying, even within brigades, even within regiments. The majority on both sides were armed with the reliable .58 Springfield or its near English cousin, the .57 Enfield, but it was not a large majority. All three Wisconsin regiments in the Iron Brigade had the detested Austrian rifle, a heavy, cumbersome thing—and some troops fought with smoothbores. (Referring to muskets, not academicians.)

At 3:00 Confederate artillery fire rose quickly, and the Union batteries answered. In McPherson's Woods the men gripped their weapons as word was repeated: "Here they come."

Two and three deep and overlapping the entire First Corps position, extending far to the Iron Brigade's left, the gray and butternut lines advanced, battle flags tilted forward. Three of Heth's brigades went in south of the Pike, followed by Scales, Perrin, and Lane of Pender's Division.

Cutler held against the odds across and north of the Pike, but south of the woods the long lines could bend around to pour fire from the flank into McPherson's Woods. Straight ahead, in front of the Iron Brigade, no Confederate lived to cross Willoughby Run. The Brigade had held fire until the Southerners reached the creek, then opened a killing volley. The Confederates stopped and fired back; both lines stood firing, but nobody advanced. On the left, the Nineteenth was taking terrible punishment from the enfilading fire beyond the woods; of the regiment's officers, only their colonel remained. The Nineteenth gradually bent back their left to face the fire, but now fire from the left hit the next regiment, the 24th Michigan. The First Corps' third division had deployed south of the Woods after the morning's battle, but now becoming outflanked it had completely given way and the Confederates were able to wrap around the south end of the Woods and pour in a decimating fire. The 7th and the 2nd Wisconsin began to take the fire from the left as they held their line above Willoughby Run; the order was given to move back to the east edge of the woods and straighten the line.

This second line traded volleys at 20 yards with the Confederates slowly pressing forward. The men used every tree as cover; still the Brigade was melting into the pages of the Death Roster. Dead and wounded lay thick among the trees. Close firing continued along the narrow line; in front of the 24th Michigan, reduced now to two hundred men, the Carolinians of the Twenty-sixth had hundreds of their comrades on the ground. But again pressure in front and unanswerable fire from the left necessitated the order given in the Iron Brigade: "Fall back. Fall back."

Their dead marking the slow withdrawal with the accuracy of a dress parade, according to General Heth, the Black Hats moved back in line of battle, turning to stand again 100 yards east, in the swale between the woods and the Seminary.

On their right, Cutler was being forced back all the way to Seminary Ridge.

The color-bearer of the 24th Michigan falls—the third killed, and Colonel Morrow tells another to plant the flag and hold it for the remnant of the regiment to rally on—three-fourths of them are now lying in the woods and in the swale—the man is shot down at the staff, and Morrow, now the last officer, lunges to support it. No, by God! my colonel doesn't have to hold the flag as long as I can—another soldier grips the splintering staff—shot instantly, and Morrow takes it; still another man takes hold of it and waves the riddled banner for an instant; he too, the sixth, is killed, and Morrow finally takes the flag and keeps it as the Iron Brigade moves back, still in line of battle, turning and firing. Back in the woods wounded men scream and foam at the mouth, made mad by the sudden shock of killing after hours of heat and quiet tension. A heavy swath of dark blue bodies overlaid with butternut and gray spreads forward from that shallow stream, up through the woods, down into the swale, across it, now up the slope to where the bleeding Iron Brigade turns again to fire, then moves up to plant their flags one more time to make a final stand in smoke and glory before the buildings of the Seminary.

7 *The Seminary*

North of the Seminary the Union lines were broken. The Eleventh Corps in the open fields north of Pennsylvania College were giving way. Their right had crumbled when Gordon's Brigade charged the flank positioned on an open knoll, and the rest of the line was caving in and falling back into the town. Closer, Rodes was finally breaking Robinson's Division. The right flank of the First Corps was uncovered, Confederates were pouring toward its rear; its right division was falling back before the lines of Southerners on front and flank. The Corps would have to retreat or be enveloped—but not before it faced the broad advance against the Seminary, from its trees and lawns the Iron Brigade's rifles blazing for the last time.

What was this slaughter for? North of the Seminary one of the worst events of the War had happened—Iverson's Brigade walked unled, veering, as Edwin Coddington says, "with a strange fatality" toward a stone wall, and were decimated in minutes by Union troops rising up and firing in their faces. Five hundred shot in minutes, lying in their rows. A general thought they had gone to ground but then discovered to his horror that they were a line of never. Two hundred killed for nothing; hundreds wounded, many crippled—freaks and amputees for life. That night survivors buried the dead in mass graves where they fell: Iverson's Pits. The bodies were exhumed after the war but only skeletons and rags and buttons remained; the flesh had soaked the soil; at the turn of the century grape arbors rose there, and their owner, Sheads, made wine with which he regaled his guests: "Sheads' Wine," fertilized and sprung from Southern flesh and blood, a liquor made from Southern dreams. Did the families in those Carolina homes know their fathers, husbands, sons, and brothers had been thus transformed?

My family once lived where wild grapes had grown for years untended. Along the back fence and twining among boughs of the trees they grew, putting forth here and there the sudden, unexpected bunch. In late August, the fragrance was indescribably sweet as the summer lay back against the maple and began to die in russet and gold.

I remember two girls making jelly, having first tasted the fruit where it grew. When grapes are still cloudy-dusty from the vines they are best. They give a fleeting, unforgettable flavor when they are first crushed on the tongue; afterward there is the sweet pulp and the sourish skin, but that one elusive taste—that is what one takes them for, cheating the winter's supply of preserves and even the birds of the air.

Mr. Sheads tended his grape arbor when the battle was forty years gone; the lovely, rolling, rich countryside had returned to its quiet and generous state. Once again young couples went up the slopes of Culp's Hill with picnic baskets, where Southern boys had come howling in long lines yelling their wildness; young men with their young ladies walked quietly in the shade at the Theological Seminary, where the Iron Brigade had poured out its last full measure of devotion with fearsome stubbornness, where Lee had pointed at the blue crowds on Cemetery Hill saying, "The enemy is *there*, and I am going to *strike* him!"

Farmers working the fields near the arbors noted that the crops always grew more luxuriantly where the Pits had been.

Iverson's boys had died on that hot day under the midsummer sun going forward as if led by a power profound and otherwise invisible, to that one terrible and delicious moment of courage and sacrifice when the soul stands up for all it holds dear, and is transfigured by its love. The Southern boys spent themselves in an elusive instant; and so their blood spilled and became an elusive essence in the flavor, the pulp and flesh and skin, of spoken history.

Red wine is the light of the high summer sun turned to flowing color. Hours and days, the deeds of the husbandmen digging and watering, even the passing of the clouds, go into the solid veins of the vines, and time teems in the stems' palpable green. Wine is for remembrance, the flesh and blood of history transubstantiated into a flavor.

It was long ago, and those who drank Sheads' Wine are dead.

But in our house there were two girls' voices. They had come in with a bucket of grapes which now lay in a tub in the sink under clear, cold water—dropped in, rolled in, lying together in a mass, in the winter to be a flavor and turn to deeds, to become the substantial notes of history. The house was again alive, circulation within as well as without.

It seems a pity that grapes are the fruit of a summer past, of childhood and youth according to an exact measure spent. Perhaps in some other world—where the flavor of the grape, its elusive essence, is born—it is not so. But here, under the lengthening shadow of the trees, man and woman fall onto the tender grass of the field and lie under the dew of heaven, and the sweet arbors grow.

Iverson's "report" covers up the whole thing; you would not recognize the massacre in it. He says, ". . . a most desperate fight took place" 100 yards in front of a stone wall. You'd think he had been there, or at least he gives no intentional hint that he was in the rear drunk. He blames it on lack of support, etc. Then he says, "I endeavored, during the confusion among the enemy incident to the charge and capture of my men, to make a charge with my remaining regiment . . . [sure he did] but in the noise and excitement I presume my voice could not be heard." They wouldn't have understood him anyway.

Iverson was indisposed during the rest of the battle.

Rodes's report says Iverson's men "fought and died like heroes." They died like sheep led to slaughter, and they didn't get a chance to fight. The distinction, ever delicate, between heroes and victims is not finely drawn here. One can add up benefits from the deaths in the 24th Michigan, but what about in the 26th North Carolina (where they got the chance to fight and die like the heroes they were); the men who died in the 6th Wisconsin just before the final rush to the Railroad Cut went down in a Confederate volley, which meant that the rest of the regiment were able to get to the embankment while the

Southerners were reloading—but what about Iverson's men? Sacrifice and slaughter are two different things. The Union dead may have died to give a new birth of freedom to the country and the world, but what of all the Southern dead? What of one small girl who dies in the front seat of a Honda, or a trainable retarded man who lives fifty years like a soft round globe in a whitewashed hall at St. Coletta's? What of us all? If there is no more than this life, then those who believe in anything other than eat, drink, and be merry are of all people most to be pitied. If there is no system of things, no large household, no economy which buys us back, then let us buy the American Illusion, all eight cylinders of it.

Just north of the Seminary building Robertson's Division had made a barricade of fence rails. Here the Iron Brigade faced the imminent Confederate assault. The last yards up the exposed slope of the rise had been expensive: many had been hit; Colonel Morrow had been wounded. With the Brigade on the Seminary grounds were the Fifth Maine Battery and the survivors of Cutler's and Stone's brigades on the right, and on the left the remnant of Rowley's Division and gunners from New York and Pennsylvania. Battery B was still on the Pike at the ridge line; the 6th Wisconsin stood with them.

The exhausted infantry and artillerists waited, seeing the long lines of Heth, Pender, and Rodes form, extending in a mile-wide semicircle beyond both Union flanks. They would be able to pour in a converging fire and overlap right and left, but the remainder of the First Corps was going to hold on as long as it could. Behind their right, the Eleventh Corps had melted away.

The long gray line came forward with shouts and yells and the ground-trembling *tramp tramp* of thousands of feet. The defenders held fire until the Southerners started up the gradual slope. As one of the attackers said later, the Union line became a "sheet of fire and smoke" in their faces, more terrible than before. The batteries fired together, blasting canister through wide lengths of the lines. The Union fire cut like a scythe, and a North Carolinian said the earth seemed to open under their front line. A Southern brigadier said only squads here and there remained of that line directly in front of the Seminary.

But they were strong men too. The lines reformed, compressed, and came again, overlapping right and left. Doubleday ordered the First Corps to withdraw; the Iron Brigade, the 5th Maine Battery, and Battery B would stay to provide cover, as long as they could. Attacking lines still were decimated by the accuracy and rapidity of fire which the Black Hats continued to put forth: one Southern officer said his whole regiment appeared to be destroyed by it. Behind the barricade, the wounded fought if they could, loading muskets and passing them; along the ridge a mounted officer rode slowly, waving the flag, an incredible sight in the sun and smoke.

Now the Corps had retired, and the Iron Brigade was alone. Ammunition was nearly gone, three sides closed off; the men were ordered to retire. "Losing men at every step," they went back in order, at a walk, filing by right of companies, then stepping into column onto the Pike, behind the fire of Battery B and the 6th Wisconsin.

Battery B on the Pike fought in a half-acre theater of exploding shells, smoke, flying splinters, bullets; they were nearly enclosed on the right, Confederate infantry was fifty yards in front and coming— still the order *"Double canister!"* was given, still the rammers plunged, the powder bags were pierced—guns sometimes fired before the lanyard was pulled as tubes overheated; the single-minded crews still pushed the wheels and brought the charges and rammed the metal, sighting, pulling, jumping back to smoking golden barrels, no matter what flew, exploded, screamed around them. (Such concentration is the essence of artistic creation.) Horses lay dead behind the guns, and men went down; now Southern infantry were coming right to the guns. "Feed it to 'em, God damn 'em," screams an officer behind the guns, *"feed it to 'em!"* The gunners fire one more blast; they limber up, fending off the gray men with their rammers, shortswords, and fists; they gallop rearward but turn again, then continue into the town.

As the First Corps made their way through Gettysburg, suffering rifle fire down streets from north and west, toward the line being constructed by Howard and Hancock up on Cemetery Hill, the woods and fields around the Seminary, and the Seminary land itself, were covered with its dead. Wounded soldiers moaned and screamed and lay and crawled among bodies, across acres littered everywhere, almost every yard, with canteens, rifles, blankets, hats, clothing, horses, cartridge boxes, packs, and everything that soldiers carried.

At the Seminary Rodes's Division would build a low stone breastwork which still stands. Across the Pike from the small stone house Lee would have his headquarters tent pitched. The cupola would be used by Confederates now. The First Corps had been driven from the field, their great commander killed; it lost half its men killed, wounded, captured—a total of 6,000, more than even Sickles would lose tomorrow in the Peach Orchard and the Wheatfield.

It had been a great victory. But not, despite the way it looked, for the Confederates. Like the perfect Galilean for whose story the Seminary stood, the First Corps had won a battle it appeared to lose. On the Third Day they would understand. The crown of glory went to their faithfulness, sacrifice, and courage in the end.

The Iron Brigade was no more. Though its survivors helped defend Culp's Hill and Stephens Knoll the next two days, and the name was kept, the regiments, mere fragments, were brigaded with others after Gettysburg. Accounts of the battle—written and circulated in the East and the South, where interest in the War remained strongest, and most of the soldiers dead and living had come from—would emphasize the events of the Second and Third days, with the names that became famous and deserved to be: the Copse of Trees, the Peach Orchard, Devil's Den; the Round Tops, the Wheatfield, Cemetery Ridge. But still the granite quarried in Montello, Wisconsin, stands with the words *Iron Brigade* at the Railroad Cut, where the 6th Wisconsin fought, and another by the rail fence on McPherson's farm; and in those woods the regimental markers: 2nd Wisconsin, 7th Wisconsin, 19th Indiana, 24th Michigan.

The Iron Brigade lost more men killed and wounded than any other brigade in the Army of the Potomac during the War. The records for Gettysburg show 171; 720; 262: killed; wounded; missing; or 63 percent. (The killed figure rises as wounded die; immediate battle returns do not show this.) The 2nd Wisconsin lost 77 percent; the 24th Michigan, 73 percent; the 19th Indiana, 68 percent, and the 7th and the 6th, each 49 percent.

But the Army of Northern Virginia had borrowed for its victory, and when the note came due victory turned to defeat. Except for Garnett's

Brigade, which reached the Copse of Trees in Pickett's Charge, the highest regimental losses in the Confederate army had been suffered by those attacking the First Corps. Figures for Heth's Division in front of Cutler's and the Iron Brigade reflect also that division's participation July 3, and its captured figure is underreported; its loss was at least 3,358 at Gettysburg. Pender's Division, not heavily engaged later in the battle, lost 2,392. Rodes's Division, not engaged later in the battle, but which fought part of the Eleventh Corps on the First Day (not losing heavily) in addition to the First Corps, lost 3,116. The 26th North Carolina, which fought the 24th Michigan from Willoughby Run to the Seminary, and advanced farthest in Pickett's Charge, lost 687 of its 843 men: 81.5 percent.

How should the quality of an army be judged? Along with wins and losses you must factor in the weights of numbers and equipment, balance the three arms of service, figure in the influence of chief commanders, try to figure how government decisions affected everything. These elements taken together, it is difficult to say whether the Confederate or the Yankee was a better soldier in the East. Over the course of the whole war, the Confederates did more with less, but at Gettysburg, when each side was evenly matched in regimental, brigade, and divisional fighting, the results look fairly even. Longstreet's two divisions on the Second Day fought magnificently; the men in Pickett's Charge seem unsurpassed in courage. But where could you find a brigade like the Iron Brigade?

Photographs late in the War show veteran volunteer Union units to be tough, tough men, not the kind any sane person would care to fight. The Yankees were stalwart, solid, and knew they were better than their early generals had let them be. The Confederates were tough and wiry, full of spirit, valorous. Each army had its character; the two are classical in opposition, each heroic in its way—the essence of neither told in passing scenes of victory and defeat. Suffering and sacrifice are the essence of great soldiers. Napoleon had pointed out that the best are used to deprivation—give him poor men, ones grown up with nothing, he said.

The Seminary at Gettysburg is doubly a reminder that in the long run victory means sacrifice—or perhaps that victory and loss are one illusion. It is an exceptionally symbolic, even graphic, location, doubly built on blood.

The Lutheran Seminary was founded in 1826 by Samuel Schmucker, a graduate of Princeton Theological Seminary, a place also associated with a battlefield. Washington's artillery was placed upon its hill for a time. The Battle of Princeton, an important one, was fought a few minutes' walk from the Seminary grounds.

But at Gettysburg a battle raged among the Seminary's trees; its classroom building became a horrifying hospital, piles of severed limbs outside its windows, graves outside its doors. One can muse upon the irony of the Prince of Peace allowing battles at his school; and one can also see him bleeding on its lawns.

Like Germans living two kilometers from nuclear installations, one can't exist from day to day concentrating on death. The seminarians at Gettysburg—the few with whom I've spoken, or rather, the few who've talked to the yearly stranger walking through or standing there, just standing there—seem not to think of the sacramental implications of the field of blood they live and work upon—despite the sacramental content of their worship and theology. But I suppose there's enough oddness to explain in crucifixion, incarnation, and testamental wine, without throwing in the Iron Brigade. Iverson's men and the 26th North Carolina might be more pertinent, though harder to understand, because their sacrifices look like sheer loss: we live in a Good Friday world, theologies of glory notwithstanding, because there is still a nearly opaque distance between us and our hopes. We live in the dark valley between question and answer, and like the swale under the Seminary it's strewn with suffering and death. The students have been taught that a faint taste meaning Resurrection is in the blood itself.

What is commonly called faith is mostly courage.

Common belief is mistaken for faith. But faith in an executed deity shatters common belief, is the opposite of belief. Belief is of this world; one faithful to a crucified God must disbelieve in the world. But belief is cheap. Nearly everyone believes—in something. We are told the devils believe. Faith is three o'clock Holy Saturday morning courage. Not many of us were born with this kind of courage. It must be a gift.

The whole idea behind sacrifice is gift. You give someone something they don't have, and it costs you to do it. The recipient hasn't earned a thing, and the only right response is to turn around and do likewise. All this is very Lutheran and those seminarians would agree with it. The problem is in telling it—to a country full of beliefs and empty of courage. We are just as desperate as or worse than general mankind, living bleak, antagonized lives in our blasted cities and fatuous suburbs—but instead of hope and faith that the self which we can see and touch will be transformed after death, we are distracted by televisions, cars, sex, and jet skis. They are wretched distractions, and we think our selves are in them. Those with courageous hope have a lower standard of living and a higher standard of dying.

The self must be forgotten: this seems to be agreed among religions and heroes. That is, the apparent self, between which and the illusions of the world there is no distance at all. What still waits to be reborn is an authentic self, beneath delusion and desire. For one thing worth having, our soul, we are not willing to give up the one worthless thing demanded, the world. Our apparent selves and the world are the same.

Being born again is not what it's cracked up to be. I think what Nicodemus was told—and I assume he believed—did not change his life. If all you want is to change your life, get born again, or win a lottery. I imagine that to be born as the Son of Man meant it would not change life but begin it.

You can believe a thousand times in a thousand tents, but still the nomad shifts about. It is like trolling at ten feet in a lake with no bottom. I think if we live life after life on earth, as Brahminists believe, then Baptists would come back again as Baptists, or Catholics, or Wesleyans—no other than they were before essentially. You can't escape the Wheel of Birth and Death by clinging to a spoke, no matter which one. The world needs no more beliefs; we've got beliefs up to the eyebrows; what we want is faith.

A soldier not outside himself with the euphoric rage of battle, but standing to it in his courage, approaches nearer faith than does the Kleenex-soaking convert. He is like the mothers, fathers, volunteers, who sacrifice daily little things for children and posterity out of love or duty; but to make such sacrifices under fire seems to be of a different order. "No greater love has a man than this, to lay down his life for his friends."

We are, of course, under many kinds of fire. Many of us face the rear, or fire a volley and skedaddle. But those who love, I think, stand to the music of the spheres. Trouble is, a fundamental malady we have is not knowing what love is or how to love. Perhaps our basic problems are breakdowns of love: do not starving children, balding men in BMWs, lonely singles, young men desperate and in jail—do they not show it plainly? Love grows crookedly on illusions. With Hollywood and Madison Avenue acting as our teachers, is it any wonder that love dies coughing in the streets?

It is well to have a thinking monument to mystery on Seminary Ridge; let them study in embattled peace. The soldiers are all gone from the Seminary, their drums distant and obscure. It is a graveyard with the bodies exhumed (though perhaps not all.) America in the summer of 1991 became a celebration without the body and blood. There is little surprise in that. The Real Presence would scare hell out of anyone trying to Get Right With God.

The Gettysburg battlefield is not only one of the most beautiful places on earth, it can be one of the most frightening. Its woods and hollows, its strange "Dutch" barns and undulating fields, its weird boulders, its sudden statues, its silent cannons, all lovely under a sunny springtime sky—cumulus white puffed here and there in the bright, clear blue—are all unearthly features of one vast graveyard. One thousand bodies were never exhumed and sent South from where they were hastily buried in fields, in woods, along streams, behind barns, under apple trees; some perhaps never found. One thousand still there. The other thousands were also buried all over the large, varied place—then dug up and either laid in the National Cemetery or sent home.

For years I had more or less wanted to visit Iverson's Pits on a dark night. Into the early part of this century, farm laborers refused to work in that area after sunset. Too many sightings of ghosts. Did they appear quietly in the twilight: a solitary man in nondescript clothes and hat, then distinguishing himself from tourists by not being there at all? Or would they loom horrible, disfigured, mad and foaming? Would they speak?

The men of Rodes's Division, including Iverson's Brigade, must have been astounded by their good fortune when they came upon the field from the north that afternoon: the Union right flank was exposed, nearly at right angles to them. Electrified by the opportunity, Rodes, who had done so well two months before in assaulting an unprepared Yankee right flank, ordered his brigades to attack. Neither he nor Iverson, whose Brigade deployed into battle line in front of Oak Hill and started forward, bothered to send anyone over the ground first to look things over.

Iverson may have been unsteady, but his men were not. On a front 200 yards wide, flags flying, a more or less even double line of North Carolinians walked forward, expecting to pass along the front of the wall and attack the north end of the Union line, which they thought was in the air. For some reason the brigade veered toward the wall. When they got somewhere between 50 and 20 paces sudden orders were barked somewhere and a solid line of arms and faces appeared; a thousand musket barrels gleamed in the sun and then flashed a sheet of fire and smoke.

Afterward the Southerners lay with their heels in line. Some had collapsed forward, the rest had been knocked backward; hundreds of them. They were hastily buried in several big rectangular holes. I have wondered whether at first, as with other mass graves in which men had been hastily rolled onto each other in layers and covered with only inches of soil, the pits emitted a faint phosphorescent glow at night.

When I got to the Railroad Cut, from which I planned to walk toward the woods through which a road goes toward the stone wall— about a quarter-mile—it was almost completely dark. Unfortunately, it had been a warm afternoon followed by a brief, heavy rain, so a low mist drifted across the damp fields and fingered through the woods. No such luck as a bright moon. Except in the west, clouds covered the sky.

A shape—or was it two shapes?—appeared in the middle of the road ahead. They or it was black, not a vehicle of any kind, not a person cycling or jogging. It seemed to drift where it was, not moving toward me in the mist, but always seeming to get closer. In a few moments I could distinguish two of them. Together they seemed to move without moving. I looked around. Monuments loomed softly in strange places. One could work oneself into quite a state. I looked back. They were still there, the black shapes. Closer.

I began to think they were two people out for a walk, though they walked in the exact middle of the road. Then I heard low murmuring as they approached: talk; two voices; a man and a woman walking. I stood still as they passed; I said hello to them. Going by within four feet of me they ignored me. (I had been motionless, standing on the bridge over the Railroad Cut, wearing khaki and a hat which probably resembled, in the fog and dark, an old campaign hat.) They must be natives, not tourists. I looked after them.

I walked on, monuments on both sides of the road faint but solid in the dark and gray. A deep mechanical roar burst from the trees and a big pickup truck, high beams blazing, screeched through a corner in the woods and came out; then it rounded another corner and came at me. The lights blinded me, the truck roared toward me at full throttle, I stepped off the road, and it exploded past me at the very edge of the pavement. I heard deep-throated post-adolescent laughter and blaring radio the instant they missed me.

I continued, back on the road, turned the corner and went toward the woods. Halfway there, I saw bolts of light illuminate the woods from inside, then veer. Oh, not again. This time a big car—radio booming, blinding high beams on—came wide open toward me. I wondered in the instant whether to cross the road. "No, you're supposed to face the bastards," I remembered. Walking toward them I stepped off the road onto the slippery slope of wet grass, as they just missed me.

I kept walking. After five or ten minutes I stopped where the road enters the woods. I should be afraid now. This is the whole point. I listened to what I thought would be utter, dead silence. Maybe the moans—moaning somewhere. What I heard were trucks on the highway, an airplane in the sky; saw the lights from houses and commercial establishments in what was visible of the town. In the distance no doubt the cloud cover glowed with the running electricity of cities. Fumes from big trucks on the Chambersburg Pike—U.S. 30—flowed into the air.

I thought that ghosts could frighten a person, or the thought of ghosts could, but not kill him. A speeding car is something else again, something to be really frightened of. But this noise of machines and the lights of countless electrical things is the most frightening: a carful of teenaged barbarians could kill one man, but these machines and fumes and lights are, body and soul, killing us all.

We ourselves are the ghosts in the road, the most fearsome creatures of this gradually settling night.

I walked into the woods, around the bend, and as I passed in front of a house I saw lights in the grass. They were small and bluish, like fireflies, but steady, and not flying. One was on the roadside. I bent to look. In the darkness I could make out only lights, not the dark bodies which seemed to be crawling slowly. All around: small lights, imperceptibly moving in the grass. Firefly larvae? Stars? Souls of the dead, Iverson's men, gone to grass and sky? Lovely, mysterious . . . lights.

Those hundreds of boys and men were betrayed by their own officers and ambushed by the enemy. And it was for nothing. Even had the day gone to the South, as their friends thought it had, theirs would have been no part. Their deaths, their lives, bought no one time that needed buying, made no diversion needing to be made. Not one minute nor one inch of ground was their gift to the South or the whole country. It was waste. The idea is nearly unthinkable for humans, unacceptable, but so it was: waste—sheer, empty, vacant waste. On the grass, the tears of their children and wives.

As they are, Iverson's men, so is Earth, betrayed by its friends, ambushed by its enemies. Waste, death, emptiness; no grass left to go to, only the stars.

I write these recollections of Gettysburg sitting by the shore of a lake, not with the long gaze of a veteran; the many older people who walk by have imparted to me the alien calm of a convalescent. They are visitors to this town and lake, and I like them. I identify with them. The lake, though overrun with motors and surrounded by rich houses, has not surrendered its purity.

It is a deep lake, hard to fish because of that and because of its very purity, and because of the motors buzzing across it, so the real fishermen fish it at night. Five miles long, twenty-seven miles around, with a public-access path the entire distance cutting through mansion lawns and parks. It is shaped not like a reflecting eye but like a goober—the fantasy of Lee's and Pemberton's hungry troops at various times during the war.

The lake is a fantasy of many sorts. Motor cruisers the size of Pentagons churn up curling wakes—boats filled with lawyers in love. In these confectionary obscenities, and behind them on water skis, glide young men who on shore wear British clothing and deck shoes, glide women as visible as Venus at sunset. The beach glistens with oily rumps. Gratifying the eye, rows of sailboats ride tied to buoys, peaceful, stately, almost quaint—a distinguished flotilla with the essentially elegant verve and decency of sail. Along the shore tourist children run slapping barefoot with tiny sunfish dangling from monofilament lines under big bobbers. One of the lake tour boats, two-tiered, built in the early part of the century, turns its wood-trimmed prow this way.

At night it is different. The fringes are silenced; there is only water like liquid glass, and a crystal sky. The celestial figures are alone. All their motion describes an arc, a circle, blue-white Polaris at the center.

These nights there is a most unusual triangle in the western sky—Venus, Mars, and Jupiter not five degrees apart. One field of binoculars takes them in. How long before such apparent conjunction will occur again I don't know—a century, a millennium, or not before this perspective of Earth, which makes them seem a triangle, is gone? But see, they are a triangle. Earth's the place for triangles; we know them when we see them. The porcelain-hard delicacy of Jupiter's moons, the rough-red affronting hue of Mars, Venus's clear improbability you could touch between thumb and forefinger—all three are there needing only stronger eyes, and perhaps a stiller mind. On a sailboat, reefed sails, one could be suspended in transparency, the feeling pupil of an eye, all else washed away from our true calling: to be attentive to the glory—blue with crowning white—of Vega, and to red Arcturus with his sons.

The universe has no economy we understand. Wonder, excess; stunning violets and reds and perfect blues, pluperfect white; unfolding violence filigreed by distance. Behind me a mother returns to a brown battered van, three-year-old on her shoulders; she shouts to a little girl who's looking down at the grass, "Whatyou think I came down here for anyway, you little shithead?"

The universe's very incomprehensibility is an infinite reserve of beauty:

> *Thou, silent form! dost tease us out of thought*
> *As doth eternity.*

We observe and name the stars; then we are shown a galaxy. Baffled by a second galaxy, we name them both, then find more; then we are shown there are more galaxies in the universe than stars within the Milky Way. Get a grip on matter, we discover energy; compute the mass of realness in the universe, and we are shown that still more, much more, invisible, "dark" matter may be out there. Discover the largest star—as a sun to sunbeams is it to our sun—and then we're shown one prodigiously heavier, and small as a stove.

Still, the universe is none too big. That young girl is in a dark seat in the van going to the house they sleep and eat in. Are all the jewels of Cassiopeia sufficient to adorn or beautify her vision? Little shithead. Up above and all around, light and unheard music cascade from every waterbearer's tilting urn, pouring streams of jewels through galaxies.

Reynolds, John Fulton; Major General, United States Volunteers; magnitude, first; color, blue with white corona; consort, Katherine: first, pure white.

8 The Town

The town of Gettysburg isn't much to look at, except in a few small areas. Some streets look dingy, squalid, cramped; the houses being right at the sidewalk implies a noisy, fumy existence. Trucks bull through the center of town, rattling windows and blowing clouds of exhaust. There are shops full of glittering plastic junk; a wax museum or two; antique gun stores. Worse still, a strip of fast food franchises elbows its way into the fields of Pickett's Charge. Since I began going to Gettysburg a subdivision has been built over the northern edges of those fields, and in front of Anderson's and Pender's Divisions. Just behind Cemetery Hill and Ridge rises the new "National Tower," where for some money you can take an elevator up and survey the battlefield (better than any soldier could have, you bet); it is a National Symbol—not of those days but of ours, showing that a confusion of minds is as protective of the sacred as is confusion of tongues. It's unobtrusive if you have a gentle definition of obtrusion. Say what you like about war; this battle has created jobs.

But it can be, withal, a pleasing enough place. It has two academic institutions, with neighborhoods surrounding them that have the smell of eastern lush vegetation and the feel of old Southern residences. As the noisy main streets become familiar, and you learn your way around the cluttery side streets, you might not wish to be anywhere else. Unless it is 105 degrees for a week running, as it was when I was there a few years ago; then all its features, like the Seminary buildings glaring bare and hot in the sun, become hideous, and you can better feel something of the evil of the place. It was and still is an Aceldama, an arena of lethal brutality and waste; until now the worst place in all of America—a Woodstock of horror; Chicago condensed.

What mad pursuit? What struggle to escape?

Though the temperature was in the mid and upper 80s, possibly 90, and not 105 during the battle, it was a hot hell to those men in wool, in the sulfur smoke. The Seminary building and the Cemetery gate must have been sinister monsters to the Confederates. The town became a dirty, ugly little maze of sharpshooters.

Impressions are not simple at such times. Confederates described the neat farms, large and well-kept barns, green fields and numerous, healthy livestock. But the working German women no doubt looked mannish, coarse, and stupid to the Southerners, whose women today still work to defy the exigencies of labor and surroundings with their looks and manner. (All of it artificial, perhaps, but those Southerners detested the absence of the artificial; it is part of civilization.)

It was no tourist spot then: the now great park afforded some hazard and inconvenience; and afterward suffering wounded men and the bloating dead lay all around. The lovely, light Christ Lutheran Church was a squirming hospital then, full of rank stale sweat and blood; on its steps where now the minister exchanges pleasantries with white-shirted and pastel-dressed parishioners a chaplain was shot dead July 1. A plaque reminds us of this.

Everywhere there are reminders to read. The oldest close-crowded houses bear the votive square bronze notices: "Civil War Building." Even now the National Cemetery is a living roster: away from the rows of Civil War markers one reads World War I, World War II, Korea, Vietnam. The town was transformed, and in a strange way plays out in plastic money, like the nation itself, its role of extermination. It is a busy, visible grid of some vast covenant with death. This distracted, lovely place, when only a little uncovered, its unconscious spread, is the fundamental question of one nation and of human life.

One must question the notion that the world is, after all, All Right, the best it could be, and in the hands of some kind Person. Every roach is a Diogenes. A toothache's more persuasive than Voltaire.

The town's economy is, in a manner of speaking, a war economy. Agriculture no longer provides the engine, nor transportation; the battle does. Perhaps instead of requesting a lottery, a bankrupt town ought to request a battle.

Every human group will of its own nature produce an economy, for we are animals both spiritual and economic. America's inner cities are an example. The general population has attempted to ignore them out of existence, consistently drawing elements of the national economy away from them. I refer not merely to the $51 billion cut in social programs under Reagan, which deprived inner-city people of some connections, or lines, to the outside. A larger, a comprehensive factor is the effort in theory and practice to keep the ghetto economy separate: to move out of the ghetto once you have money, to avoid hiring ghetto people for work outside the ghetto, to decline to live in the ghetto, to move businesses and churches and other institutions out, to route transportation so as to avoid mixing neighborhoods, to favor automobile over public transportation, and to fear and dislike black and poor people out of sheer willful ignorant prejudice. We don't forgive people for what we do to them. The young poor black man is an endangered species, and his only remaining habitat is being destroyed.

But still there is an economy in the ghetto, a war economy. Outside money comes in for fire and police; drugs and money pour in and the exchangers take their shares before they are killed; funeral parlors prosper; meager and grudging aid to the dependent children we have helped to create filters in; the young men standing on corners keep the prisons and hospitals in business: despair is a thriving industry, wherever it takes over—it produces and grinds up capital as relentlessly as its more respectable cousin. The ghetto version of the economy of death is likewise self-perpetuating; its fuel is its own body. The anger, fear, and perverted dreams of the ghetto are nothing other than American capitalism with the chrome removed.

It is not so much the system as human nature which is at fault. That capitalism runs on greed is the same thing as drug traffic running on demand: the fault is in what we are. A system of forced sharing breaks down, as it seems to have done in Eastern Europe, because of the same element, greed, as much as because of the human desire for freedom. Greed breaks systems, it breaks people; its fuel is our bodies and minds. I wonder if you can kill minds without injuring spirits.

The ideal system, which would produce and distribute goods in order to make other people well and happy, rather than in order to get more material stuff and more power for me—cannot exist on this earth. The question is, Must we make our penance so expensive? Must we make a hell of purgatory?

The essence of human economics is to exchange dignity, freedom, virtue, and contentment—for stuff. The measure of the transaction's corrosiveness is often in the amount of aesthetic blight that occurs. One need not look at the South Bronx for an example. The town of Gettysburg will do.

It is not an ugly town, but it has its ugly parts. They are of two kinds: the poor streets and the tourist attractions. Like state lotteries failing to produce better schools, there is no necessary relationship between the one kind of income and the other needed expenditure. We have an example of the "trickle-down" theory in Reaganomics, on a small scale: let the entrepreneurs come in and devastate a block with their glitzy garbage in order to make a million dollars off stupefied tourists, and the people living in the alleys will be better off.

> A sewer of a plan is this;
> All that trickles down is piss.

What happens is that taxes go up. And, of course, the townsfolk have the attractive businesses to look at.

And you have here the essence of the failure of America's press. The Gettysburg newspaper advertises this stuff, gets its revenues from the ads, is bought by the business people; this makes it difficult for the journalists to turn on them and attack a petting zoo on Little Round Top. (Americans don't read, so business must support the papers.) Likewise it's the generals, politicians, and entrepreneurs who give the news media their grist; reporters (especially the ones who want to be television stars, or rich, themselves) aren't going to turn on them and tell the truth. So what is America, if it doesn't have a free press? What offends about America's capitalism is not so much the capitalism, perhaps, as the *totalitarianism* of the system. Driving big Lincolns is little different from having big red posters of Lenin on our walls, but we find it somehow more convincing.

Gettysburg is on a balance, like the lake I sit beside to write. Its clarity is what makes it desirable—and the population around it threatens that very essence. Should this town permit salting of the streets in winter, pouring in tons of deadly runoff? Already the clarity reflects a complete ring of gaudy mansions and conspicuous marinas—but the development is still controlled somewhat. The sailboats in those marinas are part of the body's loveliness, like jewels; but the surface on some days is vexed to nightmare by the nasty buzz of jet skis and other moronic offenses. Shall they let a developer build a family park, complete with fiberglass animals, to further stimulate the economy, draw more people from the cities—make the lake more lovely? Who knows, it might inspire our schools. A dog track!—its muzzled, running beasts and greyhound-eyed developers in Gucci shoes: now that might be the thing.

How far will Gettysburg let developers obscure its painted urn of immortality? Is loveliness for sale? How much honor can you sell without running up a debt beyond repay? How much spirit sunk in the Gettysburg banks repays a hundred thirty years drawn by the developer's lash?

But I do not live in Gettysburg, it may be said; I have no interest in whether the citizens prosper. On the contrary, I live there more than most of them; and it is their very prosperity which I would see restored. One hundred thirty years of battle is enough. Can it be thought that the people of Gettysburg are better off today than they were in June of 1863? As well put a McDonald's in a cemetery, and think thereby to tame the vengeance of the dead.

Blood will have its way. We think we can plant Confederates and make the earth say money. We will find out at last that it's Confederate money.

I would like to propose a historical experiment, which unless a time machine is invented is safely unpracticable and entirely imaginative.

Let there be raised a brigade—judging by recent presidential elections it would have to be from Massachusetts or Wisconsin—and let it be trained and equipped according to the custom of the times, 1863. But let it be armed differently, not with weapons unavailable to the governments of 1863—not with machine guns, lasers, or the like, but with (it may be best for Civil War authorities to leap over what immediately follows) longbows.

That the longbow used at Agincourt had not the range of the .58 Springfield rifle-musket would be the first objection. But neither did the Springfield. Let us say the longbow is as accurate as the Springfield up to 100 yards, still deadly at 150, but nothing like a match for it at 300. Such figuring is meaningless, because accuracy does not reside in a weapon, but in the weapon and its user together. It is enough that the longbow can be accurate at 75 yards, for two reasons: first, the already cited fact that the Civil War musket was seldom used at ranges longer than that; second, the longbow, even up to 100 yards, and probably more, would have been *more* accurate than the rifle-musket.

The reason is that practice shooting was unavailable to the men. Ammunition was considered too expensive. Given that frame of mind, that 1863 economics, the arrow looks very practical. A man may practice to proficiency if it takes all summer. You shoot and fetch. A brigade of practiced marksmen facing an equal number of Springfield-toting enemies will decimate or drive them from the field in five minutes—long before their fire takes many casualties of you.

One has little idea of how difficult it is to fire a Civil War musket. It puts out smoke and kicks, so you can't see what you're hitting—or, more likely, missing: you can't correct your aim. The Civil War musket presents a problem of aiming with which we are unfamiliar because of our modern rifles: there is a delay between pulling the trigger exploding the cap, and detonating the charge. This somewhat offsets the arrow's low velocity.

The kick of the rifle makes you want to quit after a dozen shots, if you are unpracticed, and they were unpracticed.

The longbow makes no smoke. You have an unobstructed view of your fire.

There is no sound and no concussion. A dense front of two or even more ranks could fire in volley—whereas two Civil War muskets fired beside each ear of each front-rank soldier in line of battle tends to modify that line, or at least to argue for a single line at fire.

The longbow's great tactical advantage would be rapidity. In our instance, the well-trained brigade, preferably veterans, is holding the fields north of the Chambersburg Pike on July 1 as Davis's Brigade advances. Smiling until the Confederates get within 75 yards, fooling them the while by having deployed skirmishers armed with conventional weapons, the brigade whips out its bows. In five minutes— Davis's men shooting about four shots each maximum—the Up-to-Date Brigade has shot 25 times each, and Gen'l Davis is running back to Herr Ridge alone. The new brigade then executes a grand left wheel, enfilades the left flank of General Archer (a neat irony here), and *presto!* the morning's attack is repulsed, the Union is saved, and there will never need to be a General Motors.

After its battle the brigade goes back to collect its arrows—an unpleasant task, but gunshot wounds are worse—or gets resupplied by a happy teamster no longer afraid of explosions. The brigade carries its forty rounds, but need not carry more because it wins its engagements quickly. (Imagine Hancock's Corps being armed with bow and arrow instead of rifle and cannon; Pickett's Charge wouldn't have even touched the stone wall!)

The men from Oshkosh and Sheboygan would be happy, because they have not had to carry heavy rifles with hot barrels; they are not fatigued, because they have practiced archery and have developed the proper muscles; no bad weather worries; instead of carrying tools they carry a couple of extra bow strings; and this evening they can discuss poetry and economics rather than clean fouled guns. Their faces are not smeared with blackpowder smoke; they have not eaten any nor inhaled, and their hearing is perfectly intact for the evening sermonette. Finally, the soldiers do not feel stupid for having mixed up a seventeen-step loading process, and they wonder only why someone hadn't thought of this before.

It may be objected that this wouldn't have worked against the Shawnees, but that may be considered part of the point. Further, the cavalry had breechloaders and repeaters; and the Indians did not match their ferocity. Anyway, the idea is that if they had thought of some way to step out of their economy, they might have seen good results.

It may be further argued that to compare the Welsh longbow to any weapons later than Civil War is misconceived. There might have been no development of machine guns, for example, had the longbow been used in the Civil War. Put as many years and as much industry into the development of bows and solar cars as we have put into explosive weapons and the Internal Combustion Engine, and these other things might not be with us. Honda will have developed a bow that can shoot the tweezers out of a man's hand at two miles with only one foot pound of effort, and be the size and shape of a cantaloupe. Such development—or, as many English speakers correctly pronounce it, devil*up*ment—would of course have been enormously deadly by now, it must be admitted. It is the nature of the economy of military death for enemies to keep up with each other. But we may not have been as far along in the essence of all war: killing of nature, or killing the future. In this the economy of warfare resembles essentially the United States economy.

Finally, it might be said that the development of rifles, machine guns, smart bombs, nuclear weapons, and laser technology has not helped warfare solve human problems. Like the national economy, this one is baldly counterproductive—that is, destructive. Of course, as spinoffs of military development we have acquired airplanes, telecommunications, microchip technology, and the like, which would not otherwise have been so advanced. This is a consideration to be weighed.

The benefits of an economy of death are more easily acquired than got rid of. But our understanding of benefits and liabilities, of justice and injustice, of good and evil, are fundamentally confused—and perhaps exactly reversed except that things on this earth are not so neat. Our criminal justice system, for example, is well named. It allows the son of a president who plots to take $2,000 from each man, woman, and child in this country to go free while it puts into prison the son of a black man that president was elected to serve for stealing a television worth $200. I may be exaggerating; the black man may go in for less, and a television isn't really worth $200. At any rate, the disproportion is roughly correct, while the cost to the nation on each end is underestimated.

The sum of the matter is, we are destroyed by our desires. But our minds are imprisoned by them; each of us lives in a totalitarian state unless we are free of our desires; and our desires determine what we call pleasure and pain, justice and injustice, good and evil. No plan or perspective outside our own exists in minds made up of what we want. No wonder the question is difficult to argue, and God does not fit its terms. Only something outside these terms can satisfy our need, rather than our desire, but what is it, and how might we know it?

> Heard melodies are sweet, but those unheard
> Are sweeter; therefore, ye soft pipes, play on;
> Not to the sensual ear, but, more endeared,
> Pipe to the spirit . . .

The town's founding holds a strange coincidence. James Gettys, who made the town, took to wife a woman named Mary Todd. This would be odd enough without the fact of her actually being related to Lincoln's wife.

There may be a unity of things we do not glimpse in common hours. It may be that a music seldom heard drifts among the stars, sweet beyond all measure, grand and subtle, terrible and comforting; that even in our small events its soft incline plays out mysterious harmonies; that somehow all will yet come right—and that we have been paying the wrong piper.

Meanwhile the town, surrounded by its brede of marble men, dances to the mechanical drummer on the corner.

9 Higher Laws

You can't expect much good character from those in power. Power is more than most humans can bear; its tendency to corrupt has been a byword for centuries, though nobody wants to believe it. But the good side of this is that today's public barbarism doesn't in itself mean the American people are morally defunct. A less-distinguished list of mediocrats than the public officials of 1863 you could hardly find—a crowd of small, narrow, greedy, pocked obscurities. The great man Lincoln stands above the sea of Lilliputians as Saul stood a head above the Israelites, but he could not run the country or win the War alone. How was it done? The mother, sister, father at home, the man in the ranks that Whitman found to be patient, generous, courageous, undaunted, true—they did it.

Where are the solid, humble brave of today? Where are the honest, patient, and true? Watching television.

By power I don't mean only Congress and state house. I mean the commercial interests that won the War and profited by the War—the ones who manufactured miles of cannons, mountains of percussion caps, cities of ordnance crates, rivers of buttons; spectacle frames, needles, steel pens, forage caps, stirrups, revolvers, pocket Testaments, playing cards, combs. How could the Southern Confederacy break away from a power that manufactured 90 percent of North America's bayonets and toothbrushes?

The commercial powers of the North picked up the war that Lee dropped. Now their yelling, wawling progeny are everywhere in our faces, in our ears, in our brains; and you can't flood the market with material without driving down the stock of spirit.

In one of Gettysburg's seedy drugstores I heard the constant loudspeaker bringing to my attention the news that thousands of people wake up at night startled and in pain: leg cramps. The commercial advised that I protect myself against this ugly eventuality by buying whatever it is that counterattacks it. One more bottle to have in one's plastic cabinet.

The poor slobs who manufacture this stuff, and manage the stores that sell it, aren't making the real money—for what that's worth. They probably drive old Plymouths and bring home Wendy's hamburgers to eat in front of their big-screen stereo televisions, sad without knowing it. The ones driving the BMWs are the advertising agents who create our need for their product; the lawyers who defend them against us, each other, and the government; the executives who package the "news" these sad ones watch; the sports figures and actors who entertain them; the televangelists who motivate and reassure them; the underworld: in short, it is not the material of free enterprise that gorges itself on money, but the spirit. Our enemy is not the plastic VCR, but the powers and principalities, on earth and above and under the earth, which have engraved the VCR on our hearts, that we fight against. When we're not watching television.

America needs a massive mental garage sale. Get rid of all the pernicious junk—all-day TV, Beverly Hills, and so on—and use the proceeds to buy some mercy and equality. Clean up the place.

A battlefield is usually littered with trash afterward, and somebody can always be found going around to collect it. In Gettysburg some of this stuff is in public museums and some of it is in commercial establishments. At the Adams County Historical Society you can view a cylinder. (The finder of this cylinder, an informative label tells us, became an educated man and used it to store diplomas. It is not identified as a probable holder of maps, used by an officer. Just a cylinder.) You can view a wooden spoon and fork, old bullets, a powerful telescope, swords, a Confederate revolver in bad condition. All of it is interesting in one's weaker moments; the items bemuse you, as if you *should* look at them because they're there. It's always interesting to look at things that aren't made out of plastic, whether they were used by Charlemagne or by Hiram D. Biddle, 6th Mass. Infy. An interesting thing is that most of the stuff is Northern, since the Federals brought the most stuff to the battlefields. Items made by Northern factories and circulated in a proliferating commercial world. Who won the War? And who lost?

Duty is the field of glory. The correspondence of Robert E. Lee is full of references to duty. It is the most beautiful word in the English language, he said. Considerations of duty are everywhere among the soldiers, to a degree which suggests it was widespread in society and not a meaningless abstraction inculcated by a regular military establishment.

The world is different now. While duty might still be an ideal at military academies, the people of America have lost vision of the abstraction upon which duty rests. That abstraction is *posterity*. During the Revolution the word appeared often; now it's gone. And no word replaces it. But duty rests upon it because *duty* is always a requirement made by the future, often without reward for the doer, and often entailing sacrifice. The sacrifice is made for those to come. Today those to come are sacrificed, for our pleasure.

This hasn't worked very well. We are sacrificing unseen multitudes, perhaps ourselves, but our pleasures are desperate and trivial. It would be well to remember that duty is a thing not only to die for but also to live for. Life affords marginal fun with gross misfortune at the center, except in childhood, normally. But Americans have not accepted this. Blessed or cursed by voluminous natural riches, we have come to think not like Russians, Kenyans, Indians, Egyptians—or any other human breed except Americans, to the effect that we can pursue happiness and normally get it. America was an acre of dubloons to a European ragpicker stumbling upon it, and an acre of dreams to which he raised his life. But now all that great glory is spent, and America is a geriatric debauchee rolling downhill in a Japanese wheelchair.

We knew it in 1980, but we thought a patriot was someone who says, Let's forget the bad things and live as though nothing's wrong. Let the critics, the naysayers, be called unpatriotic. We want eight years in Hotel California. But the course of duty would have been to look at things the way they are, and to try to save some of the future for posterity. Better to have stopped kidding ourselves and come to terms with what we had. Perhaps with self-denial—*sacrifice*—we might have saved a little; at least we might have tried to work compassion, justice, honor. They were the things, along with duty, posterity, sacrifice that made the dream worth dreaming, that made America the hope of dignity and liberty, and not the world's marketplace and playground. Our poor need the evidence of things hoped for, some substance of things unseen. But we have sold out, for trinkets—that old Manhattan once again: as Hosea says,

> You have changed your glory into shame.

The greatest robbery of posterity—and we pretend to have such righteous love for the helpless unborn—is the poisoning of Earth. We are rightly outraged at the Eastbloc countries which have created toxic sewers of their land and of our air, while we go on with our cars and convenience and plastic packaging, consuming and abusing much more of the earth per person than anybody elsewhere. As if we were Adam and Eve put in the garden of America, not to tend it, but to use it up and fling the refuse to the skies.

The earth is our physical correlative of the moral universe. We outrage it, and it shrivels into ash around us; we violate its commandments, and our sins are ground to metallic powder in the cup we drink.

Perhaps the world is not so different now.

The laws of nations are not the legislations of their rulers as much as the forces they are governed by. The former are mere human statutes; the latter may operate from somewhere higher, or lower. Ultimately every nation is "a government of laws, not of men."

That was Lincoln's belief, courageously ventured in his Second Inaugural Address, in which he said the war was brought "to both North and South" for the evils they did. Whitman says it at more length in writing that the causes of the war were strongest, not in the South, but in New York, Pennsylvania, and Ohio. There, he said, the malfeasance which saturated public office brought about a disaster as surely as violation of a natural law brings death. Tell me,

> . . . does that Star-spangled Banner yet wave
> O'er the land of the free, and the home of the brave?

or over an ill-kempt sleazy graveyard of the patriots' dream?

One usually defines a nation by boundaries, but that is not the definition that actually obtains. A nation spreads across time more than space. What had Colonel Vincent to do with the abominations spoken of by Lincoln and Whitman? But life is expensive; there is always a rude demand for sacrifice.

The individual person is not defined so much by spatial bounds and features as by time and memory. What if a human being were like a nation, and each life were but a field of memory? If, as the Brahminists have it, the soul marches on through life and life, what cure is there for memory but sacrifice?

The higher laws form no capitalist economy. They operate against all selfishness, and all their services and gains are made for free.

This country rejoiced that communism failed in eastern Europe, but now capitalism is looming to take over. We should look at the total effects of capitalism as we practice it. Going at the present rate, it—or rather we—would destroy the world in an unrestrained rampage of that earthy megapower, human selfishness.

The earth, however, will probably be able to kill us first. It is not unwise to look for other worlds. But there is no good to that unless it is to put new men and women onto them. Old worlds for old people, new worlds for new.

But how to make the new person? It should be plain by now that we can't do it by ourselves; we have too much invested in the old. Still the tragicomedy goes on. We fight, we kill, we die; the constellations wheel, and stars flare through their apparitional appointments.

Johannes Kepler thought the universe is governed by harmonic laws. That seems at least as good a guess as any. What is scientific theory, anyway, but human perception? As such, it is a succession of human hopes and fears, a parade of myths, the one that works today replacing yesterday's.

The Harbor

The harbor steeps in salt and intense sun;
there are no wings and no inflections in the air.
The dry boats are eggshells suddenly run
aground from the world having moved somewhere:
tipped, they ship sun on a saline crust;
they are dust and dust of dust.

Their captains, owners, crews were mastodons
who lumbered to their graveyards under sail,
having felt the water bulging like a bomb,
having seen the sudden swollen eye of the whale:
their hearts slammed shut from terror and stayed clamped
a bleat before the sun burst like a lamp.

Gods and goddesses have slipped their shifts,
shed their faces, sprung their quantum leaks,
and poured like leaping leptons through the rifts
of probability; Orion has become a geek.
All that once was navigated fell
when they proved constellations don't constel.

What are our signs? Where are our prophets?
When our Lord Jehovah breaks the seas
we dry all the way down to the gates of Tophet
and there like water we pour to our knees
and swirl swiftly toward the dusky hole.
What's science but the navigated soul?

What's science but a prophecy of how
the soul will next unplug its silver plug?
The mind is a toy ship, a little plow
abob that somersaults when Atlas shrugs,
watching for a hand, or a trace of blood,
as it drifts upon a draining flood.

I think we should stick with Kepler until the universe we hear conforms to him. It would signal, not a new grasp of the universe, but an

improvement in the race, when the universe we know conforms to the highest laws we feel.

Once some years ago I visited the house where Jenny Wade was killed. The young woman was making bread. A stray bullet, if one can term it such—and how utterly destroyed most of our defenses are if we admit that *any* bullet can be stray!—fired by someone wantonly perhaps (for snipers had good, odd guns, and heavy sights to match them), burst through the door and through her back into her heart.

Many times I've passed the marker telling Wes Culp's story—but not his secret. The site of the wagon-making business where he worked is identified in town. A little while before the War he left and went not many miles into Virginia, following his Gettysburg boss, and worked his trade. Behind he left some friends, of course, and the hill—Culp's Hill, named for his uncle—which many times he'd climbed to hunt birds not many years before. When war came, he joined the army of his new-beloved state.

On his way with Lee that June he came across a wounded Yankee by the road, a friend from Gettysburg, who begged him close and whispered something for his friend to tell a girl, if he ever should get back to Gettysburg—some word of love, perhaps; it was for Jenny Wade was all young Culp said. Wes was killed on Culp's Hill.

> Bold lover, never, never canst thou kiss,
> Though winning near the goal—yet, do not grieve;
> She cannot fade, though thou hast not thy bliss,
> For ever wilt thou love, and she be fair!

Jenny Wade was the only civilian killed at Gettysburg, and, presumably, the only one who had a message to expect. How appalling when the clearest incident of design, or so appearing, should be cruelest; or is there some economy of heaven here? If Ovid had been told of this, our summer heavens would show, perhaps, not Cassiopeia or Cygnus, but Virginia and her Lover, rapt in endless harmony, great and delicate, imperishable in the wheeling light and soft, soft music of the stars. No less indelibly are they inscribed on the battlefield: are the fields of stars greater than these fields? The distances among galaxies are mere brush strokes on the chalice of this place. What they, or He who made them, did here—its glory wrapped from mortal eyes—is painted on this living place more sweetly than in any rhyme.

But their bodies lie in Gettysburg. There is no distance like the hum of horror in our minds. The only sound we have for it is prayer, the kind with silence at its core.

In the Seminary Chapel when the windows are open and the breeze is right, you can smell dairy cows. Having been for a brief time and in a small way a dairy farmer, I have felt there was something right about it—a chapel built on blood and therefore in a way hallowed, but fragrant with the alfalfa of earthly fields. A place Martin Luther would have liked. ("God milks the cow.") But since 1863, American popular religion has moved to the factory.

In the previous century American "evangelicalism" tried to make the world more just for others; now it tries to make the world more comfortable for itself. That certainly is progress of a sort. But it is a perversion of faith. Faith is like the Iron Brigade fighting to the death in McPherson's Woods; popular American religion is like Iverson behind the lines with his bottle. Luther's evangelicalism might not condemn drinking from a bottle, but it does try to avoid living in one. Our religion, in the pagan tradition of most religions, looks like a system for trying to get what we want and being comfortable with what we have—and with what others don't have. Even a casual reading of the New Testament shows that this isn't what the Galilean was talking about.

But literalists aren't casual readers of the New Testament. They read it like you'd read a bicycle-repair manual. The Fundamentalist Principle is that the words in the Book are direct from God and without error, and the Book is applied to life with a vengeance, the way you'd have to apply "Ode on a Grecian Urn" if you thought it was supposed to be a guide to making scooters—or rather, to making one kind of scooter, the only kind anyone has a right to make. It doesn't seem to occur that many other books read and applied with the same blind religiosity might yield the same or better results, in the practical sphere. But the universe isn't a bicycle factory.

I wandered into a public lecture in the Seminary Chapel this spring and heard Dean Lawrence Jones of Howard University. At one point he said, "America is not, never was, and never will be a Christian nation." This has not been an unmixed blessing. But I suppose he meant "Christian" in some ideal sense.

Perhaps there cannot be a Christian nation, even in the ideal sense, or especially in the ideal sense, any more than there is Christian popcorn or Christian trout. To try to conceptualize an institutional nature for them is, like trying to bite your nose, an amusement which puzzles other people.

But as I said, this is not an unmixed blessing, because one would want at least the *ethics* which go along with Christianity to have a restraining effect upon a people's desires and actions. There is a prophetic element in biblical religion that condemns desires as being illusion, to use the Eastern viewpoint, and establishes connections between actions and consequences. America has taken too little care of this again. We have thought that by mouthing moral laws we can escape the consequences of them—as if they were pieces of practical American advice rather than a quantity of fire.

Human actions are too confused in their motivation and too multifarious and unpredictable in their consequences to admit of righteousness. Our efforts must be more heroic and our assumptions less grandiose. The greatest human good has the attendant of evil; likewise human evil can in greater hands produce good. The questions a chapel on a battlefield poses are, In what sense if at all is the kingdom of God really within us and among us, as the New Testament says, and, What should we do?

Though assuming to ourselves every freedom we can imagine or invent, we may have forgotten the greatest and most significant freedom of all—the freedom of God. "God's sovereignty," a favorite phrase in literalist circles, surely does not mean that God is boss, according to rules we establish for Him. It means that He is free—and being God, uniquely and absolutely free.

The universe, a British scientist said, is not only queerer than we suppose, but queerer than we *can* suppose. The element of chance, which is an irreducible problem in human life, is the threshold of God's absolute sovereignty. It is a most frightening place to us; it is also a height which we cannot ascend. Chance is the boundary beyond which even the devil cannot pass. We fractured beings have no control there, whether by reason, prayers, or supposed righteousness. The highest laws are mysteries to us. Chance is where religion ends and faith begins.

The lecture in the chapel ended and a hymn concluded the program: ". . . Give us wisdom, give us courage, for the facing of this hour." Then we went out into the jarring sunlight.

10   The Peach Orchard

There are no larger fields
than these.

—Thoreau

Arguments can be made for Sickles's decision to march his corps into the Devil's Den–Peach Orchard–Emmitsburg Road salient. Harry Pfanz has compared the actual elevations of the Peach Orchard with other areas of the Second Day's field, and proved what on-foot observation shows: the Peach Orchard is a significant elevation. From the Rose Farm, for example, Kershaw's men had to go uphill—the slope is steep enough that from behind the rivulet north of the farm you can't even see the peach trees. From the Peach Orchard you have a long view of the field of Pickett's Charge, all of which is quite a bit lower. The land slopes down toward the Trostle Farm and toward the main Union line; from the Confederate line on Seminary Ridge the Peach Orchard appears as an eminence.

But while this kind of observation supports Sickles's concern about the high ground at the Peach Orchard, the tactical question is larger, concerning the relation of the Peach Orchard to other features. The chief other feature to consider is Little Round Top.

When you visit Gettysburg you are impressed by the size of the battlefield, especially if you've visited Antietam, so hideously small. Gettysburg's size is partly actual: the Union line *is* about three miles long, and the Confederate nearly twice that. But part of the size is only apparent, resulting from disorientation. As the battle becomes clearer, the field becomes smaller. Nearly all the First Day's battle could have been seen from nearly anywhere along the First Corps line. (The apparent size is increased by there being more trees now to obscure the lines of fire.) What becomes really striking is the omnipresence of Little Round Top on the southern half of the battlefield. You can see its bare jumble of stones and monuments from the end of the path in front of the Virginia monument. Alexander's guns along the Emmitsburg Road (aimed at the stone wall and the Clump of Trees in order to support Pickett's Charge) must have been placed *en echelon,* not only to crowd the most metal into the sharpest angle of fire, but also to try to diminish the effects of enfilading fire from the glowering Little Round Top. From the Wheatfield the nasty bald spot is *right there*. And in the Peach Orchard you're a sitting duck.

Sickles should have been more concerned about covering Little Round Top, as he was supposed to do, than about occupying the Peach Orchard. That hill was a castle; the orchard was a knight.

But the question, as Sickles wanted it put, was whether his occupying that forward position saved the Union main line by wearing out Longstreet's attack well in advance of it. This deserves consideration, and of course has received it.

Sickles's presence so far forward was a surprise to the Confederates, making Lee's attack plan, based on earlier observation, odd. (That plan betrayed a dumb lack of attention in the first place, typical of the poor staff work and general lack of coordination during the Army of Northern Virginia's worst-run battle.) Longstreet apparently was frustrated and irritated enough by the unexpected situation that Hood's suggestion of a flank move by Law's Brigade—similar to Longstreet's own rejected flanking idea—struck him like a horsefly.

That idea, to send Law around behind the Round Tops, is quite relevant to a discussion of whether Sickles's move was the right one. Only a freak circumstance of people's minds—the kind of thing that makes visitors wonder about Providence, fate, the intervention of the gods—prevented Hood from sending Law into the Union rear. There were Union troops just at hand there, and Longstreet might simply have lost a whole brigade. But it's interesting to think about what might have happened if Law's fighting Vincent's Brigade *behind* Little Round Top had drawn in more of Hood's Division and shifted the *schwerpunkt* of Longstreet's whole attack from the Peach Orchard to somewhere east of it. Then Sickles's move would have been a catastrophic blunder, the results of which never could have occurred had the Third Corps stayed where it was in the morning. Had Sickles stayed where he had been put, Longstreet would have attacked across the Emmitsburg Road and never looked around behind Little Round Top. So one may argue might-have-beens against Sickles as well as for him.

Lee's order of attack was obviated by Sickles's new position, so why didn't Longstreet simply take the bit in his teeth? Who knows. He may have consulted with Lee again before deploying for the attack. In any case, Lee's manner had already insulted him perhaps. Longstreet was conscious that daylight was running out. He was too prudent to put a brigade where he couldn't see it. But why wasn't he over on the right, where his offensive began? He thought the real coordination problem would be at the orchard.

Coddington dismisses Sickles's claim of wearing out the Confederate attack in front of the main Union line. There was no main Union line behind Sickles, he observes. Coddington knew a good deal more than I do, but I am still tempted to consider Sickles's argument. It seems that for two reasons it's still valid, despite there being no Union line yet on lower Cemetery Ridge. One is that Cemetery Ridge itself was there, a natural fallback position. There was no fallback position behind it. The other consideration is that the Third Corps and its reinforcements were able to fight a retreat in depth, as Reynolds had planned to do the day before; the defensive line was fluid and was therefore hundreds of yards deep. Artillery fought behind the Peach Orchard, for example, fell back to the Trostle farmyard, then fell back to the hillock behind that. But once pushed a few yards back from a Cemetery Ridge line, there was no place to go but a Confederate prison. A Union counterattack, back up the eastern slope of the rise, piecemeal as the reinforcements were arriving, would have had less chance of retaking the Ridge than a coordinated attack of two-thirds of Longstreet's Corps would have had of taking it in the first place.

I think an attack on the Third Corps at the lower end of Cemetery Ridge would have had a chance: no formations broken by Devil's Den; good artillery positions on Warfield Ridge and the Peach Orchard; Longstreet's splendid veterans attacking in depth on a narrow front; and it was Lee's plan.

Quite possible, nevertheless, would have been a repulse of that attack without the grinding up of seven Union brigades. Meade would have been sending reinforcements before the attack hit, because the Confederate approach would have been visible longer. The reinforcements would not have had as far to go, and may not have had to be thrown in piecemeal and in confusion. Artillery and small-arms fire would have been effective before the assault landed. And Vincent and Ricketts still would have gone straight to Little Round Top. Which was better, the long battle which occurred, or one throw of the die on Cemetery Ridge?

Chances are, the Second Day would have turned out the same, with less killing. On general principles, Sickles was wrong. He disobeyed, if not explicit orders, then the intentions of a superior who knew what he was doing. He uncovered Little Round Top. He exposed his men along a position too long for his corps, with both flanks in the air. He could have lost the whole works; he probably threw away many men's lives.

I am interrupted in writing this by a concentration of mallards. The bench where I happen to be sitting on the lake shore is surrounded by noisy, outraged males. Now a female comes up from the lake. (I am on a ridge of two or three feet above lake level.) She comes up Bench Ridge and the males advance. Her noises are also angry, but deeper. The males around me—iridescent deep blue-green heads; deep blue chevrons along the wings; crisp, thin white collars indicating branch of service—deploy and advance. Everyone shouts orders—privates and officers alike, as in the fighting at Devil's Den. The female raises her own battle cry and makes a stand, assisted perhaps (I can't see) by a drake. But the larger battalions go for her, beaks like shovels lowered nearly to the ground. Two in particular, fresh out of military school, press the attack, followed by the others. Around my bench, like Achilles and Hector around Troy, of course, they chase her, never quite close enough to bayonet her. She retreats to the edge of Bench Ridge. The drakes re-form at the Bench line. All is quiet.

Now she's back with five guys, and it looks like trouble. But only she attacks, and she's driven off easily. There is some discussion, and the army moves off.

I had thought this fortuitous battle—not as grand in numbers as the ant battle at Walden, but more splendid than Desert Storm in all its

glory—would help me with my point, that Sickles's bungling impli-
cated a lot of men and women, because the ducks were waddling
around in a way I saw no logic in—sheer bellicose confusion. But it
was *I* who didn't understand what was going on.

Any soldier at Gettysburg then knew more about the battle than I
do now, even without having any idea of what units were where or
who else was doing what. Knowledge is an arbitrary thing. I once had
a colleague who always claimed perfect confidence in his competence, no matter how little he knew about what he was doing. In his
mind it was an entirely valid claim.

Just as in our minds we know the battle. Professor Coddington's
knowledge of the battle was magisterial, and he did know and understand, in a way vastly larger than any participant in the battle; but
what Civil War buff would prefer the knowledge in *The Gettysburg Campaign* to the experience of one person in the battle? Coddington himself would have given all he had, I am sure, for that pearl. There is
knowledge, and there is knowledge; and there is knowledge.

Many Civil War buffs acquire all their knowledge in hopes of coming closer to the particle of experience they want: what it was really
like to be there. Why? (I would wager that, if one could count all real
Civil War buffs, their number would not exceed the total number enrolled in the Federal and Confederate armies.) But alas, one kind of
knowledge does not transmigrate into another. So who knows
whether all our talk about the battle has anything to do with what the
battle was about—or even whether those who were in it had a knowledge of what the battle really was; was their knowledge, or is our
knowledge, any key to Lincoln's knowledge?

We are even more ignorant of the limits of our knowledge than was
my colleague, but this is not to say that there is no knowledge. There
are knowledges. The limits I refer to are those boundaries between
knowledges. We assume that one kind will get us another, and that
what does not exist in one field cannot exist in another; and that an
answer pertaining to a certain field must lie in that same field, or in the
same terms the question is stated in, rather than in another field.

I was told in school that ducks enact instincts, and they don't know
it; but I didn't know as much of what was going on with these ducks
today as one of them. None of us knows the answer to the larger

questions my observation of them raises. Shall we assume, then, that there is no meaning and there are no answers?

But I was about to say that Sickles was a murderous bungler. Some people think the Civil War was particularly characterized by such fellows. The word SNAFU, however, was not invented during the Civil War. I think, in fact, it's the Hebrew word for "postlapsarian."

War is interesting to many of us, not because we like weapons or crave adventure, but because we have questions about life. War is life highlighted, accented with pressure. Here in Sickles's move to the Peach Orchard salient we have, in vivid terms, compacted into a few terrible hours, what Augustine called the *massa damnata*—the group lostness of the human race that puts us all at the mercy of the mistakes and evils other people and nature commit, that implicates all of us in widening circles of tragedy. Sickles's men made no decision to put themselves into that uselessly dangerous position. Now, each of them may have deserved it, or may have had their lives's paths set out in that direction from the day they were born by a wise and kind Providence, like the people in Thorton Wilder's *The Bridge of San Luis Rey*. But, like that book, the battle can only suggest the possibility, not prove it, nor convince many.

We translate our bafflement at this into the question of unfairness, and in our minds this synthesized question rules out there being a kind, wise, powerful God.

Unfairness as a concept has limitations. We cannot trace fairness very far, or control its many variables. Our favorite, "first come, first serve," is an example. What could be more unfair than to give most to the first?—the one with the most reliable car, with the inside information, the one who is the healthiest runner, or whose mom made him wake up earlier, or the guy who showed up by accident? Unfairness is easier to identify in practical terms when it involves oppression, selfishness in power; but the theoretical problem is merely raised to another level.

We expect to fit one kind of knowledge into another; we expect to put God's thoughts into our little heads.

A private named Archibald Duke was shot in the leg during Barksdale's advance to the Emmitsburg Road. After the fighting his brother,

J. W., came to him, and Archibald cried out, "Thank God! My prayers are answered. I have asked Him to take me in place of you as I am prepared and you are not." Leg wounds were often fatal during the Civil War. The big soft lead bullets mangled bones and veins, leaving little for the surgeon to reconstruct; and when a limb was amputated (usually the measure) the soldier's chances of surviving gangrene and infection were not particularly good because sterilization methods were not used. Archibald Duke did die.

J. W. Duke was spared miraculously. Before Barksdale's attack two men were needed to take down a fence. The Union skirmish line was 50 yards from that fence, and Federal artillery had it covered. There were no volunteers, and men ordered to go to the fence refused to obey. Finally the company's captain, who had been personally ordered by Longstreet to send the men, singled out Jim Duke and another man. "We will be killed," Duke said to the other man. But they went. They ran to the fence, took it down, and ran back—untouched. Pfanz speculates that perhaps the Federals wanted the fence down too, but thinks the escape was unlikely nevertheless. We don't like miracles that come about mundanely; they're too hard to believe. Of course the miracle, if there was one, may have been not for J. W. Duke but for Mears, Woods Mears, the other man. Kind of hard to rule out Mears.

That's the trouble with fundagelical miracles; the rest of us appear as supernumeraries in them. Most of us, however, believe that God is secretly on the side of the fifth business folks, the ones buried without names on their headboards, the ones never found in the woods or mentioned by anybody (as if mention were immortality—a pagan notion), the ones evidently forgotten by God. Who knows? Archibald Duke's prayer and his brother's escape may have been the means for saving poor Mears; also we don't know what Jim Duke did with his escape, if anything. Maybe he would have been better off going unprepared. The only thing we really know is that Archibald was a genuine hero. It might not require supernatural intervention to save the brother of a man like that.

Maybe Archibald was a pain in the neck, a self-righteous, teetotaling ass, and his brother Jim, who gave evidence of courage if not valor, was the solid one whose brother should have taken note of his example. No matter. Archibald was willing to lay down his life for someone else. Not willing in the abstract, but positively willing; a Christ-like act. Brothers, friends, lovers, parents, Christians, Muslims, Jews—all of these have been similarly willing. A man dives into the icy Potomac to save passengers of a crashed airplane, keeps doing it until he drowns. Ducks do it. We call it heroism in humans on the assumption that for us it's not an instinct, but perhaps it is, or was.

Now there was a soldier who died not far from Archibald Duke, on the other side: Bucklyn's Union battery, in the Peach Orchard facing the Emmitsburg Road; in it Private Ernest Simpson. Private Simpson was the battery's clerk, a noncombatant, who should not have been up at the orchard with the battery. But he had received a letter from his parents: they disapproved of the girl he wanted to marry. He went out to the battlefield to die, stood among the cannoneers in the shot and shrapnel. A piece of hot iron took off his head.

One act was willing self-sacrifice, another was suicide. Both required a kind of bravery. But it is not bravery that is to be praised; rather, courage. So I vote for Jim Duke and Woods Mears, who were afraid to die but did their duty. No rewards for them, no escape for them—just tragedy, a place they didn't deserve to be in but couldn't get out of. They happened to survive, but that is another story.

An associate of mine tells me now and then about his life. I avoid him when I can; perhaps I am irritated at his helplessness. He has been married for over twenty years to an aggressively frigid partner, and, I assume, the man himself is normal. He could have discovered this fact about her ahead of time but she was too righteous to let him. He is Catholic by background, as he has told me several times to explain, as he sees it, his previous lack of ethical and biblical knowledge; ever since their brief courtship his wife—a born unromantic faultfinder, and a conservative Protestant by upbringing—has lectured him on right and wrong. As a result he is now worthless in his own eyes, and resorts to me with his troubles. A fine expert she is on right and wrong. My associate has read the Bible four times through, looking, I imagine, less for comfort than for a way out, and has found none, but has picked up some comfort along the way. She has not read it once. Still the lectures go on. And still he buys his secret once-a-year *Playboy;* meanwhile at home, he says, she holds forth on the evils of sexual exploitation. Capable of having children, she has used them: You can't leave me, she has said, because of them. (I imagine them to be perfect wrecks; he says they are not.) In his mind he invents a lurid parody of the love and happiness he wants. What obscene, servile lives we lead. He appreciates my listening to him, perhaps especially because he seems not to listen to himself. I tell him he lives the tragic vision, but he has a technical background. I cannot reach the Catholic in him; he has not been reformed but buried. In quiet desperation he will carry his duty with him to the grave. And perhaps come back as a bee. How could her life be other than equally tragic?

Such mere existence is typical. We have either a bleak house, or poverty, or ill health, or failure: the soldier's moments in a battle are emblematic of most lives in this world. It is not what we had bargained for; but then again, it was foolish to have thought we could bargain. Our circumstances are the fields we battle in. We may have volunteered, we may have been ordered: but we are here. Privates Duke and Mears could not improve their circumstances. A soldier drinks, perhaps, and talks and swears and gambles; he reads and writes letters, takes comfort from his pipe and tobacco; he studies his Bible and carries other favorite books; he gets what food he can, what sleep he can, what protection and relief he can; he loves his friends like brothers; wishes he were home. That's about it. A better brand of toothbrush won't make much difference. In the end he will be measured by his courage.

Is my acquaintance a fool? Is he ignorantly brave? Is he courageous? I wish I knew, as I wish for him a miracle. I don't wish to be in his place, but in the current market, are there miracles without sacrifices?

I also think, however, that a God for supernumeraries would take care of Ernest Simpson. Was his death mere adolescent moodiness, or did he show a kind of courage? He died perhaps not so much for his love but, like Haemon in Sophocles, to defy and strike his parents. "The enemy is *here*, and I am going to *strike* him!" Or in his eyes it may have been refusal to obey the rules, to play the tragedy; but a characteristic of tragedy is that it cannot be escaped, only compounded. He might have married someone else and lived a happy life.

Or appeared to have. If Ovid had had his fate to work with, perhaps Ernest Simpson would now haunt the Peach Orchard, entwined with the woman he loved, two branches from the same blood-soaked roots. Whose heart does he not haunt? Who died to save *him?* Or was he more prepared than we'll ever be? War is an excuse for fate. Its fields are maps of bafflingly unreadable design. Or are they nothing but randomness—as the universe itself appears to be?

A Roman Catholic in 1863 would not have wanted to bury Ernest Simpson, a suicide, in consecrated ground. But the brave have consecrated it far above our poor power to add or detract, and they are more forgiving. My associate's wife would condemn Ernest out of hand. He certainly was not a *Christian.* What was he, then? Is there no place for him? Is Ernest Simpson dead as earth, while people like this woman sing hosannas in heaven? My two friends, the lines could as well be bitter:

> *Bold Lover, never, never canst thou kiss,*
> *Though winning near the goal—yet, do not grieve;*
> *She cannot fade, though thou hast not thy bliss,*
> *For ever wilt thou love, and she be fair!*

At Gettysburg it began to show that despite the great Confederate advantage in generalship early in the War, it was the Union which had the richer chest of excellent officers. There could hardly be a better example than General Andrew Humphreys, who commanded the division posted along the Emmitsburg Road just north of the Peach Orchard.

His grandfather, Josiah Humphreys, had designed the U.S.S. *Constitution.* The General himself had been an outstanding topological engineer in the regular U.S. Army. Like Meade and Lee he worked on Mississippi River projects. But he had not fought in the Mexican War, had resigned during the Seminole War. He had been a staff officer for McClellan in 1861; for a time was the chief topological engineer of the Army of the Potomac; then got a brigade to command in April 1862, and a division that summer, which he commanded at Antietam, Fredericksburg, and Chancellorsville. After Gettysburg he would serve as Meade's Chief of Staff, then command the Second Corps (Hancock's Corps at Gettysburg). Charles Anderson Dana, an Assistant Secretary of War, said that Humphreys was "the great soldier of the Army of the Potomac"—a statement which, though leaving out consideration of Reynolds, Hancock, Buford, Joshua Chamberlain, Warren, and so many others, is a mark of the respect Humphreys eventually commanded.

He was not a magnetic person, like Hooker, or a commanding, charismatic figure like Hancock—and his troops had no particular affection for him on the morning of July 2, 1863. He was a strict disciplinarian and wore glasses for reading. In his fifties, he was considered an old man, though energetic and not gray. He kept himself unusually neat and clean, with his "continual" washing and his constant supply of white paper dickies. He had charm for those who respected character, however: a man entirely without vanity, in a profession strutting with prima donnas. He was courageous, skillful, intelligent. He was a man to depend on with your life, or to go fishing with.

Best of all, he was known for his "distinguished and brilliant profanity," and was a prodigiously loud swearer. Sometimes what you want most of all is someone to do honest verbal justice to life. The notion that a person can express as much without resort to all the resources of English is sadly erroneous. We have been misled by all the dolts who swear without imagination: it is like giving a palette to a thousand children and, when not one produces something like a Michelangelo, concluding that painting is vulgar or unnecessary. The artists put away childish things and mount up on wings of splendor into the ether of maturity. With uninspired clods one feels that thought within the framework of such monotonous vulgarities exists and is expressed through a glass darkly, but with a genius like Humphreys it is face to face.

So with a character like his in general. When you look for a friend, what you want is an actual person. Many self-consciously religious persons would not miss church on a Sunday if their souls depended on it, or pronounce an oath if it would save a regiment. A gathering with these folks seems perfectly normal if there is no one to compare them with. But imagine Andrew Humphreys walking into the room: one would suddenly see that the others are faint and watery, and he is the only one in deep, sharp color. The only one with a shadow. His cleanliness is that of honesty rather than self-defense. Some people's goodness is so superficial, flat, pious, and persistent that it almost makes you tired.

Good profanity is euphonious and startling, like any artistic language, or interesting personality, or honest faith. A distinction might be made between the profane and the obscene, profane being an offense against religion or God, and thus ruled out of speech; but while in general this may be a good principle, it is too restrictive when holy things are on one's tongue. And its application mustn't be too widespread: what would we do with most of our religion, and what would happen to us? The god of common religion is easily offended, but the Great Spirit has higher sensibilities. In fatuous excess and nasty temper it is our own tenuous touch to the holy that we impair, and thus violate the Commandment. It should be remembered that the greatest crime in history was perpetrated to shut down blasphemy. No, let conversation and religion be frank and essential.

E. P. Alexander, Longstreet's Chief of Artillery, called the artillery battle centered on the Peach Orchard the severest such fight he'd ever been in—and he had been in Antietam's "artillery hell." The casualties among the gun crews in the fighting at Gettysburg were much worse even than at Antietam. They fought at a range of about 700 yards, in the open except for a few of Alexander's guns behind the trees along Seminary Ridge, on more or less equal terms. There were seven Union batteries at the Peach Orchard salient—forty-two guns in a solid L along the Emmitsburg Road and across the orchard. Alexander developed eight batteries, though the number of guns actually engaged with the salient may have been as low as thirty, according to Pfanz. The Southern gunners had the advantage of converging fire. The shooting went on for an hour.

The idea was to knock out some of the Union guns preparatory to the infantry attack. If the Confederate idea was to trade artillery for infantry, the thought was a good one—but if they planned to use Longstreet's Corps' artillery again soon, it was not. In an even contest, Union artillery generally dealt worse than it received. Their metal was better, and they had been able to afford practice. A good third of the Confederate's fuses were faulty. It was difficult for the Southerners to learn that their valor and self-conceived personal superiority could not stand up to Yankee brass and iron. The Union crews and officers were very good; there was no lack of valor there.

Union infantry were exposed to all this fire. They lay down along the road as Confederate solid shot and shells flew over them, exploded over them, struck among them. General Hancock thought it is the "severest test of discipline" for infantry to lie exposed to an artillery bombardment. Most batteries were using the fearsome solid shot. The idea in counterbattery fire was to dismount the enemy's guns, and solid shot was the way to do this. However, some Union sections tried canister against the enemy's crews, and the Confederates fired many shells. One of these exploded, sending a piece of hot shrapnel into a soldier's cartridge box, driving it into his body and igniting the cartridges "like firecrackers"; in horror his friends watched the "quivering" body, and put their faces to the ground. Shot and shells would strike short, and come bounding toward them.

Spherical case looked like solid shot. Shells were oblong; fuses for both were usually screwed in after the flammable material contained in them was trimmed to the proper length according to the estimated range. Flame scorching the end of the fuse would travel and ignite the black powder inside the iron projectile. This meant that even when fuses worked right, it was a matter of estimating correctly, in order to have the missile explode at or over the target. Not all fuses were designed to be lit by the cannon's detonation. One of Alexander's men grabbed a projectile with a faulty, burning fuse and managed to get the fuse out with his bare hands.

The Trostle barn, unmistakable with the brick design on its peak and the hole from a shot, still stands, along with the house. Visitors often recognize them from one of the famous postbattle photographs, showing dead artillery horses lying in the yard. The batteries here fought the artillery duel, then were attacked and their positions overrun by Southern infantry. Lieutenant Colonel Freeman McGilvery had command of several batteries here, including Bigelow's and Phillips's.

As Bigelow's Battery unlimbered, a Confederate spherical case shot exploded, killing one man and sending a piece of iron through the

lung of Lieutenant Christopher Erickson, a native Norwegian. Bigelow sent him to the rear for medical help, not knowing exactly what
the wound was but correctly judging it to be serious. A while later
Erickson was back, saying he was ready to get to work. Bigelow assumed he was all right. The Norwegian borrowed someone's canteen,
drained it, and set to. It was typical of McGilvery's batteries that day.

At first Bigelow's and Phillips's were at the Wheatfield Road,
roughly on a line with the north edge of the Peach Orchard. McGilvery was attempting to plug an infantry gap with artillery. The Third
Corps had been spread too thin: Humphreys's Division waited along
the Emmitsburg Road, beginning at the Klingle Farm a few hundred
yards north of the Peach Orchard and stretching up to within 250
yards of the Codori barn, which still stands in the field out in front of
the center of the Union line on Cemetery Ridge. Sickles's other division, Birney's, was supposed to cover a line from the Peach Orchard,
through the Rose Woods and the Wheatfield, to Devil's Den. All together it was a 1.5-mile line, twice as long as the one Sickles had been
assigned on lower Cemetery Ridge, with rough ground on the left—
and both his flanks were floating. The whole travesty developed because Sickles had wanted the Peach Orchard's high ground for artillery; all right, now there was plenty of Union artillery at the Peach
Orchard—with too little infantry to support it.

Birney's three brigades were being overwhelmed: Ward's Brigade in
Devil's Den and DeTrobriand's in the Wheatfield by Hood's Confederates, and Graham's Brigade in the Peach Orchard by McLaws. The
Fifth Corps had come to the rescue at Little Round Top, and the Second Corps at the Wheatfield, but all the left of Birney's line had been
shattered. Now Kershaw's Brigade of McLaws's Division was coming
at the Rose Farm and the Peach Orchard; there was another brigade of
Confederates to back them up, and it was clear that Graham's men
would not be able to stay in the orchard long. At about this time
Sickles was wounded; Birney succeeded to command of the corps and
gave Humphreys the desperate order to withdraw his whole division
from the Emmitsburg Road back to Cemetery Ridge.

The effect of all this was to leave McGilvery alone. Some of his
batteries were moving back as Kershaw's men came across the Rose
Farm and up the rise toward the Union guns. The cannoneers worked

feverishly, in the peculiar crash and silence of batteries, the crews knowing their routines and going about them with little need for shouted orders—hands and faces slick, sweat soaking their grimy shirts in the glaring heat. On the right, Barksdale's Mississippi Brigade had broken the west face of the Peach Orchard salient. Just before one battery had pulled out, the man who handled the rammer, John Kraus, had his foot shot off by a Confederate shell; the loader looked at Kraus, expecting him to crumple to the ground—but instead the maimed man shouted, "Damn you, what are you waiting for; put your charge in; I am going to have one more shot at them leg or no leg!" The other man shoved the charge in and Kraus rammed it home. Such was the fight of the Union artillery in the Peach Orchard, typical of the determination which perplexed and enraged the Confederates.

But worse was yet to come. Barksdale had attacked later than intended, too late to support Kershaw properly, but when the attack came it relieved pressure on the South Carolinians attacking Bigelow's and Phillips's batteries. McGilvery ordered them back to the Trostle Farm buildings. A battery that had been ordered out just ahead of these two, Clark's, had fired 1,300 rounds; one of its guns had fired 241: the sustained use had enlarged the touch hole from .2 to .5 inch diameter.

Phillips, seeing the batteries on his right pull out, their horses getting shot, prepared for the move by having the prolonges—heavy ropes wound at the end of a gun's trail—uncoiled and strung out straight behind the guns. When he moved back, one of his guns was taken off "by prolonge": its horses had been brought up, but in the half-minute required to hitch the gun, all of them had been shot down; the crew refused to abandon the piece, and Phillips helped the men pull it over the lumpy field.

At this point Freeman McGilvery became one of the great Union figures at Gettysburg—and all of Bigelow's Battery with him. Bigelow was the last to pull out, from the left of the Peach Orchard. He was being attacked by one of Kershaw's regiments on the left and front, one of Barksdale's regiments on the right; at the same time he was under fire from the Confederate batteries. Bigelow knew that if he took time to attach his guns to the limbers and have the horses pull them out, the guns would be out of action and nothing would stop the

advancing Confederate infantry—probably within a 100-yard distance—from shooting down all the horses and drivers. So he had
the whole battery retired by prolonge. As a few men guided with the
ropes, the others loaded, rammed, primed, and fired the pieces. The
recoil would roll the guns back. In this way they reached a fence
corner just across the lane from the Trostle house.

A gate stood open at the corner. The other batteries had passed
through and were moving back across the Trostle fields toward Cemetery Ridge. Bigelow shouted orders to move his guns one at a time to
follow them, when McGilvery rode up and told him to stay where he
was, and sacrifice his battery if necessary.

The whole Union line depended upon McGilvery's thinking and determination now, as it would upon the courage and skill of Bigelow's
Battery. Humphreys's Division was hundreds of yards to the north,
retiring slowly toward Cemetery Ridge. The Wheatfield, just to the
south and east, was lost; between the two was a quarter-mile hole
with nothing in it but retreating fragments of units. McGilvery told
Bigelow to buy him some time while he gathered whatever artillery
he could to make a line along the east side of the Trostle land.

The place where McGilvery collected his line is marked today by
several cannons; it is a ledge of ground near Plum Run, affording a
good field of fire. While he was hauling units into line there was
nothing to protect him from the oncoming Confederates except, in
that fence corner a couple hundred yards forward, Bigelow's six
guns—where the picture of the dead horses was taken later.

Bigelow had a field of fire of only 100 yards. The ground ahead of
him sloped upward, blocking his view and that of the Confederate
infantry. But almost immediately they were over the rise and coming
at him. Four of his guns fired double canister, then reloaded with
triple charges. One section (that is, two guns) was crowded and had
little field of fire, so Bigelow ordered them to pass behind the other
four, go through the gate, and try to save themselves. One piece went
through the gate and turned over; while the crew was righting it the
other crew, not desiring to linger, took the horses and gun over the
stone wall behind the battery, a feat not possible for ordinary human
beings except under the stimuli of the Rebel Yell and a regiment of
.58–caliber bullets in the air.

A gun crew's officers usually remain mounted. Bigelow and his horse were wounded as the Mississippians crowded from the right, within yards of the cannons, which were now being charged up to the muzzles with canister; each time a lanyard was pulled the Mississippians in front were blown to pieces. The others would hesitate, shoot at the officers and gunners, then come on. All horses of the number five gun were down. The chief of piece two used his last charge, fired, and was shot. A squad of Confederates aimed at Lieutenant Erickson, still mounted, valiantly fighting the weakness and dizziness from the hole in his chest, and fired; hit five times, he fell dead.

Bigelow's men were surrounded on three sides. A South Carolina regiment had worked its way through the woods on the left and came out firing. The attackers in front remained at bay but shooting; on the right the Mississippians approached within a few yards, loading and firing deliberately. Now the fourth side was closing. Some Mississippians had come all the way around to the battery's limbers; as a color-bearer stood up on one of them waving the red Rebel battle flag, others rested their rifles on the chests and wheel rims and fired at the backs of the cannoneers. But McGilvery had made his line.

Bigelow looked back and saw the row of Union guns and ordered his men to pull out. Confederates were right in among the crews of Lieutenant Erickson's two guns, and the gunners couldn't battle them off. Another piece had no horses left; the remaining piece had lost its horses some time ago. The men got out as best they could, leaving twenty-six killed and wounded.

Captain Bigelow reeled in the saddle, and a few yards back from the gate he fell to the ground. His bugler, Charles Reed, and his orderly, John Kelly, lifted him back onto his horse; all three were mounted and the Confederates were almost on them, but they had to go at a walk in order to keep their Captain on the horse. The Confederates were otherwise occupied, or declined to shoot, or some uncanny factor intervened again, and the three managed to get back toward the Union guns of McGilvery's line.

But they came right into the line of fire of the 6th Maine Battery, lanyards taut. Kelly rode off; Reed held both horses' reins with one hand and his Captain with the other. An officer galloped out from behind the guns and shouted at them to hurry, but Reed answered that they could not hurry; go ahead and fire. The guns Reed was in front of were not loaded with canister. It was said that the bugler did not flinch at the concussions or as the shells rushed past him. The two survived. Thirty years later Charles Reed received the Congressional Medal of Honor.

We still have the Trostle Farm, and the photograph's dead horses. Many other horses were left wounded and maimed, all across the fields from the Emmitsburg Road and the Peach Orchard back to the farm buildings. They stood, according to one soldier, "upon their maimed limbs regarding us with a silent look of reproach which was almost human in expression."

Part of war's betrayal is accepted willingly, as when soldiers enlist or permit themselves to be drafted, and part is suffered in ignorance. Bigelow's men didn't ask Dan Sickles to move his corps out more or less contrary to orders and expose them to three crossfires; nor did Longstreet's men ask to be ordered into an ill-conceived, mismanaged slaughter. But war and life are like the Battle of the Peach Orchard, as McLaws called it. "The battle fought . . . was not the battle planned," in Harry Pfanz's words. Unanswered reproach rose from grieving homes North and South.

> Weeping, sad and lonely,
>   hopes and fears, how vain.
> Yet praying when this cruel war is over,
>   praying! that we meet again.

North of the Peach Orchard, General Humphreys had been ordered to execute the most dangerous movement in tactics: a withdrawal under attack. Not once but twice. First, Birney ordered Humphreys to refuse his left in response to the pressure of Hood's attack. Then, as Kershaw and Barksdale attacked the Peach Orchard, the order came for the division's withdrawal to Cemetery Ridge. Humphreys did not know that the corps's left was in ruins, but he did know that in addition to the fighting on his left there was a major attack coming at his front. It was Anderson's Division, A. P. Hill's Corps; their turn had arrived. (Evidently it was Anderson's Division, not Longstreet's Corps, that was to attack *en echelon*, right to left.)

Humphreys was outraged at this order. Not knowing he had no support on the division's left, he wanted to hold out, and felt certain that he could. He did not want his men shot down by the hundreds retreating in the face of an advancing enemy. But in any case, he was not going to let happen what was almost inevitable in such a withdrawal: that it degenerate into a rout. He held the division to an iron discipline, retiring a few paces at a time while the men loaded, then ordering the long line to turn and fire. Humphreys himself, riding a horse dripping blood from seven gunshot wounds, and his staff rode back and forth making sure his orders were obeyed. Sometimes Humphreys rode *between* his line and the enemy. When his horse was finally killed by a shell fragment, Humphreys borrowed another and remounted.

The men may not have needed the provost guard of seventy which Humphreys had strung out behind them. They made a fighting retreat; they were going back to take up a line, not fleeing; they didn't feel like or act like defeated troops. A New York private took the time to remove a bloody bridle from the horse killed under his colonel; but shortly after presenting it to the colonel he was shot. The color guard of the 11th New Jersey had been ordered to plant the flag; then in the confusion the lieutenant who gave the order forgot them. When he remembered them and ran back through the smoke, he found them still there—an island in the storm of bullets and shells, a tableau in smoke with the Stars and Stripes flying huge over them.

The whole division turned twenty times, in Humphreys's recollection. In the retreat the 11th New Jersey, turning, firing, loading, walking, lost 60 percent. The withdrawal of Humphreys's Division, like the stand of Bigelow's Battery, was an act of concentration. Condensed into an hour or two, the challenge of earthly life: a relentless barrage of fatal distraction.

The division left its dead and wounded covering the ground from Emmitsburg Road to Cemetery Ridge, but it did not panic, it did not run, and the great Confederate wave was wearing out, was losing men it could not lose, and Meade's reinforcements were coming. Through the rest of the War his veterans remembered General Humphreys riding in the storm along the lines, calm and iron-eyed, his voice loud amid the tearing volleys, ordering, cursing, encouraging; unhurried and intent—and to them he was "the great soldier of the Army of the Potomac."

11 *The Round Tops*

The thinking in quantum physics today is that the observer affects the phenomenon: which slot the electron goes through is determined by the person watching. Could this "discovery" have been made in any other century? I don't refer to the technology which made the "discovery" possible, but to the frame of mind which made it inevitable. There seems to be a personality in an era, and all branches of thinking become aspects of that personality. Historians, like physicists, are especially aware of the influence of the observer. The logical consequence of this is, on the one hand, deconstruction as a literary theory, and, in cosmology, a revival of the idea that the universe is not actual but apparitional. Not that such a conclusion is necessarily wrong. Hindu philosophy has been saying all along that the universe is apparitional. The difference, and the depth of our problem, is that the Brahminists say this illusion should be overcome, transcended—but today we simply describe the universe as not actual, or determined by us, and let things go at that. It's the difference between courage and despair.

There's nothing new in saying that we often find what we want to find in history, and it's clear that we remember what we want to remember. For instance, who was right about how far the 15th Alabama got in their attack on Little Round Top, and who was right about why that regiment retreated when it did? In both cases the two colonels, Joshua Chamberlain of the 20th Maine and William C. Oates of the 15th Alabama, disagreed. Neither was an ungracious partisan, but their memories and impressions differed—each in favor of his regiment.

Oates insisted that the present marked line at the spur of Little Round Top is *not* the limit of Confederate advance, that his command pushed the Maine men back to a second line behind it. Colonel Oates claimed a clear memory of being near a large boulder behind the present marked line—a memory transfixed by the horrific sight of one of his men bayoneting a Yankee through the head. Colonel Chamberlain wrote that groups of Confederates did penetrate his line, and that sometimes there were more Rebels around him than Maine men. Perhaps the difference here is that the lines were at times so jumbled, so interpenetrating, that each colonel could have had a different idea of where his line was. "I say our line is here!" "Be damned! *Our* line is here!" kind of thing.

Somewhat more problematic is the conflict between Chamberlain's certainty that his regiment's bayonet charge threw the 15th Alabama into flight, versus Oates's statement that he gave the order to get out of there on the run *after repelling* the bayonet charge. Of course, Oates gave the order based on some confusion: the appearance of sharpshooters and a company of the Maine men on his right flank. His claim that he retreated through a line of dismounted Union cavalry in his rear lends plausibility to the idea that the order was precipitated by panic, brought on by the bayonet charge and the flank volley. (I have found no written evidence of Union cavalry in that place then. When Sickles's Corps went into position on the left, Buford's cavalry had been ordered off the field to refit in Maryland—Buford having operated without forage or sufficient horseshoes for some time now.) On the other hand, Oates says his men collared three troopers. Presumably they were palpable. Could Oates simply have made a mistake, thinking of the cavalry there on the Third Day? Or were some of Buford's men still around, either stragglers or, like some of that division's troopers on the first day, stubborn men staying to fight with the infantry? It seems not unreasonable that *some* cavalry would have been around on the left flank of the Union army, with ammunition wagons parked only several hundred yards away.

The melee of battle engenders strange confusions and controversies. It is known, for example, that a Confederate lieutenant colonel surrendered to someone of the 20th Maine, but to whom? Was it Reed, as the officer himself and Oates both claimed, or Chamberlain, as Chamberlain claimed? How can this one be solved or reconciled?

These cases are not terribly decisive of anything, and nobody is lying about Watergate here, or about being in or out of some loop. But how are we to know what really happened? Can we ever know? Did the participants really know? What does it mean to "know"? These are not modern questions, but there is a modern answer: nobody knows—nobody as opposed to Somebody. Some questions aren't knowledge-able; the "God question" is one. Just as medievals thought they proved God's existence ontologically, we think we prove his non-existence epistemologically, in effect. He exists because of what must be; he doesn't exist because of what we can't know. What's a little silliness now and then?

The problem gets serious when one becomes involved in it some way. You go to Little Round Top and hear somebody telling a group of people that the 20th Maine faced two-to-one odds and won anyway. Now, there's no question, even in the mind of Colonel Oates, that the Maine regiment was a hard-fighting crew. But suppose you have emotional ties to Alabama, or you live in Wisconsin, Indiana, or Michigan? Then you quibble.

As an Alabamian, you note that the Fifteenth had marched 28 miles since waking at 3:00 A.M. It was in the mid or upper 80s on Thursday, July 2, and humid. The men were fatigued, hungry, and needed water very, very badly when they arrived on the field south of Gettysburg. Ordering the regiment's canteens gathered, officers sent out a group of men to find water—but then the regiment was ordered forward before the canteens got back. (The water detail was captured a little later.) The importance of this should not be underestimated. Then the Alabamians encountered the fire of United States Sharpshooters (that weenie Berdan's men, who could put ten shots into a five-inch target at 200 yards; decent infantrymen must have feared and despised sharpshooters). The Fifteenth lost at least two men killed before the men in clever green, sensing that pretty soon they would get shot back at, lit out and didn't stop until they reached the other side of Round Top, and found another place to wait quietly in ambush. Then the Alabamians climbed Round Top, difficult enough today even with the paved path, *then* were ordered to go back down and attack the 20th Maine, waiting behind rocks and trees and *up the slope* of Little Round Top.

Now we can get to the numbers, remembering that the Maine regiment should be multiplied by a factor of, say, two because of its position. The Twentieth was 386 officers and men, computed by Busey and Martin *(Regimental Strengths and Losses at Gettysburg)*, based on reports of Chamberlain and others. Oates says his strength was about 400; elsewhere he said 500. Does this variation put other statements into doubt? Busey and Martin put the Fifteenth at 499 but note that 22 water carriers, Company A, and an unknown number of men who had not been able to keep up over the 28 miles and hot sun were missing from that total. So the biggest regiment in Hood's Division, 600 men sometime before Gettysburg, may well have had only 400 men on the field. If this is so, the Twentieth had them pretty well whacked before the word Go.

Oates says that in the attack his men were fired on obliquely from the left by one or more regiments to the right of the 20th Maine. (The Confederate regiment next to Oates was very small.) When you add the men in snazzy green to Chamberlain's total, you find that, unless he actually fought only Chamberlain's left companies, Oates *might have been outnumbered.* Twenty-eight miles; perhaps no water; uphill.

The purpose of all this is not to detract from the Twentieth but to give proper credit to the Fifteenth. Those Alabamians were splendid fighters and sufferers, and perhaps only the 20th Maine or some few other regiments like it, and as intelligently officered, could have resisted them. *You* stand at the base of Little Round Top and look up.

When you read accounts of the battle between the Twentieth and the Fifteenth, and stand in that small area, and realize that perhaps 30,000 bullets were fired there, you wonder how anybody could have survived. Losses were Fifteenth, 81 killed and wounded; Twentieth, 110 killed and wounded (which suggests that Chamberlain did fight two regiments)—with missing and captured added, 34 percent and 32.4 percent. This is grievous. But look at the 2nd Wisconsin: 77.2 percent; or for all of Meredith's Brigade: 63 percent. Now one sees why, though the deeds of the 20th Maine are not to be denigrated, veterans living in the South and the Midwest thought the Northeast, with its publishers and political influence, was taking more than its share of glory.

The stand of the 20th Maine and the 15th Alabama's attack constituted a dramatic focal point of the battle, and as such deserves all the attention it receives. But though the 20th saved the day, it was, as Bruce Catton observed, a day that needed a lot of saving, and it was a battle that is almost infinitely interesting because there were constant possible turning points. McPherson's Woods, the Railroad Cut, Cemetery Hill, Greene's Brigade, canteens, Hood's pleas, misunderstood order in the Peach Orchard, McGilvery and Bigelow, Ewell, Reynolds, Lee, Jackson's death, Brawner Farm. The list, even of events during only July 1–3, could become very long. It was a decisive battle where many things were decisive.

Why is it that in a battle where so much depended upon so many individual acts, one can get the feeling that something beyond human action took part? For instance, a Confederate sharpshooter almost shot Joshua Chamberlain. Twice he had the Yankee colonel in his sight; twice he *felt something wrong* and decided not to. What subtle influence? Neither he nor Chamberlain doubted that influence. Why didn't someone decide not to shoot Vincent, or Hazlett? Why, in fact, slavery, and the War? Uncanny experiences make the problem of evil more complicated and acute.

The joker in this deck is the human mind. It is our concepts of free will, predestination, evil, divine goodness and omnipotence and omniscience that do not work together.

The Christian soldiers fighting over Little Round Top would have had their own difficulty in trying to reconcile concepts of free will, evil, and so on, in the Bible which gave them direction, comfort, and strength. There are two horns of the dilemma. One projects from the notion that everything in the Bible is inerrant and directly from God. You're busier than a cat tidying up on a tin roof, then, trying to explain all the contradictions and nastiness in the Bible. Who says the Bible is inerrant? Why, the Bible says so! Unless one is an American, one wouldn't buy a brand of soap on such logic. If it be countered "Of course! It's beyond human understanding," then anything illogical could be afforded the same defense. There is another problem with biblical inerrancy: it has no practical existence. Let us say the Bible is inerrant; but it does not exist for us by itself, apart from human reading. Which reader, that is to say, which interpreter, is also infallible? If the Bible were infallible, we'd never know it. The concept is vacant. Getting two theologians to agree on an interpretation is like convincing two ducks to kiss. The odds for Pickett's Charge were better.

The other horn of the dilemma is liberal interpretation, of the kind where culture or reason or individual intuition—a pietistic variation—are normative, instead of Scripture. While the Bible isn't used as a textbook, or a manual for small-engine repair, in this view, it provides no reliable standards of spirituality or wisdom either. There are no standards. This liberalism has no weapon against fundamentalism, and no weapon against itself.

Liberalism and fundamentalism are rationalistic. Their means for interpreting the world and Scripture, for knowing good and evil, and the medium for receiving God's dictated word, is none other than that splendid mechanism that made up good, evil, omnipotence, goodness, omniscience, and now can't put them all together. For the ideas in this little round top, whether they come supposedly from an ancient book or from a social program, people are willing not only to die but to kill.

In order to make a simple illustration, let us pretend that the men of the 15th Alabama are fundamentalists and those of the 20th Maine are liberals. The "fundamentalists," typically self-serving, find that slavery is by gosh in the Bible and so it's right; the "liberals" bag the Bible on that score and try to make everyone else conform to their concept of what's good. At some point, both say, you've got to stand up for what's right. That point is Vincent's Spur, on Little Round Top. Who wins? Neither idea, only the side with more guns, or better ground, or smarter leaders, or fresher bodies.

The average Southerner didn't fight to preserve slavery any more than the average Yankee fought to abolish it. Each fought for pretty much the same things: freedom; preservation of home, government, rights; for the flag, for the country; for adventure; out of hatred, fear; for duty. But really, most joined for none of those reasons either. Most of the volunteers enlisted because of an inner necessity that neither they nor we could understand.

There is an alien yet subtly human mystery here, creating a comprehensive beauty, subsuming horror and bravery alike, rising over the known causes and events of the War; transforming courage and contingency, accident and virtue, lifting their effects toward the beauty that sustains the stars.

12 The Rose Farm

Explore thyself. Herein
are demanded the eye
and the nerve.

—Thoreau

If one were to choose to serve in someone's brigade with the idea of taking the mold of its general, it would probably be Kershaw's Brigade. Joseph Kershaw was a lawyer and military man; returning to South Carolina after the War, he became a legislator and jurist. His reports are characterized by a graceful decency and restraint. He was a fine Southern gentleman, "gallant and pious," according to McLaws; "cool, [and] judicious."

His wartime photograph shows refined solidity and a handsomeness not quite independent of trustworthiness, but also inseparable from that quality of dash without which he could not have been the consummate Confederate brigadier he was. Courage illumines his light blue eyes; his voice of command inspired courage in his men.

That he was a highly intelligent officer is clear from what he did when his brigade reached what we might call the jumping off point, after that long, wasteful march into position which Longstreet so thoroughly bungled, perhaps more or less wanting to. His whole corps marched four miles to cover one, under a hot sun, suffering delays while questions and orders were being relayed, taking a couple of hours to do it.

As Coddington observes, Longstreet's attack on July 2 couldn't have hit Meade at a worse time—Sickles just having gone into place but not braced, and Little Round Top being temporarily uncovered—still, the attack was supposed to have occurred at about noon instead of late afternoon. Longstreet, neither believing in Lee's plan (rightly) nor wanting to attack without his third division,

Pickett's, hadn't started his corps from its camps a few miles west of Gettysburg early in the morning, as Lee had expected him to. Then when it became clear that the corps would have to countermarch to avoid being seen by Union signalmen on Little Round Top, Longstreet agreed to McLaws's wishes and idled Hood's Division while McLaws marched past them in order to preserve the order of march, when it should have been reversed to save time.

But there was a problem between Longstreet and McLaws. Longstreet may not have been so solid a man, in his view of himself, as his solidity in battle might cause one to believe. The tall Georgian (not "burly," as he has been described) was somewhat temperamental, it seemed, and needed to think highly of himself. He was very able, that is true; he was Lee's "war horse," in the Commander's words; but at Gettysburg he gave Lee a lot of guff few other commanding generals would have tolerated. Longstreet was right and Lee was wrong, and perhaps Lee had some intimation of that; but Longstreet's balkiness once the orders had been given look a little like insubordination. He was not the villain Early tried to make him out to be after the War, attempting to cover his own (Early's) mistakes while also discrediting a non-Virginian; Longstreet had not been ordered to attack at dawn, as some claimed later. But he was slow. He was dismayed, discouraged, and angry.

McLaws would have none of it. *This* Georgian, who was the burly one, had been highly competent all during the War; he was reliable and intelligent. But, if the judgment Freeman made in *Lee's Lieutenants* is correct, Lafayette McLaws never improved, never developed with the War, so at Gettysburg he seems uninspiring. Freeman also points out that the general's apparent lack of brilliance at Gettysburg was "no fault of his own." Certainly it's hard to fault McLaws; his division performed superbly. Barksdale's charge would be hard to equal for color, *élan*, and success; and Kershaw succeeded in a Herculean task. During the Chickamauga campaign McLaws was relieved of command by Longstreet; McLaws demanded and received a court martial, which vindicated him. But he never was returned to his old division; Kershaw was appointed to its command, which he retained until its surrender during the Appomattox campaign.

On July 2 Kershaw came to the edge of the woods on Seminary

Ridge, where the road from the Wheatfield and the Peach Orchard comes west to cross it, and stopped short. He had been told his brigade would emerge at a point opposite a farm and a peach orchard a quarter-mile ahead across the Emmitsburg Road; he was to deploy and move forward to occupy the orchard, so that artillery could be placed there for the corps's attack on Cemetery Ridge, where the Yankee line was. There would be nothing in that peach orchard, except maybe some Yankee skirmishers.

A reconnaissance had been done many hours earlier. Lee had sent a few mounted men out before dawn; they had ridden all the way to Little Round Top, found nothing but Yankee cavalry down around there. Shortly after they left, Union infantry came and occupied Little Round Top; but they were withdrawn about midday, so that Sykes's Fifth Corps could occupy it. It was between these two occupations that Lee had someone look again. And of course Sickles didn't waltz out there until midafternoon, so that, not keeping a constant watch in that area, Lee and everyone else assumed the Yankees were dull enough to end their line on lower Cemetery Ridge, short of the Round Tops.

There had been other problems too. Before Longstreet's march, Lee, McLaws, and Longstreet had gathered to talk. Lee showed McLaws how he wanted him to position himself and attack, tracing a line across a map. Longstreet came over and said, No, *this* is how I want your division placed. It was exactly at right angles to what the commanding general had indicated. Lee, no doubt forcing down considerable irritation, said, No, I wish it to be exactly opposite—and traced the line again. Longstreet went away angry at Lee, not only for *this* happening in front of a subordinate he didn't get along with, but for Lee's rejection of all Longstreet's advice; Lee was angry at Longstreet for his insubordinations and delay; and McLaws was madder at Longstreet than he was at the Yankees. He was working for a boss he despised, who he thought was "a great humbug." In a letter to his wife written July 3, McLaws referred to Longstreet's behavior during the previous afternoon and evening: the other Georgian was unusually off balance, McLaws wrote, going around giving contradictory orders to everybody, and in general being "overbearing." (Interestingly, Longstreet wrote that at Gettysburg Lee was off his usual balance.)

These Confederates were not getting along. I think it had important consequences. Longstreet stayed with McLaws's Division to direct the Corps' battle, instead of going over to supervise Hood on the Yankee flank. This was due to no chumminess toward McLaws. Probably he considered McLaws's position central, as his would have to be the division actually to break the Union line—and it was in the middle of the attack, because Anderson's Division of Hill's Corps was supposed to go in on McLaws's left after the First Corps's offensive developed. But perhaps Longstreet also trusted Hood, and wanted to stay with McLaws to make damn sure he did what he was supposed to. So when Hood sent his requests to turn the Yankee flank, there were delays in getting Longstreet's responses. (Longstreet may actually have received those requests in McLaws's detested presence.) When he finally rode over to Hood, Longstreet's refusal was as petulant as it was regretful. He was still mad about everything.

Longstreet could have changed Hood's orders; he had already changed the whole Corps' plan of attack because Lee's orders, after all, wouldn't work: they made no sense once the new Yankee position had been discovered. Given the results of Longstreet's battle, it seems justifiable to consider Hood's alternative.

But imagine Kershaw's startled expression when he looked out of the woods and saw all those Yankees where there weren't supposed to be any. One would give Los Angeles to know what this Southern gentleman's first words actually were. The place was bristling with artillery; Federal batteries and infantry were stacked along there like cordwood; one line extended off through that farm toward the hills to the right, and along the Emmitsburg Road there was another whole Yankee division. It looked like those Yankees meant business. He suspended the order to go out and deploy, and instead told his men to file off the road behind the treeline and stay under cover. Then he went to ask McLaws for further orders.

McLaws couldn't believe what Kershaw told him. Went to look. Wait a minute here.

Some time later a message came from Longstreet back on the line of march, asking why the attack hadn't opened. (Clearly, the original plan called for McLaws to attack before Hood.) McLaws sent a temperate reply to the effect that, as he would be attacking superior numbers in position, he required time to revise his dispositions.

What? You can imagine Longstreet's reaction. Spurs his horse forward.

And there they were, thousands of Yankees. For once the boys in blue had the advantage of surprise in a Confederate attack.

In the two hours or so that passed while plans were changed and Hood's Division attacked Devil's Den and Little Round Top, Joseph Kershaw had plenty of time to look at the long blue lines and think. He was to attack straight ahead: that farm and that orchard full of guns.

When he went forward, he sent three of his regiments toward the Rose Woods across the farm, while two others were to veer north, ultimately at a right angle to the first three, and take those guns that would be enfilading his main line.

The plan was good, and it worked except that one of the orchard regiments misunderstood an order and instead of capturing guns opened a hole in the brigade's attack. Eventually Kershaw's Brigade fought in two parts, in the Wheatfield and across the Trostle Farm. On the way to the Wheatfield his men had crossed the Emmitsburg Road, the fields in front of the Rose buildings, and the woods, exposed to artillery fire and a brigade of Yankee riflemen in the woods.

The often-reproduced photograph mislabeled "Dead of the 24th Michigan" shows Kershaw's dead South Carolinians lying in front of Rose's Woods.

I've walked the fields in front of the Rose Farm many times in the last few years, trying to imagine the viewpoint of the South Carolinians: the big hill off to the right, beyond those woods; on the left what looked like a hill or ridge with a peach orchard and stretching away on both sides from it a solid line of blue artillery crashing; straight ahead a big stone barn and a stone house. And then perhaps nothing—or what? The next thing you know, you're a tourist, and it's the twentieth century? All the people you knew look different, but feel the same; this place has a meaning about it, a sense of purpose you didn't feel before, a shadow of divinity, a beautiful place—death, yet everything still here as it was; distance and time immense yet close; of all the strangeness what is most strange is the familiarity. Or, as in Tolstoy, a change to the pale blue and clouds of heaven? Or nothing? *Nothing?*

In the grip of all this space, time, and intention, those men, one thinks, should have been as reverent and still as monks. Fat chance. A Union captain was shot as his regiment pulled back through the Wheatfield, pursued by Georgia infantry (which followed Kershaw), who had just forced them from the Rose Woods. The Northerners there had exacted a terrific toll for the passage, using in a relatively short time most of their forty rounds. As two soldiers helped the blue captain away, he was shot in the back and killed. One of his two men leaned over the stricken captain for his last words. What he heard in a few seconds was a stony Georgia drawl: "Go to the rear you damn-yankee son of a bitch."

Rose himself got callous. Becoming tired of bodies being buried all over his farm, he dug up an officer buried near his door and left him to rot behind the house. (Fine stone buildings they were, "but the coarse louts that live in them!") Not a worthy steward of the treasure given by the gallant Kershaw and his men. A representative man of our times, though—what he did with spade and shovel we have done with self-interest and willed ignorance; we have interred something dark into the nation's fate, and into our souls. They churn in our hearts, they jibber in our dreams; our poor we will always have with us. There is in lack of gallantry a most perfect hatred of one's self.

Recently I spoke with a staff person at a VA hospital. Based upon her experience, did she believe that more Vietnam vets have killed themselves than died in Vietnam? "Oh yes, but even more don't get counted—the ones who kill themselves passively, with alcohol or drugs." I asked what the men are like. Reluctantly: "I'm getting tired of many of them. They use the system to get medication and attention." (You mean the system that used them?) Why all this, do you think? "I suppose because they didn't get any appreciation when they came back from Vietnam. Poor self-image."

They weren't accepted *for what they did*. Most of us don't get thanks for what we do. But they needed someone to tell them wrong was right. "The world is startlingly moral"—certainly the world we hold inside our heads. The vets weren't fooled, this time: they were had, they were sent to do a dirty job and they got dirty; they became the country's executioners, scapegoats, and lepers all at once. They have been ignored.

This is exactly how we deal with our millions of poor. They are lower than "gooks," "dinks," and "slopes"; they are nothing at all. Dead and buried in the streets.

The Rose Farm is a grave. Once I heard a Civil War scholar leading a group of tourists out from the Rose Woods and across the fields which on July 2, 1863, were in clover; his voice carried to where I stood at a fence, trying to make out the information. I heard nothing except bits of sound from across that grave where rows of bodies lay, the syllables confused and distant, small, sounding like several people talking all at once, a confusion of many voices moaning round across the deep.

13   *The Wheatfield*

Colonel Edward Cross commanded a brigade in Caldwell's Division, which was sent from the Second Corps to help Sickles hold his line against the developing Confederate attack. The brigade deployed into line of battle facing the Wheatfield, in the center of that part of Sickles's front which extended from the Peach Orchard to Devil's Den.

There had already been fighting near the two ends of the Wheatfield; two Union brigades, after a hard fight, had been pushed from the stony hill on the Wheatfield's west edge by Kershaw's South Carolinians. To the south, Anderson's Georgia Infantry and Robertson's Texans had dislodged the Union line extending toward the Wheatfield from Devil's Den, and most of Anderson's Brigade occupied the stone wall extending halfway across the south edge of the field. DeTrobriand's Brigade was still falling back from that three-foot-high wall, contesting a Confederate advance into the Wheatfield itself. The right half of Cross's battle line would strike that stone wall; his left two regiments would enter the woods that protruded 150 yards into the southeast corner of the field.

Colonel Cross always wore a red silk handkerchief around his head when going into battle—had done so on the Peninsula, at Antietam, Fredericksburg, Chancellorsville—but today was different. On June 28 he had asked Lieutenant Hale of his staff to take care of his belongings after the approaching battle, for it would be his last. The lieutenant, hiding his nervousness perhaps, made light of the request. But on the morning of July 2, as the brigade began its march toward the fighting at Gettysburg, Cross asked him again: See to my belongings, will you? because I won't survive this fight. Nothing further came up during the march and the anticipation of the battle, and Hale assumed it had been forgotten. When the brigade was ordered forward with the rest of the division, Cross as usual asked the lieutenant to tie the handkerchief around his head. But the silk handkerchief Cross handed him this time was not red; it was black.

General Hancock, the Second Corps commander, rode up to Colonel Cross as the brigade marched from Cemetery Ridge. "Colonel Cross, this day will bring you a star."

"No, General," said Cross, "this is my last battle."

When Hancock rode away, Colonel Cross looked toward the Wheatfield, deep in thought, then roused himself, mounted his horse. "Mount, Gentlemen," he said to his staff. Cross rode out in front of the brigade and led the line, flags flying, toward the Wheatfield.

The 1st Texas and the 15th Georgia waited in the woods on the brigade's left; Anderson's men loaded their rifle muskets behind the stone wall. The Union battle line would take the wall obliquely. The brigade halted in the Wheatfield; Cross and his staff dismounted and passed to the rear of the line.

He was on the right, in the open field; before ordering the charge he wanted to check on the left regiments in the woods. Walking into the trees, behind his 5th New Hampshire, he was shot in the abdomen at 45 yards. (The Confederate soldier who shot him took his aim from the ten-foot-high boulder on the east side of the Wheatfield, at the southwest corner of two battlefield avenues; you can recognize it by a cleft running horizontally two feet from the top. The Confederate was killed by Sergeant Phelps of the 5th New Hampshire; the sergeant was killed in the subsequent fighting for the Wheatfield.)

The Wheatfield seems to be a rather small place, considering the thousands of men who fought back and forth over it. It was a very confusing battle; toward the end of it a Union regiment's colonel heard from one of his men: "Colonel, I'll be damned if I don't think we're facing the wrong way; the rebs are up there in the woods behind us. . . ." The Wheatfield is in an angle between the wooded Stony Hill and the extension of the Rose Woods going along the south and around the southeast. "Tige" Anderson's Georgians fought three times there, and Kershaw's Carolinians twice, or rather continually, succeeding at last. First DeTrobriand's Brigade defended that part of the Union line, then Caldwell's Division (Cross, Kelly, Zook, and Brooke); after the Confederates finally won the battle for the Wheatfield and advanced toward Cemetery Ridge, Longstreet's offensive had worn out and Union reinforcements had arrived. The victors, Anderson and Wofford and Semmes and Kershaw, all retreated back through and out of the Wheatfield in the face of Crawford's fresh Union infantry. So it remained in Federal hands after all, despite the Confederate success.

Wave after wave had trampled the wheat, advancing, firing, sometimes at very close range; sometimes fighting with bayonet and rifle butt, pistols and fists; first one side advanced through the smoke—the Irish Brigade with its emerald flags—then the tattered red flags from Georgia or South Carolina; then, with shouts for New York or Pennsylvania, a line would advance through defeated, flag-cased troops: so on it went, until two thousand men lay bleeding in that hot July pandemonium. It is a small field for two thousand shot men. And any sense to it is hard to discover.

One soldier wanted to take some of the grains home; it was a different, good-looking kind of wheat they didn't have back in Michigan—but he had to move before he could get any of it into his haversack. Instead, most of the human bodies got sent home, except those that were taken up to the new cemetery in the fall, and some in the woods that were never found. These were not a new strain of wheat; they have fallen with the same desperate nobility and confusion through all recorded history and perhaps will fall until the human world ends. Sophocles on the Aegean heard it long ago.

When you walk across the Wheatfield it is useful to let your imagination take over and to think of yourself as a soldier in a line about to capture one of the cannons. You feel no danger, only a single-minded invulnerability—as you should, for this is typical of soldiers actually in battle. Like an irresistible force you step to a silent barrel and commandingly strike your palm upon it. What you hear is the faintest tiny *ping*. You are flesh, perishable as the wheat of the field: one blast and your thin membranous guise disintegrates.

In mouldry windrows they lay, grains of wisdom winnowed from the chaff of time, growing roots to distant waters. When Crawford's troops came to that field they could hardly walk without stepping on those bodies lying grotesque, or peaceful, squirming, moaning, begging for water; Plum Run was lined with shot soldiers bleeding in fluting currents—Bloody Run, they called it then; a trodden field sown thick with pools and smears of blood; soldiers coughed and gurgled their own blood. Rifles, knapsacks, jackets, caps, and blankets littered the field everywhere; bayonets and cartridge boxes, Bibles, books, and toothbrushes, haversacks and photographs; on a rock a stream of blood.

What universe is looking in? Who had seen around Colonel Cross a theater whose actions had not yet materialized here? Who or what told him, what voice or muffled drum had he heard? What we see, and know, what we discover and remember, are matters of attention. This universe is not without windows. Its walls are membranes to many rooms.

Colonel Cross exemplified the burden of humankind. In those quick hours he knew tragedy. Through no fault of his own, but because of who and where he was, a cosmic finitude took aim at him. There was no escape, no appeal to a justice outside this jurisdiction: his hopes, his future, ripped away, and passionate, substantial life to aery thinness beat.

Americans have never believed, as a culture, that we could not get what we want, that unhappiness can be a fate—and so the underclass, in whom the tragic vision is itself visible—darkness visible—is shut aside. Likewise in our homes we won't believe we aren't the children any more, that we have been assigned a mirror outpost with a bullet in its gaze, that death listens to our prayers and tucks us in at night. We will not accept the duties of despair without a bigger house and larger car. Americans learn not that life is tragic but that time is money. The tragic voices tell us, You cannot have what you want, you mustn't have what you desire. We will not listen.

And so the wisdom which is born as grief bleeds upon our hearts drop by drop, cries answerless in the streets, lives on cereal and television, coughs in alleys rancid with the sputum of neglect. We live like atheists.

Our popularly imagined heaven is a fantasy. We want to be diverted from the core of tragedy, which is not death but separation. We imagine that we will all be as we once were (when?), and be there together. We already have that here, however, under less intense circumstances than consciousness of eternity, and we still can't get along—but never mind, it will work out there, *up there*, and so we'll stay forever. But recently I was told of a man and wife who learned from their doctor that they both had inoperable cancer. As they clutched each other and looked into each other's pale eyes the man cried in agony, "I'll never talk to you again!" The depth of his realization was cosmic. It was not that the husband didn't believe in life after death; he did—but he knew something of the distances in heaven. Not as we are, shall we remain; never *this* man, with *this* history only, shall meet *this* woman again. And he could do nothing about it—not tithe, not buy masses, not even *believe*. He had made the mistake, at most, of being born. The soul may be renewable, but *we* are not. When the silver cord is broken, indeed a man's thinking ends. How differently shall we know each other then?

Meeting in a pagan heaven would make a mockery of life and death. The tragedy must deepen there, before our vision opens.

Pilgrims to Medjugorje want more than healings; they want a sign of God. They want to know that He is, that He knows us. Most of all, I believe, they want a glimpse of His beauty. With that, all else can be borne. It is, perhaps, the goal and culmination of life.

Colonel Cross got his miracle, his star, but not his deliverance; he had the casual knowledge of the convinced, but no rescue. What he knew, he knew. *That* he knew is the hope beyond the corpse. To hold the substance of the question of pain, one universe is not enough. The pain itself, we feel, gets its orders from elsewhere; the world we see is just a corporal in some army of the night.

We rightly trust that love is the closest thing to beauty. But it is the campaign of the world to make us deny our faith—so that we might live in this world and no other. The just are rebels in this world. We were made for a revolution. Its result is to be more fundamental and astounding than the turn from night to day. The world itself must be redeemed. Our want is beauty, a sign of our living God, though we breast the terror for it, though the cramped and crowded air is contagious with bullets.

Colonel Cross's will obeyed the orders of his corps commander; his fate took orders from higher up. Belief in fate, in a sense-to-things that binds coincidences, is a banner in our minds that calls all experience to rally around it, name it Providence or karma. We remark not at the troops who flee but at the remnant round the standard in the smoke: they are enough, they hold the line—and at the end what side shall keep the field no one in time can say. A messenger or two in blue or gold or gray will do; we march by intimations. Thus courage is the primary virtue.

Were we really made to live as we do, in such despair? Do we really care about what preoccupies us all day long? How closely do our minds' conversations parallel our mouths'? Day by day we talk like permanent residents, about our houses, schools, and cars; what the prices at the supermarket are or what goes on in Hollywood or Washington; when what we really hunger for is some glimpse into our own depth of soul, and that of others, into some grand green avenue toward God. It is as if we had been to heaven once and spoken with the Master of the Universe—beheld His glory crowned in white unending light—but now we speak each day among the weeds of our minds as if some implacable overseer listens for each serious word, has forbidden everything with honesty and meaning. The meanest desperation is to divert our eyes from desperate sights—chiefly our own lives whose condition is defeat and boredom. Our economy is geared to this, an industry of paltry satisfactions, addictive—truly a consumer society, consuming us before we get the shock and presence of mind to pine for Eden; a remedy within our grasp, yet overwhelmed by trivia. The tragic vision has been rewritten for television. One honest sentence straightly spoken would annihilate a plague. Perhaps it takes a lifetime to discover it—a small price, at today's rate—but instead we choose the steady, small attrition of our irritating lives. *Courage!* The cruelest overseer is our worldly self, our uniformed opinion of ourself. Instead, what rather should we think we are, that angels, intimations, ghosts, and unnamed mysteries speak to us? Do they not say we are capable and worthy of more than this? Unfurl the colors! One blast of solid purpose, spirit, hope would sweep this ennui and junky visibility away. Now that the American achievement has become material merely, the nation is chaff for one idea, one belief. Like Moab we will disperse with our belongings among the willows, all this obscene frail edifice actualized to plastic dust in the wind. No wonder any group with sincere belief can call the multitudes. The willingness to die is itself an arresting power that commands our piddling minds. The currency of our economy of death is fear of death, which is really fear of life; our wish for the materials of production prosperity is a self-inflicted capital punishment indeed. We cannot bear the thought of death, we who understand that we have not lived; that is two deaths, one at the end and now continually; and there can be no courage in those who have no life to give. Cross's last words were a lament for his "poor, distracted country." Who can receive a second birth except those who have lived a first?

I think there is a constellation in the northeastern July sky called the Wheatfield. At its angled corner is a blue-white star the size of seven suns, and at the opposite, in distance ten degrees, is a red star like Arcturus, receding from the solar system at a speed nearly that of light. Within the borders of its five stars there seems to be an empty field of night sky. But look closer with a telescope, and two thousand stars and nebulae come forward to view. It is a vast and fertile field of violent creation, glistening like summer wheat in the spray of its own light. Each has its history and color; the origin of each belongs to some corner of the heavens dark to us, and the light of each comes to us from a time and place beyond memory, the distance irretrievable. Look deeper, and you break through out of our galaxy, into a field at first as dark as time; stare in still silence, ignoring the bright missiles across the face of your gaze, and up from this opaque field rise galaxies with graceful arms, to whom the distances between our stars are like mere breaches between atoms. White and musical, flowing streams of red and blue and silvery purple, they are huge and glorious and terrible in their rushing beauty, seeming not to move at all except by the turning of our earth. They watch the ages out, our earth's even shorter than a single campfire's flame, great clouds and choruses of them. There are more of them in that small field of ten degrees by ten than there are stars within our galaxy. Theirs is majesty that overrides our speculation. And past them, through them, what universes?

14 *Walking*

I have traveled a good deal around Gettysburg, mostly on foot because I am impatient. There are other ways to travel the battlefield. You can drive the roads by car or motorcycle, of course, and bike or jog them. There are equestrian trails, you can fly over the battlefield in helicopters, and, for there is no depravity to which humankind may not descend, the possibility of snowmobiling must be admitted. Walking is still the best way. Traveling on foot at Gettysburg is like one imagines walking on water to be: you have to be attentive but not too attentive.

The Peace Light Memorial strikes me as something somebody in the 1980s would have thought up. It's a kind of imposition, like adding a scene to Shakespeare. Because it's a big structure and highly visible, and seems to state a good wish, you go look at it. But the battlefield speaks for itself—interprets itself, as Luther says of Scripture. The field and Scripture are similarly revelation, though the Bible has the advantage of portability. Both have given rise to interpretation, error, inspiration. The relationship of past to present is an issue in both.

There was a scribal error on a marker tablet in front of the Whitworth guns at the Memorial this year:

McIntosh's Battalion
Hurt's Battery Hardaway's Alabama Artillery
Two Whitworths Two 8 Inch Rifles

Someone in repainting the raised letters and numbers on the tablet made the 3 into an 8.

(An 8-inch rifled cannon as opposed to a 3-inch would have been a hell of a field gun.) This would disturb a literalist of the physical battlefield. There are, in fact, quite a few errors on markers. Another one at the Peace Light Memorial says, rather poetically, "The first hot skirmishes of the battle had crackled across the fields ahead on the morning of July 1." *Hot skirmishes* indeed! Decisive, costly action, upon which the battle's issue depended. Regarding a portion of it, near the Railroad Cut a quarter-mile or so in front of the Peace Light Memorial, a marker says, "the 84th and 95th New York assisted by the 6th Wisconsin made a charge on the cut. . . ." *Assisted* indeed! The dispute is whether the New Yorkers got there at all before it was over. One could not be a battlefield literalist, if such an aberration were possible, without losing touch with what happened. A literalist might say of the Hardaway Artillery tablet that the markers are inspired *in their original condition*, and simply deny that the others contain any error, and in fact condemn historico-litero critics as being un-Gettysburgian—but it is a characteristic of the true Civil War buff to thirst after the real thing, to know no rest until he or she rests in fact. "Any truth is better than make believe," writes Thoreau. Likewise we are all essentially spiritual beings, whether we read Chuck Swindoll or Shirley MacLaine, and the neat lie of literalism removes us from the real thing and leaves us with a thirst that *will* not be slaked.

The Peace Light is an eternal flame—or as close to one as piped gas lets us come; at dusk it can be seen even from the Seminary. It would be a good place to read a newspaper, if one has the habit of reading them, because you can't read the times except in the light of eternity. Habitually I walk the fields of Gettysburg, however, in a news-free zone for a week or so at a stretch. I do not read papers or magazines or listen to the radio; I have still not fully digested the news of July 1–3, 1863, and worry that anything put on top of that wouldn't be truly appreciated for what it was until a little more of the 1863 news is comprehended. It is not lonely to be thus without radio and television, or not so lonely as it is to be with them; you have the Eternal Company of 160,000 men and women, 50,000 horses and mules, and yourself—the latter alone supplying enough reason for vigilance and deliberation.

I have noticed during the past ten years that there are large animal holes in the turf along the Railroad Cut. One must be careful; one could break a leg in one.

There are holes south of the Peach Orchard, too, smaller ones. Still smaller ones—about 800 of them in one 14-foot board in the Trostle barn—were found at the time. There were 80 in one rail on a fence along the Emmitsburg Road. And, of course, there were thousands of them in bodies. In all areas of life except the spiritual, we consider holes to be evidence of something rather than of nothing.

I wonder if you could go in a hole at the Railroad Cut and come out another below the Peach Orchard, or if you could get a hole in you in 1863 and come out the larger end of it in 1991 with a broken leg. Holes may be one of the clues to distance. There may be a pattern to holes, but it is well that we can't map them on our own terms, or we would have another literalism. At any rate, God presents highly evidential silences in this world, and when you enter one of them, I think, there is a good chance you can come out another.

Crossing the Railroad Cut one is struck by how mental a thing it all was—the decision, the willingness of the 6th Wisconsin to charge, the success of the charge. The War itself was a war of words: secession, tariff, slavery, states' rights, black Republicanism, free soil; symbols: the old flag, home, family; and for both sides an idea: freedom. Like little boys, we let things come to fists. Little boys, or "monsters of the deep"? Humanity will prey upon itself.

It occurs to me that Christian literalists read their Bibles astrologically, rather than astronomically. It would be well to value education more; certainly there are better ways to read.

War is about thoughts and words. The translation into physical acts, into killing and blood, into emotions, is an odd and problematic thing. It is especially difficult for Americans to consider the connection, for the country as a whole seems not to believe words and thoughts to be very important. But how the world's fundamentalists read their holy books during the next one hundred years will be a matter of life and death for millions. We must learn to read in the best light.

McPherson's barn in the early, clear morning is one of the most beautiful of Gettysburg's sights. Sunlight strikes pure white off the barn. Its old stones below the white boards give it quaintness and solidity. The barn sits in substantive calm.

> *Cold Pastoral!*
> *When old age shall this generation waste,*
> *Thou shalt remain, in midst of other woe*
> *Than ours, a friend to man, to whom thou sayst,*
> *'Beauty is truth, truth beauty,—that is all*
> *Ye know on earth, and all ye need to know.'*

Leaning on the Virginia rail fence at the corner of McPherson's Woods, I have to reassure myself that I am actually here. And if so, the memory must stay palpable for months, perhaps years, before I return again. The place has not changed, these beautiful fields and this green shade; but the memories have deepened, and play upon each other like the mottling leaf shadows on the ground the Iron Brigade stood upon, and fell and bled upon; and I have changed, and America has changed.

I myself am somewhat tired, less hopeful; my dreams have subdued. If I know more, it is chiefly that I know so little. I have more responsibilities and more duties; perhaps they cloud my sense of responsibility toward the universe, if such exists. But I am also the same, and I believe this is so because of more than conscious memory. I am still sentimental. I still fight the War.

Like me, our country is closer to judgment. It is living like an angry senior citizen who has forgotten to prepare for birth. We should all live—countries and individuals—not as though we will die but as though we will have to live again.

I believe there is an America, but it is dead on the field. I hope it is not too late for some hand to pass across it: for the bones to rustle, knit together, stagger into flesh and close up in a battle line behind that earlier flag. America's hopes have been replaced by fantasies; its dream has become a lust for brass, rather than a vision of the future—

though more and more it is an *aes alienam*. What must awaken first is memory. Meanwhile the battlefield is itself perennial and pure, with the litter of generations crowding at its margins. It will sleep a while longer, or rather we will, while its figures blue and gray pace the fields of memory invisible.

The Iron Brigade monument at the corner of the woods gives figures for the 2nd and the 7th Wisconsin regiments. For the Second, 302 present, 26 killed in action, 155 wounded, 52 missing: 233. They defended a regimental front of about 60 yards when the afternoon attack finally came. The Seventh, with 370 originally present, defended 35 yards, losing 39 killed, 103 wounded, 52 missing during the whole battle. During the War the 7th Wisconsin enrolled 1,714 men: 1,029 originally mustered in plus 685 recruits throughout its service. Of these, 172 were killed in action, 100 died of wounds, 762 were wounded, and 124 (a very low total) died of disease: 1,157. Such was the economy of courage. We see what they paid, but the gains are not in yet, or visible. If one's soul had to depend on one unit, North or South, the Iron Brigade would be the one—as the Union depended on it at Gettysburg. It was the right choice—assuming a choice was made. Did Providence put them there, or did those stalwart, valiant men simply come forward first and strongest, staking out their line and planting their bright, tattered Stars and Stripes, and the three blue state flags with the word "Forward"? But if it were one afternoon of life you wanted, a sunlit advance to echo forever, perhaps you'd charge with the 26th North Carolina. For "about an hour" the 26th North Carolina and the 24th Michigan faced off in those woods at 20 paces, then two days later the Carolinians almost reached the wall in Pickett's Charge.

There were nearly 7 million bullets fired during the Battle of Gettysburg, for 7,610 killed outright and 26,358 wounded. Wiseguys point out that it took a man's weight in lead to kill him. But the killed and wounded weren't the results of that battle, they were the cost. We are the results. We are their victories and defeats. One's own devil shoots straight; our question is only who and what we will die for. Posterity will be our beneficiaries and victims. Perhaps these Gettysburg men will lend us their valor.

The walk to the upper end of the woods is steep, and ends at the Reynolds marker. His orderly, Veil, said at first he didn't see a bullet hole; the lead had entered behind, at the collar, and passed downward. There was no blood. As he pulled his General's body back toward the advancing Union line, Confederates only yards away shouted, "Drop him! Drop him!" but he braved their fire and the Iron Brigade swept in. Some time later Charlie Veil paid a single visit to Katherine Hewitt, who gave him his most prized possession: a handkerchief she had been embroidering for the general. I think she left the convent never to return to another. The man who ordered up those uncased blue flags wouldn't have wanted her to stay.

"Not fare well, but fare forward."

Noontime sunlight strikes the new brown paint of the Virginia memorial's statuary. Until a few years ago the color was the metal's own weathered gray and green. The stateliness of the monument, and the majesty of Lee, are not impaired by years or color—but I wonder whether Lee would have liked wearing the butternut of his troops. He would tent, rather than live in houses, for the sake of his men. (But even this has its legendary aspect; the owner of the Gettysburg house used by Lee and his staff said that her things were handled rudely.) Still, Lee would not dress like his men, "Lee's Miserables." It was all right for Grant to dress like a tramp, in an army where every one had plenty of clothing and equipment, but it would hardly have done for Lee, when all his foot soldiers were in rags. It made everyone feel decent; he dressed for them.

In an army of finely attired generals (the contrast with the men being apt, some would say—symbolic of Southern society), Lee was not a dandy like Stuart; his elegance was the surpassing kind which rests on simplicity, expensive simplicity. Though not really rich if you subtract Arlington, which perhaps should not be subtracted from Lee's mind, Lee was nevertheless aristocratic. His was a gracious aristocratic manner, yet that graciousness did serve to remind that the condescension came down from afar.

One might have reservations about his generalship at Gettysburg and elsewhere, but it cannot be doubted that Lee was one of the world's great leaders. He was larger than a general, as all great captains seem to be—as Lincoln seems more than a president. A glorious leader is seldom a servant, however, and that sort of leader is expensive. One is better off with Calvin Coolidge than with Napoleon. But Lee was revered by his men, a reverence so strong its impact is still felt. The very reason for Lee's not being properly evaluated as a general is his greatness as a leader. At Appomattox his men crowded near just to touch his horse. It should also be noted that others stayed away, glad the damn thing was finally over.

His presence is still radiant at the Virginia monument. For years I could not regard it without emotion. Then at one point I understood Pickett's point of view, and would have none of that murderous glory. Now I think of Lee as a representative man: at the same time saved and a sinner, both grand and small, good and evil, noble and ridiculous. Late in life Lee was observed to attract the attentions of young women. Once as he talked to several while he was mounted on Traveller, the horse kept sidling and backing and nearly rearing in a way that made the rider appear dashing; the observer noticed that Lee was surreptitiously pricking the horse with his spurs. Beloved Traveller? This was the man who reproached others for using their horses too roughly—and the man who ordered the frontal assaults at Malvern Hill and Gettysburg. Any criticism of Lee is bound to prompt outrage, but such outrage does no justice to Lee's grandeur. Human greatness cannot be unmixed, purely virtuous, cannot be the perfection we attribute to God and the angels. Our greatness lies in mastering our own natures, which are, if not fallen, at least flawed or imperfect. Lee's grand effort all his life was to be master of himself. Though the self will out, in ways unseen, it is to Lee's credit that he to such a high degree succeeded. His father, an impulsive, irresponsible man, was Lee's chosen devil, and at all cost he wanted to win out over that devil. In his personal and public lives he succeeded; how many of us can say the same? He may have appealed to the ladies, but he was never unfaithful to his wife. No responsible revisionist will ever get to Robert E. Lee on his family life. Not willing to fall into weak destitution after the War, as had his famous father after the Revolution, Lee took a job as president of a small, half-dead college as a way to support himself and his family—but, more, he chose this work, rather than the many meaningless luxury positions he could have had, for the sake of the South and of posterity. The South would need well-educated people if there were to be a future, and his former faithful soldiers needed the chance that education might afford them. Credit is due to Lee more than to any other person that Washington and Lee University is one of the best schools in the country. It has been said that what Lee did during the War made him famous, but what he did *after* the War made him great.

Still, he remained a Southern man. We cannot expect someone to forget, but rather to transcend, his circumstances. Lee *was* a Southern aristocrat, and he had his views on black people. He was unable to transcend these views as Lincoln did; nevertheless, Lee treated people with respect, so far as he could, and with decency. He did not really forgive the North; but who can expect more than he accomplished by his actions? He may not have liked Yankeedom any more than anyone else, but by his example he was instrumental in the South's reconciliation—to the extent that it did reconcile. His lack of complete honesty about his earlier views on slavery and secession appear to be self-serving, but this too worked to undercut ideas that still weakened the Union. America could hardly ask a better man from the hand of history: even his faults give us strength to make of ourselves something better than we are. "Pick up a musket; we need all true men now."

In the military aspect of Lee's character, however, Light Horse Harry Lee, the impulsive genius, had his say. "His name might be Audacity." This greatest of Civil War generals also made the greatest mistakes. Such an observation should not be upsetting to anyone except those who, in effect, make heroes impossible to follow, by ascribing to them a perfection the heroes themselves, in their daily struggles, would have thought absurd and irritating. If Lee was a greater general than any of us, shouldn't we accept his own analysis of Pickett's Charge? "It is all my fault."

In a mythic sense he was certainly the greatest general of the War. After Lincoln and Washington, one might well be most inspired by Lee. Is not saying this enough? Must we also say the man was perfect? What dishonor to a man who spent his life in keeping down his imperfections; as if he hadn't had to fight at all, as if his courage and endurance faced puny adversaries! As if his war had been a short desert storm and not a lifelong civil war! The man we take our inspiration from was the human, imperfect Lee, not the statue on the marble block—and that, not the statue, was whom the soldiers followed. They knew him, and the faithful followed him to death, disease, starvation. Partly, they made more of him than they should have; but choose a captain in some dim and distant future to assail the fiery gates of hell—who would not follow Lee? It is the *man* who'd strike them, not a copper figure, tarnished green and thickly painted. It is the *man* we follow, not in heaven already, but striving like most of us, the man whose last words were not words of one who has arrived but words of one who moves on, expecting more enemies to meet and more green and sunlit fields at last to win: "Strike the tent!"

The figures at the base of the Virginia monument—Lee's pedestal does not rest upon them; they stand freely in front of it—are the ones for whom the memorial is really inscribed: *Virginia, to her sons at Gettysburg.* Meant to depict common occupations of people in the state, they represent the average uncommon genuine Confederate—who never failed to excite the full attention of Union soldiers if captured, as if they had dropped down from the moon, or materialized from some other universe, which in a way they had. After Pickett's Charge the Northerners were surprised at how thin and abject their captives were; they were legends already then, as enemies often are, though the Southerners had no such idea of Yankees. We would be as profoundly wondering as the Yankees were if those Confederates would step down from that monument one day while families stood snapping pictures. But we would have even less ability to understand them. The quiet childhood origins of their language we would have no comprehension of, though we use most of the same words. Suppose after uselessly trying to talk to us, they resort to singing, perhaps a sentimental war song like "Somebody's Darling." A few of us might snicker; most of us wouldn't even be able to follow the syntax.

More likely it is we who'd talk to them, and try to show them what life is like now—my, how the world has changed, though we have no idea of how. Show them a van; give 'em a ride on a motorcycle! Now *this* is really speed! Scared, huh? Fly 'em to L.A. We could do them much more harm than they have done to us. They might be impressed by our airplanes and boom boxes; there may not be a Thoreau among them. (In fact, there would not be many, for to him "only the defeated and deserters go to the wars, cowards that run away and enlist.") But after all, though the past always seems a ceremony of innocence, it is they who invented the present, and we are progeny of their deeds. We naively think that people in the past were less capable than we are or, just as naively, that we are pygmies standing in their monumental shadows. (We have Thoreau's cold comfort: "Shall a man go hang himself because he belongs to the race of pygmies, and not be the biggest pygmy he can?") The people of each age believe themselves to be at once superior and inferior to those gone before. Lee abhorred Light Horse Harry and emulated Washington. He escaped neither. Today we wonder how those people managed to do all they did, with inferior tools and no deodorant. But sufficient to the day is the evil thereof.

Taking Lee as a superior military authority, one is tempted to speculate on a Union counterattack after the failure of Pickett's Charge. Lee prepared for one. Did that mean he feared it, or desired it? Was it something he would have done, or something he expected Yankees to do? As Coddington points out, it would have taken hours to organize a counterattack, if indeed one could have been organized out of the crazy quilt of Union corps fragments; and where to attack—over the same fields on which the Confederates had been decimated trying to get across? Haskell wrote that one large army can't simply *destroy* another one like it. Civil War battles were not decisive, in that spectacular sense. Lee wouldn't have to destroy the Union army to win the War at Gettysburg; another Second Manassas would do. As Lee had predicted, the new Union commander would make no mistake. Meade turned the War. Now it is industry, population, technology, determination, time: courage has become endurance. There is no mistake any more about bravery, when endurance is the staple of character. This is modern war.

The sun has passed the center of the sky. One must walk on.

The little pyramids of solid shot are gone from the long line of cannons on Seminary Ridge. The iron slabs they used to rest on are there, empty. Perhaps some "collectors" discovered how to pry them up, and soon cannon balls started disappearing as fast as relics of the True Cross, though for less reason. If the vandals had had an attitude of reverence, the loss would be less irritating, though as absolute. In a German town I once got into a tour behind an American couple who, before looking at a thing or walking many steps, went first for the postcards and inquired for the ones picturing things they would see. As nineteenth-century Americans were sentimentalists, collecting emotional tokens of experience, so we are *materialists*, with the similarity that the memento has sometimes displaced the moment. But the "collectors," if such they were, were into objects merely and—the perfect image of materialist civilization—should be made to wear them around their necks; and if Dante was right, they will.

Children playing on the cannons are a different thing, and are to be encouraged. It had not been discovered yet in 1863, but that is what cannons are for. Many of the birds of Gettysburg have made their nests in cannons, an extravagant use in terms of material expense, and inferior in architecture to a tree, but as an instructively casual affront to human pretensions and preoccupations, it's a good use. One wonders whether the young birds that fly out of the Parrotts and three-inchers are rifled. One wonders whether, as seashells carry the sound of the sea in them, the barrels still contain the howl and growl of battle.

Once I found an actual shell on the battlefield, on a farm over which Law's Alabamians advanced on their way from Warfield Ridge to Devil's Den, now grown up partly in trees, but some of it still in fields. I had to stand and debate transmigration of the soul with a staunch, unretreating bull to get it. The shell is green and brown, a turtle shell rather than an iron one, easier to carry as to weight but more substantial as to suggestiveness, and wholly appropriate (my acquisitive nature told me instantly) as a souvenir of Gettysburg. I still possess my shell and am ashamed to say I behave toward it as would a college student or a collector, though I have reason to believe I shall be parted from it one day.

The apparent unity of things leads me to wonder whether today's immune-system epidemic corresponds to a breakdown in our mental and spiritual immune systems. In the body and mind, a compensating reaction can set in with a vengeance. This does not mean that the disease will not still be fatal, or that the reaction is necessarily benign.

One of the most virulent commercial bacilli was spread by American ships first, and now European and Asian, carried on the bodies of technological objects of amusements, convenience, and profit; the bacilli are as numerous, indeed as ubiquitous, as fleas on rats, and as invisible to our attention. We ought not be smug or self-righteous about this; nobody is safe.

Commercial amusements are so tawdry, giving the impression of having been thought up by not very intelligent little boys whom one should pity. Gettysburg is full of such commercial establishments, which I will not describe or name, in the expectation that future obscenity laws will be more stringent than the present ones. We must not fool ourselves that the persons in danger are indiscriminately active heterosexuals or homosexual males. No; the ones most at risk are children, for families are least immune, and the innocent are led in by their jaded elders. The Gettysburg establishments which offer such enervating debauchery are not camouflaged, they are advertised. From miles out of town one can read billboards which could be attractive, one might think, only to the seediest blownout reprobate. But no; they attract vacationers from the nation's suburbs, families with clean faces who go to church in heavy numbers. For these, indeed, are the nation's most infected population. The flashier individuals—politicians and movie stars—make the tabloids, but the gas chambers of the nation's soul are places with nice lawns and central air.

These Gettysburg establishments, it is argued, boost the economy. What economy? The life-forms around new establishments should be the first consideration, but of course they are not; the value of an economy is judged—now that our immune systems are shot—not by the benefits to the human and natural environment but by the size of the machine. And we have bought all these huge katzenjammer implements on credit; pretty soon we're going to owe *somebody*.

One avoids these commercial establishments in Gettysburg like the very plague, but casual contact is sometimes unavoidable. One walks past, averts one's eyes, and shudders. All this on hallowed ground?

The National Military Park Visitors Center has people who don't look at you like you're crazy if you want to know what kinds of fences were on the Trostle property in 1863—and they will be able to tell you or know how to find out. It is an oasis of sane people in a world interested in other things. The exhibits present a rich minutiae of how the soldiers lived, fought, and died. You see what they wore (long underwear even in summer, though cotton instead of wool), how they camped, what they ate. You find exhibits of papers, diaries, tracts, and books—mostly Northern, because they had more money and materials, were in general more literate, and were more willing to pack things a Southerner wouldn't tote. Writing sets were sold, consisting of stationery, metal pens, and clay (CSA) or glass (US) ink bottles in a box. Soldiers had a good deal of time on their hands, despite the several hours per day of drill, and some "longed more for something to read than for something to eat." They had cards, chessboards, checkers, backgammon, ivory and wood dominoes; songbooks, accordions, fiddles, "Jews' harps"; they whittled, played quoits, ran races, wrestled, played baseball games; they organized plays, concerts, even balls; some regiments were filled with practicing religious men, some had almost none. The weapons they used are well preserved at the Center: they look new, serviceable, shiny, and lethal. Union officers had good swords, made in the North, in England, even in Solingen, Germany; Confederates, a notice says, carried swords showing "unskilled and rudimentary manufacturing techniques"—hand finished—and scabbards made of iron, copper, or even wood instead of steel. The Nashville Plow Works, it might be noted, made swords. Confederate canteens were wood rather than tin. You can see how a Napoleon twelve-pounder was loaded and fired, and how a company of infantry would shoot. You see a section of wood water pipe used in Gettysburg in 1863. You can see the four small wooden chairs General Reynolds tried to sleep on the night before the battle. You can buy books, maps, tapes, and postcards. The Center houses a map and manuscript collection. Often I run into regiments of schoolchildren from near home; to all of us alike it is new, fascinating, unbelievable, and real at the same time.

You go outside into the natural light and see the Cemetery. There lie the men who shouldered those muskets, fired those Napoleons, carried and ate the hardtack, wrote letters to sisters, mothers, wives, and sweethearts. There in concentric half-circles are the Union dead, identified by state. Still there. Men you read about, like Stevens of the Iron Brigade—their bodies lie at your feet, and the men of the 1st Minnesota who ran out to stop that Confederate advance—name after name, state after state, there under the grass in the quiet; they are real, yet the mind can hardly comprehend: the War didn't happen in books after all; it happened *here,* and to *them.* Giants in the earth, average height about 5' 7". Buttons, rotten scraps of cloth, perhaps some bones remain—but where are *they?* Why seek we the living among the dead?

Crossing the parking lot south of the Visitors Center and following the walkway you approach the crest of Cemetery Ridge. A statue of an old man seated, looking out over the field of Pickett's Charge, an eloquent work of art; his shoes are as solid as his gaze is deep. Not to youth alone belong the "long, long thoughts." Woolson, from Minnesota, the last Union survivor, seeing it again . . . *Long ago, long ago, long, long ago.*

What did he think of it all, when he went back? Did the veterans at those encampments walk the fields absently sometimes, or fall into gazes, or was it still too close, like yesterday, to them? Time is a distance in the mind. In dreams there is no such distance. To the immortal, invisible God, what could time be, then; what will it be to us?

One night I stood near there, on upper Cemetery Ridge. It was a clear night, stars sprinkled across the sky. To the southeast, city lights made a lurid, dull glow. There on Cemetery Ridge, the statues tall and strong and dark, it was quiet. The only perspective to have on things is that of starlight—or of a moon sliver large and low in the sky, so that one realizes it is there, at a specific distance, orbiting this planet riding in the universe with its thin, smudged film of air. The stars are below us as well as above, at depths we can't imagine, some of them so huge they would fill the orbit of Jupiter if their center were at the sun, and some as heavy as these but the size of a meadow. We would fight different wars if we fought in that light. But what are light years and time to the One who is all times and places now? The lines go forward into cannon fire once more, a young man takes up his flag anew, the infantry die and rise and fight again, for time is but the chariot of

Arjuna, and all the universe a field of jeweled fire. At one word of His it could be changed, renewed, or pass into beginnings again; youth and age are the same—Antares newly blooms and Hercules tries his longbow, the dead reclaim their ancient rights and walk unwounded by the sea. All that dark intensity is only the other side of a dry moon. The light of Albert Woolson's gaze has reached the upper fringe of Seminary Ridge, and dawn spreads over the battlefield.

The Peach Orchard changes every year, because peach trees don't last long. Criticize the Park Service for truancies elsewhere, you must credit them for keeping the Orchard alive. Every twenty years you must replant, so that every twenty years a new company stands there at attention on their chancy eminence, legs in bright white wrappings like Zouaves, ready to drop their future fruits onto the earth. The first time I was there I wondered whether they were the same trees.

The Park Service has allowed the battlefield to change, but the change is only visual; it deceives only the casual observer. One goes to Gettysburg to see deliberately, to front the essential facts of life and death—and these do not change. When you see that this year the Service has begun to put up more fences as they were during the battle, so that things look a little different, you realize you are older.

A battle is a book of time. Why else do we refight it and preserve it? The changes of a lifetime happen in a splintered orchard; the questions of a thousand minds converge on it and reduce the terms. A thousand hearts lie buried there among the small leaves and deep roots, their loves and energies dismantled. Birds suspend a theme of vigilance in flight; fields of fire settle on the mind like snow; ghosts arise: Are your loves and aspirations worthy of your life, is your life worthy of its hopes? Do you wear with honor this azure mantle?

Ghosts? If a man die, shall he live again? What love shall he have left behind? For the dead among the cannons and peach trees there is no going back; rather, it is for us, the living, to imagine what happened; for them it is only forward, to find what all are looking for. Where we cannot see—in *nothing* yet, if anywhere—there remains a residue of the past more faithful than our conscious lives.

We are ourselves ghosts who haunt the places of the past; still it is we who are haunted. What is this longing that refuses to let fall its standard in the storm of our desires? What love is this, that pipes through our age, lets all lesser things kill us, that we might be its own at last? Perhaps not all pain comes from evil. Perhaps we are kindly condemned in this world, loth and struggling to escape, devoured by a frenzied ecstasy of alien passion. We are one thing and no other:

> *for ever wilt thou love . . .*

At home in Ohio the dark-eyed girl awaits him, as he lies blackened here in the sun—yet she awaits not that corpse but him, wanderer in some universe undreamt of across some grassy border—and she wanders through years of empty rooms with curtains rustling in warm night windows, past visits to a gray-stoned grave, through a family and sickness, and death in dusty taffeta, still sought as much as seeking, wearing a scent of promise.

> There is a future, O thank God,
> Of life this is so small a part,
> 'Tis dust to dust beneath the sod;
> But there, up there, 'tis heart to heart.

The afternoon sky is clear, a skein of faded blue across the frame of being. Little shadows speckle the ground, shifting across the cannons; the sun's warmth draws a nectar of years through the trunks and branches. Fruit ripens and falls.

> No more the bugle calls the weary one.
> Rest, noble spirit! in thy grave unknown.
> I'll find you and know you
> Among the good and true,
> When a robe of white is given
> For the faded coat of blue.

While leaning on a fence along the Wheatfield Road just east of the Peach Orchard, I resolved my focus onto a tourist who was filming me. He was filming some cows at the fence, actually, but I was chiefly sensitive about me. Like the "primitives" who believe a photograph captures one's soul, and gives the shutterbug power over it, I wondered whether it should be legal to film somebody candidly, especially while thinking. George Washington and Robert E. Lee went to war for less.

But I wonder whether a film such as the one shot of me could be developed *enough* to show ghosts. Images of the past? Is the past like the human unconscious mind? and the world of sunlight like the conscious? If one looks at Gettysburg will the invisible, with long enough exposure, resolve into visibility? Could all distance so resolve, from one mode into another? Or is it a higher consciousness only that can look at these things without being blinded by all the light?

I would like to see that fellow's film projected through a clearer medium than we have at present, and with better illumination.

Crawford's Pennsylvanians charged across the Plum Run valley between Little Round Top and the Wheatfield, pushing the tired Southerners back at last, on the evening of July 2. Earlier, at the south end of the valley near Devil's Den, Robertson's Texas Brigade had charged. One section of Union guns swept the low place with canister, piling red, mangled bodies. On the open slope of Little Round Top, all along the west side of the little valley, fighting for the hill roared among rocks and stumps. (The west slope of Little Round Top had been harvested of timber, as if in preparation for the battle.) Plum Run ran red; the little vale became called the Valley of Death.

Now it is a green and pleasant place under a blue sky, with wild-flowers sprinkled along the narrow road, where cows wander in their peaceful plod, looking up with their full-faced stares and tranquilizing unconcern. They were bred, I think, for their pacifying effect; their milk is a distillation of their serenity. What hell there once was amid this nourishment, what raging mayhem! And now, one walks at peace with earth and grass and sun, the paved lane clumping beneath one's heavy hiking shoes—all of it as present as it was then; with the sense of the place's dreamness being just behind a light, pervious sheet of air. For the place, though tranquil, is somehow bizarre. The rocky, bald hill to the left, with its weathered gray spire and figures along the top, and cannons; at the lower quarter Devil's Den, the anomaly from

Mars or the moon, a nasty jumble of druidic rocks. The vale has the look of something strange. Even now, when the Valley of Death seems to be a secluded shelter from the violent and senseless world, one can hardly help thinking of the shepherd's psalm:

> *Yea, though I walk through the valley*
> *of the shadow of death,*
> *I will fear no evil:*
> *for thou art with me;*
> *thy rod and thy staff*
> *they comfort me.*

There is no irony; it is too solemn a place. Like an ancient dale of Arcady, the place has a terrible awesomeness if one is still enough; it has the bare elementalism of a sacred grove, but it is not pagan—only humans are pagan—rather, rawly divine. It is a stony amphitheater, where you feel, when you are quiet, that God can hear your every word, every thought. It is the Valley of Death.

Walking up the southeast face of Little Round Top you step over ground where men crouched behind rocks to load their rifles. Somewhere here, a man went out that night to bring water to the wounded—and was after a while shot down, out of plain meanness, perhaps, or sport. There was, some say, a grumbling mutter of curses that night in Devil's Den, men angry at having been, if not defeated, beaten. You walk across the 83rd Pennsylvania's front, step onto the paved lane, pass Vincent's Spur, and walk in the shade up to the crest of Little Round Top.

If it is evening, the day's last buses might be there. A hundred junior high schoolers from a conservative private school in Ohio, perhaps, the girls in skirts and the boys climbing the rocks in crisp white shirts and dark trousers. Among them dodge children who've come with their families, and here and there a baseball-capped old man listens again to a son-in-law: "See that tower in the distance? That's Camp David, Maryland." A tour guide stops with a family: "Here brave young Vincent fell, and leaning over him, Hazlett received a bullet in his brain." The Confederates had a sharpshooter's rifle that weighed thirty-two pounds—a fat octagonal barrel and tube sight. Farther on, "The man on this plaque is Colonel Patrick O'Rorke, an educated young man, brave as a lion—killed right here, where you stand. Oh, it's all right, touch his nose, it's no sacrilege; it will bring you good luck—he was Irish, after all."

I am an amateur at Gettysburg; I love to eavesdrop on the tour guides. I envy them. There was a man at Chartres cathedral, when I visited a few years ago, who made his living giving talks to tourists. All his income came from what we hearers chose to donate. He was living as he wished, as his genius prompted him, Thoreau would say; how weak he showed the rest of us to be. The man at Chartres was eccentric from long solitude, and finicky, but he could have stood with Vincent and O'Rorke.

We do our work like penance, building purgatory from scratch, by the sweat of our faces, a race of unbelievers. Who decreed that we must mitigate our lives by selling them an hour at a time in trivial pursuits, to get a living—a living death, that is; what tyrants do free Americans obey? As if you could buy time without selling eternity. Who will stand on their rocky eminence and face down the slavedrivers?

You look at another marker: "1291 enrolled, 1098 engaged"—sounds like the college I attended—"284 wounded, 51 killed, 14 missing." Their odds were better than ours. These days, most of us are missing.

It is becoming dark. The last tourist bus left half an hour ago. The sun has slid its orange edge behind South Mountain. Shadows down in the Valley of Death below have flowed together. The cows have gone. Now young lovers sit on rocks, looking at the western sky as if at the very same spot together, holding hands, as young and unmoving as the statues gazing at the blue mountains, but more eternal. Why is it lovers gaze after the setting sun, rather than at the rising? Is it an instinct in the race, a knowledge of what follows? There is already a poignancy in young love which, like a silent gaze into that darkening valley below, intimates a wisdom soon to be forgotten, and depth where there is not length.

Sitting on a rock near the marker for Patrick O'Rorke is a man in khaki trousers and khaki shirt. Bearded, tan from much walking, he slowly smokes a pipe. Barely I smell the dark, sweet tobacco, a trace of old Virginia in the still evening. He stares at the rocks and field below; one old hiking boot he props on the stone in front of him; holding the pipe loosely like an idle pen, he rests his elbow on his knee. What veteran is he, what does he see with that perennial unmoving stare? Has the battlefield changed for him in all these years, as the thin blue smoke has risen and drifted from that old briar pipe? I drift away from him, a wounded phantom in his dreams, ascending the years again.

15 Culp's Hill

God himself culminates
in the present moment.

—Thoreau

One of the most pleasant lines of advance at Gettysburg is a route beginning at the school on the east side of town, going up and around Culp's Hill, and back down to the school. In addition to its virtues, the route has an academic framework of apparent purposefulness and circularity. It is, however, a very independent study, interdisciplinary in its content, a crowded classroom but with high individual attention. Having done it only alone, it is difficult for me to say whether it is a route better taken with a companion or in solitude. There is a certain sacredness about the journey, or the classroom, which warrants deliberation as to appropriate tactics.

While a solitary person is more sane in another's company, according to the usage of company, he is more trustworthy alone. Or perhaps the sanity of nature is of a different sort from that of human company, being more filled with signs, symbols, portents, wonders, and explanations. It is altogether a more articulate associate than many human ones. Among people, one is either in union or confederacy with them or at odds; but in nature, by either the limitation or the capacities of our minds, one sees one's very self, in all its minute dearness. It may be true that only in human company do we find our human identity, but surely it is an alien identity, and in any case it would be silly to think one receives one's soul from the congregation rather than from God. We are both less than and more than human.

The first spring I took the Culp's Hill walk I was entirely on foot for a week in Gettysburg. It is the best mode of travel there, even when it involves walking among fumy traffic in town—which does at least focus attention on the rest of the walk's value. It is certainly the most economical, involving least waste. In a car, one passes the actual details of life in exchange for mere abstractions, time and distance. It is too bad we have managed our details so poorly that we can't afford to walk everywhere we go. Unfortunately, it is only the rich who can expend the time: it is true that the rich get richer and the poor get poorer. One thinks falsely that a long walk is a blank space between points; it is the points which are usually the blanks.

The mind notices and retains everything. No blade of grass or premonition goes unseen or unrecorded. We *need* never pass this way again. Experiments have been done in which subjects have been left in a room for ten seconds or a half-minute, and then set down elsewhere and asked to make a list of everything they saw. The list, of course, is very short, even though the room was filled with objects. But under hypnosis the same subjects can recall the smallest details of the room—including texts of whole newspaper articles taped to walls too far, it appeared, to be read by human eyes. Thus the blind, like Milton and Homer and Dark Raftery, if their attention has been focused, sometimes have seen so well. Knowledge is a matter of attention; vision is a matter of concentration. In this sense perhaps all knowledge, as Socrates said, is recollection. Perhaps the very distance between God and ourselves is a function of attention.

If one were attentive enough on Culp's Hill, maybe one could see, behind the limpid, regardant, statuary deer, the solid forms of Confederates and the backs of aiming Union men, and officers pacing back and forth. That first spring I saw seven deer, silent forms, like wise spirits, materialize into my vision and then like notes on a score trace in unheard music their route to human invisibility. Likewise perhaps we are surrounded by more than the ton of insects in that one-foot column of air rising a quarter-mile above us, or the microorganisms huddling their universes beneath our feet; we live in a grander, if less palpable, continuum than that. (I have noticed this morning, finally, the small head of a creature swimming near the shore where I write of Gettysburg; it has been observing *me*. He or she appears too mammalian to be a turtle, and seems to swim too much for fun. An otter perhaps, a little Nessie: it was here all the time; where did *I* come from? I try to tell it, Not all humans are from Chicago, just as it tells me, Not all of us residents are turtles.) We are surrounded by a cloud of witnesses; while we wish we could interrogate them, they are observing us. The statues on Culp's Hill are wondrously attentive.

I think we might be able to hear them as well as see them. And if we hear them—their songs, for instance: if we listen to "Juanita" or "Home Again" from the band book of the 26th North Carolina, would we hear not only that desideratum we call history but also perhaps—and they are one—ourselves as well? I think the spirits that observe us walk in music. Bright-eyed in their military coats, standing in their graceful gowns, do they long for us as we long for them?

You start by walking the road behind the school. On the left are brigade markers, C.S.A., and on the right you will see a tablet headed, "Wesley Culp's Message." It has a photograph of the broken stock of the rifle made especially for him. He died on Culp's Hill within sight of the house where he was born. One is tempted to think we all move in similar circles.

The cycle of birth and death, for all its industry and trouble, seems in a way self-generated and pointless in itself, like a wheel spinning in mud, and in its own blind whirl separated from the more fruitful economy of the soul, which perhaps, if it weren't heavily concentrated here, would like to pull out and go on about its business. Wesley Culp went to Virginia to make and sell carriages, yet in the end traveled less than he had supposed, and on foot. Our lives are all probably such irony as this. We are, after all, in school, and irony is a Zen of understanding.

You continue into the beginning of the trees at the base of Culp's Hill, cross the creek on a low stone bridge. You may meet a jogger rigged out in neon, and momentarily reflect that America is going to bedlam in a fanny pack, but the morning is too new for this, and the woods ahead too freshly available in their delicate, faint green, and you may shed all negative thoughts and all lesser fears as older peoples would have shed their ordinary clothes upon entering a temple. If there is a Presence, it is here and now that you will know—but probably will know it by your own ineffable joy, in sweet confederacy with nature. Only with the easiest carelessness can one approach the green altar. The just saunter to heaven.

The road to the summit is circular, which is correct. Too direct a path is wasteful of the pleasures and the phantoms along the way. You would miss most of the trenches, the white-blossomed undergrowth, the monuments to courage that are the best preparations for so practical a goal as the view from the tower at the top.

Still on level ground you come to Spangler's Spring, where men from both sides crept for water. It is housed now in stone and circled by iron and pavement, but the spring still gives its water, through all the years from its unseen underground passage—"what's water but the generated soul?"—clear as ever, unless we have leached our conveniences far enough down into the earth; it is the drinkers who have changed.

(From where I sit by this large, spring-fed lake I can see no fewer than eight American flags, within several hundred yards. We are some old last inheritor toiling from flag to flag, trying to remember what they stood for, defending them like weasels but barely able to recall our days of freedom, light, and courage. The flags here are thick enough for two brigades in battle line, but where are the soldiers? Sitting by their televisions again; all that beauty spent.)

As the road ascends, you pass the long, low mounds that Greene's troops made with their picks, shovels, and bayonets. It was a wild night, July 2. Southerners at first cautious in the dark, not knowing how many troops had left these Union lines to go help against Longstreet; some of the best Union troops in a thin line—here Greene's Twelfth Corps men, and on the northeast face Wadsworth's from the First Corps—both firing at rifle flashes and keeping covered when they could behind rocks and trees. The Northerners had artillery, cover, and position; the Southerners as usual had a raging valor—but this time they had poor generalship, too. Ewell, convincing Lee to let his corps remain so far around the Union right, couldn't even get half his guns into action; he had no plan or timing for his assaults; some of his generals conducted things poorly. At Gettysburg the Army of the Potomac's officers fought their best battle; the Army of Northern Virginia's, their worst. The excellence of many Union officers had been masked by the ineptitude by their commanders in chief, until now:

Greene, Wadsworth, Cutler, Dawes, Webb, Hays, Humphreys, Hancock, Gibbon, Chamberlain—in fact it seems that so many of them were fine soldiers. It was not a hapless army that got kicked around by Lee until Grant fed in enough men to clog the Southern cannons. It was perhaps the best army in the world: What other men could have been defeated, been betrayed, made to look foolish for so long, and still know themselves, still believe in themselves, still be willing to die for their principles, still *know* that they would win? During the Seven Days battles, when the Army of the Potomac was falling back from blow after blow by the wild, attacking Rebels, a Southern officer heard one of the Union camps one night singing "The Battle Cry of Freedom." From that point on, the officer said later, it was "all uphill." Another veteran of the Army of Northern Virginia said many years after the War, ". . . never disparage the Army of the Potomac; it was the greatest army of the age—with the exception of one, that modesty forbids me to mention."

The Southerners came yelling, firing, climbing up the hill. By midnight it was given up, hopeless from the beginning. (The Union right had been refilled by troops returning from battle on the left. Appropriate to the shape but hardly to the grim defense of the Union line, two brigades on the far right were commanded by Generals Candy and Kane. (Only someone who lived through the American 1970s and 1980s would mention that.) Up the road, monuments mark the deadly progress of the night. But now they are part of the woods, a deepening of them perhaps, a depth of human time and human struggle—a union, now, of human heart and meaning with the loveliness of nature, making a beauty unapproachable by other means. There are no larger fields than these.

To some extent the walk is work. It should be remembered that to a degree at least the Southerners' battle was "all uphill." Having marched for miles, they then were ordered to attack McPherson's Ridge, Barlow Knoll, Seminary Ridge, Devil's Den, Little Round Top, the Peach Orchard, Cemetery Ridge, Culp's Hill, Cemetery Hill. With the stalwart Army of the Potomac on these places, there were, perhaps, no steeper fields than these.

Twice I have come upon heavy columns of Boy Scouts on the roads of Culp's Hill, foragers out on both flanks messing around in the woods, stragglers making agonized faces in the rear, adult file-closers marching them along. The only thing missing is the dead guys. Like a ghost I pass among them going the other way, marching to the same distant drummer, accomplishing the same distance, however measured, to the same view, however far above.

The lookout tower at the top of the hill is built of girders like a picked-clean skeleton; it shudders with hollow metal music as you stamp the waffled stairs. From the platform at the top you see gentle hills and soft green forests everywhere. From there they all look pretty much alike. The first time I climbed it, about twenty years ago, I had no notion what was where. Unless you know exactly where to look, the monuments on Cemetery Ridge are too small to be recognized. I took photographs in every direction, not knowing but that one of them might be Round Top, or perhaps, is that one Cemetery Hill? A height or promontory is not itself enough. The world's bibles have done damage as well as good. It is the hands and eyes that scale them, and the spirit of the heart.

In the distance you can see the huge, long range of Appalachian hills called South Mountain. From there the Southerners came; through them they would return. Immediately in front stands the ancient cemetery gate—a house, it was, with door and windows, through which mortality passed; to the left extends the line of monuments on Cemetery Ridge, over to the half-cleared loaf of granite called Little Round Top—and of course the "National Tower" raises its nasty buttocks practically in your face. It wasn't there twenty years ago, and by all the saints it won't be there in a thousand. Only the spring woods will be there, and some ancient monuments perhaps, like calm sentries from a vanished time—no orders came to withdraw.

Clanging down the steps, one thinks of what Buford was supposed to have said to Reynolds as he descended the steps of Old Dorm's cupola: "There's the devil to pay." And so now, the woods are lovely, dark, and deep; but there are bills to pay out in the streets. Conscious that your time at Gettysburg is limited, you walk through the woods again. You savor every second, savor it like nectar and ambrosia; never will you use your free time for some asinine vacation with a tour group in London or go camping with the nation's suburbs in

Yellowstone—ah, but next year it may have to be, so drink this to the depth of memory, save the fragrance of it in your soul, and stop your grumbling. "Mankind is in love, and loves what perishes."

A half-hour or an hour later on Cemetery Hill you walk among the guns out on the forward slope. Early's Division attacked here in the evening of July 2, driving in among the gunners, who stood their ground and fought with rammers, handspikes, pistols, even fence rails—a German battery, says Coddington, "punctuating their blows with the mouth-filling oaths of the enraged Teuton." Other Germans, and non-Germans, part of the Eleventh Corps that Jackson's attack had surprised and overwhelmed some weeks ago at Chancellorsville, ran at the first shots. The Army despised "the Germans." It seems tidy to identify people by their classifications, but that was the Southern mistake. There were native Germans in the Iron Brigade.

Here on Cemetery Hill the consonant-clotted *Schimpfwörter* and the wielded spikes and fence rails reduced the Causes to their lowest terms. The army of the nation that broke their eggs by the large end was defeated by the heroic defense of the army of the nation that believed eggs must be broken at the smaller end, and the world, perceived by both nations to be somewhat oval-shaped itself, has never been the same. It is a human tendency to be thus flippant at a cemetery.

But rather than go through the gate, you walk down the north face of the hill in the soft spring sunshine. Some years ago I watched a little girl roll over and over and over down the hill, laughing all the way. Such monuments, after all is said and done, are the better ones.

Americans do not fully appreciate what happened in the Civil War. The nation was destroyed. Visiting its greatest battlefield is like witnessing a funeral pyre—but whether a new phoenix rose from its ashes, or something somewhat less, is in question. The best of both North and South was destroyed, as if the patient, sick unto death, died in the operation. Better would have been a regimen of changed diet than the violent alternative of such an operation as was performed, but the patient had no heart for it. And the War came.

The Union won the War, but its ideals died in a long, slow burn of racism and industry. Lincoln was America's last Lincoln. He could not be elected now any more than *Walden* could be televised. The South without its racism, the North without most everything but its ideals—now that would have been a Union worthy of the War. But what came out was the very opposite, a triumphant industrial state on its way to commercial totalitarianism, with a hardened, practical indifference to an unfree underclass. If this picture is too bleak, there will surely be enough voices to correct it. What is wanted more are actions to belie it. The Union manufactured six million uniforms during the war, or something like—no matter; very few are left, whereas the men who wore them long since are in their graves. Still we will not learn that men like that, and women like that, cannot be manufactured. America came out of the War a shabbier man in more elegant clothing; what we need is a new fashion, the main element of which is a new person to wear it—or rather the old one, cured of the disease and the illusions. For this what company or engineer can we turn to?

One thinks of Christianity first of all, or at least the American churches. But this is where the very failure has been. The Constitution was formed with Presbyterian church polity in mind, as it seems to me. Nineteenth-century evangelicalism had much to do with anti-slavery. Thus two pillars of America rest upon the churches. But today the churches have retreated in the face of a bizarre, self-righteous, literalist consumer fantasy. The laws and culture of America are becoming abjectly secular because the dominant religion is itself pagan. It has the piety of a religion and rants a parody of Christian theology, but nobody is fooled: reverence for God as God, transcendent mystery to be adored and worshipped, and respect for other human beings and ourselves, have been sloshed away. What is left is a Stepenfetchit god, and people who are either conversion fodder or condemned substandard furniture; and this is paganism in its sewerage form. No redeeming virtues or culture, either, but a *danse macabre* at K-Mart with Guns N Roses on the speakers. The mainline churches cannot retrieve the initiative or even defend their lives as long as they keep turning and running. They move their headquarters to the seats of popular religion, not to invade, but to capitulate. Are they afraid to fight this popular religion, which is little more than an attempt to show that the Church of Christ is not really different from, but the same as, the rude and vast illusion that honks its brainless slogans in our face? A great argument for Christianity is the devil's efforts to suffocate it—witness now the influx of American fundagelicalism into Eastern Europe, when there were more Christians in Russia and Poland than there are in the USA; what couldn't be destroyed by Czarism, Leninism, and Stalinism is now in more danger from American capitalism and its priests. You fight a pagan with a pagan, and the pagan always wins. What father if his son asked for bread would give him a stone? But the Russians asked us for a cup of cold water and what have we sent them? A commercial American paraphrase called Living, but really Dead. What confessing churches rise up in indignation? Where is Luther? Where are the mouth-filling oaths of the enraged Teuton?

It will be stormy today. A low ledge of clouds is piling over the horizon, heavy, ponderous. The lake where I sit and write looks not as blue and calm as yesterday; though the sun still shines, the water has taken on a steely, slate-gray chop. I had not noticed how the year has turned. I remember like a vision of eternity a spring morning walk on Culp's Hill—while here the jet skis growl on a darkening flood.

16 *Pickett's Charge*

We are all sculptors

and painters, and our

material is our own flesh

and blood and bones.

—**Thoreau**

Pickett's Charge should have another name, but nobody has thought of one that will stick. "The Pickett-Pettigrew Assault," "Longstreet's Second Assault," and "Longstreet's Attack on the Union Left Center" do not have the handy dash of "Pickett's Charge."

Pickett actually commanded only one of the two and a half divisions which made the attack, and his authority did not extend beyond his own men. The "charge" was a running, yelling attack only at the last and in part; most of it was a mile-wide walking advance of about fifteen minutes over open fields. But it cannot have a merely technical label, because Pickett's Charge has a mythic significance. However, the myth is not large enough, and needs some correction or enlargement. As is true of the War in general, the courage and poignancy of both sides is essential to the story and tragedy.

Pickett's Charge is an emblem larger than words of a grand and valorous forlorn hope: the wide fields in the hot July afternoon, long lines of gray with red battle flags flying, shot and canister tearing through them, smoke, and the actual, legendary Rebel Yell. This was all true. The soldier who on July 2 exclaimed, "Oh, Captain! Ain't it beautiful?" would have been—perhaps was, if he survived—speechless as the long lines of Longstreet's and Hill's men came out of the trees in parade order and swept toward the waiting Union lines. It was even more hideously splendid than that.

Cemetery Ridge, where the Union line waited, is only a gradual rise in elevation, and it appears almost flat from across the fields. Similarly, Seminary Ridge, the Confederate side a half-mile away, is gradual, perhaps ten to twenty feet lower than Cemetery Ridge in relation to the fields in between. Seminary Ridge was wooded, and the Confederates could assemble their troops along and behind it unseen; Cemetery Ridge was generally open, with a noticeable clump of trees at one point—and this was chosen as the focal point for the attack. The Union men sat and lay forward of the ridge crest, behind low stone farm walls or improvised breastworks of dirt and rails, or along a fold in the ground. They were more or less visible, but one of the important and surprising factors in Lee's planning is that the Southerners did not for a moment believe that Cemetery Ridge was being held by so thin a blue line as the one they were able to see. At the clump of trees there was only one brigade in position; another brigade to its left; and the Union line presented only regimental depth along the brigade fronts. Surely there were heavy lines of reinforcements behind the crest. Of equal concern were the Union batteries visible all along that crest. Lee had his batteries concentrate on the Union guns there at the center of the line, and also on the heavy support lines behind the crest.

But there were no support lines behind Webb's Brigade, at the stone wall which made an angle about 200 yards north of the clump of trees, and Hall's Brigade at the trees. Confederate gunners cut their fuses to explode over the crest, and havoc was done there to caissons, horses, and Meade's tiny headquarters—while the troops in position were generally spared. The metal flew over them, exploding either at the batteries 100 yards back or over the crest. Two mistakes were made by the Southerners, then: one was to assume the Yankees would not dare hold the center of the ridge with so few troops; the other was to assume too quickly that their forward line was not seriously manned, and therefore to conclude that there was even less there than two brigades. Another mistake was to underestimate the importance and ability of the Union units right and left of the focal point. On the right of Webb was Hays's whole division; on the left, another Second Corps brigade and a couple of First Corps brigades. These troops would be very well handled by Union commanders: as the Confederate mass came to the focal point, these troops to right and left would swing out like two gates and take the Southern flanks in dense, murderous, and nearly point-blank crossfire. There was some preparation for this: two brigades on either Confederate flank and somewhat to the rear would move forward to support the main line, catching any Union flanking attempts in their own flank fire. But on the right the two Confederate brigades didn't go to the correct point. (This shows that what looks easy to us now—getting troops in plain sight of the objective actually to arrive at the objective—was not at all easy; and it highlights one of the phenomena of the attack, namely, that two divisions in long lines, starting a quarter-mile apart from each other at different distances from the focal point and with different angles and maneuvers to march, actually joined, and struck the clump of trees together.) On the left the two support brigades never got started properly; and units that actually advanced in the main line on the extreme left did not get into the intended position, and Hays's flanking movement and fire easily shattered them.

But on paper, the idea of Pickett's Charge was not so stupid as it appears to us now. Two brigades on each end would support the flanks. The two main divisions would attack on a four-brigade front, with three brigades immediately behind them, and one or two more right behind that, guaranteeing great depth at the crucial point. Artillery would first concentrate on the Union guns there to weaken their ability to cut down the infantry where the attack went in; then batteries would move forward with the infantry in support. Finally, the ace in the hole was Stuart's cavalry, which would sweep into the Union rear from several miles back, causing confusion among the Union wagon and artillery parks and scooping up the disorganized, fleeing troops ejected from their lines by the Confederate artillery and infantry: no indecisive victory this time.

It is questionable as to whether this would have worked even had everything gone right, for the factor Lee never seemed to consider with enough seriousness was the Army of the Potomac. Could it not withstand an attack of three divisions on its center, even adding artillery and two or three brigades of cavalry? It could move reinforcing troops quickly along its interior lines, while Lee could not back up his attack with any speed at all—hours. But mostly, something Lee still would not believe, even after those two days of battle: the Northerners in that line at the center would fight like absolute hell. Lee said he thought his men could do anything, and so they could, except for superhuman things like surviving cannon blasts and mistaken planning; but the Army of the Potomac had men like that too.

Still, what those Southerners did seems nearly superhuman.

As it turned out, things did not all go right—and they had to *all* go right, even for what slim ephemeral chance might have existed. Ultimately this was a mistake of pride too. One can almost see Lee's failure as a Greek-style drama in which the hero, Lee, is victim of his own hubris. But of course the tragic heroes were Pickett's and Pettigrew's men; they suffered out of proportion to their mistake. It is they with whom we identify, upon whom we look with pity and fear. Lee committed the sin but did not suffer the punishment, and in any case the punishment would have been deserved, not tragic. This is not to say that his conduct afterward was not noble, mythically so, riding among the returning survivors alone, exposed to artillery fire, admitting it was all his fault, and calling upon them to stand firm.

In effect, though not in words of confession, Lee realized his sin of pride. It was after Gettysburg that he became a great man and a great general—brilliantly fighting Grant's "overwhelming numbers and resources" in 1864, making Grant lose more men than Lee had in his whole army. Not that this should be exaggerated beyond the human level either: Lee still wanted to attack after the Wilderness; but he had learned something about possibilities.

On this afternoon his men would have to be superhuman. Their supports would not be there. The coordination Lee thought could be achieved, that "proper concert of action" which failed on July 2, was supposed to happen in the face of Union resistance. Lee knew how difficult movement and coordination were, dependent upon couriers and interpretation of orders, and foot power. It was a proud blindness to think that all this could be done in the faces of those Yankees. The one coordinating attack, Ewell's Corps against the Union right, had started and ended too early to prevent Meade from reinforcing his center when Longstreet advanced. The cavalry might have struck at about the right time, being able to move fast when the artillery bombardment ceased—but what about the Yankee cavalry? Already before Gettysburg it had achieved overall superiority, but that possibility couldn't even be imagined in the Army of Northern Virginia. Lee finally planned a Napoleonic use of cavalry, but the assumption that the enemy's cavalry could simply be fooled or ridden over was a mistake Napoleonic in magnitude—as was the charge itself. And could the Southern artillery, with its inferior numbers and equipment, hope to knock out the Federal guns?

Lee certainly was aware of the disparity between his and Meade's artillery—and it was somewhat acknowledgeable, resting substantially upon Northern factories and not only on Northern skill and valor. Assuming this, one must conclude that Lee was willing to trade chess pieces. He would not need his artillery as much to support the assault as the Yankees would need theirs to repel it. He feared their artillery more than their infantry. Let us both blow off all our long-range ammunition in a huge cannonade; there will be little left to shoot at my men as they advance. What batteries I can demolish, I will demolish, even at the cost of some of my own. Lee's lack of concern over whether he had enough artillery ammunition further suggests this possibility, as well as perhaps overconfidence. There was not enough to adequately support the attack.

Lee's plan worked to some extent. Union General Henry Hunt, Meade's Chief of Artillery, who had control of a large artillery reserve independent of any infantry corps command, knew what was coming and understood what had to be done. He went among his batteries telling them to aim and fire deliberately. His tactic was to focus the whole works on one Confederate battery at a time, pulverize it, and move on to the next. He knew an infantry assault was coming, however, so he wanted to conserve long-range ammunition. At the center of the Cemetery Ridge line, where the attack would come, Hunt's plan was foiled. It was the area of the Second Corps, and General Hancock would have none of the batteries silent along his corps' line. It demoralized the infantry, he believed, to have to lie under a bombardment without the booming of their own guns telling them the enemy was getting it back.

Except for the reserve artillery—and there was dispute about this—the batteries in an army belonged to the corps they served with, and therefore were considered to be under the orders of the infantry commander (who also outranked the highest artillerist in the army.) Hancock ordered the batteries along Cemetery Ridge, which Hunt had ordered to conserve ammunition, to resume firing. Farther down the line McGilvery, part of the Artillery Reserve rather than the Second Corps, refused to obey Hancock's order. When the attack came, his guns and those of Rittenhouse on the ubiquitous Little Round Top finally opened up and tore at Pickett's lines, partly enfilading at long range, dropping maimed bodies all across the half mile. But in the center, the Confederates were amazed at how little artillery fired at them during most of the advance; the long-range stuff all came from left and right. Not only were the Second Corps' batteries out of long-range ammunition, a dozen or so guns were pulled out and were not replaced before the attack moved forward. But when the Southerners reached canister range—about at the Emmitsburg Road—the Union guns opened up and did murderous work. Hunt said later that had his batteries been able to save their long-range ammunition for the infantry, the charge would have been broken up before it reached the Second Corps line. Hancock knew infantry, but it is hard to dispute Hunt's opinion that many fewer Confederates would have reached the stone wall.

Hunt had no equivalent counterpart in the Army of Northern Virginia. Pendleton, Lee's Chief of Artillery, exudes down through the decades an irritating impression of incompetence. On July 3 he didn't know what his batteries' supplies were, and he had not provided for sensible resupply. He neither possessed nor sought authority to coordinate the artillery of all three army corps. The responsibility, therefore, for the inefficient use of guns on July 3 was his, Hill's, Ewell's, and Lee's. Longstreet had Lieutenant Colonel E. P. Alexander, the Chief of Artillery for the First Corps—an intelligent, perhaps brilliant, young man; personable, honest, honorable, articulate, and, like most great captains, a war lover, who once in an action aimed a gun himself, taking great satisfaction in his having been able to follow the curve of the landscape to drop a shell into a building with sharpshooters in it; at South Mountain he borrowed a rifle in order to shoot long range at some Yankees. Alexander wrote, in two versions, one of the most interesting, fair, and winning reminiscences of the War. His *Military Memoirs of a Confederate* (1907) is a formal, restrained volume; his personal version, written for his daughter and less reserved in its judgments and personal evaluations, was edited and issued more recently as *Fighting for the Confederacy* (1989).

His writing shows that the earliest cogent critic of Robert E. Lee's generalship was not a Northern partisan. (Of course, Pickett himself may have been the first real critic, a more gallant Virginian than whom could not be imagined, and Longstreet of course.) Even the first published version of Alexander's memoirs is full of implied criticism, though its main focus is the artillery. *Somebody* was to blame for these things: Hill's batteries using up long-range ammunition in a silly duel at 11:30, and not being able to support the afternoon's charge by shelling the Union flank attack on its left; the idea that Confederate artillery—in open, lower positions—could "suppress" the enfilading Union batteries on the elevations right and left was accepted (by Lee); most of the firing was done by guns "parallel to the position of the enemy" while "56 guns stood idle" elsewhere; Lee's concave line was not used to enfilade the Union batteries, especially on Cemetery Hill; the infantry support on the right was allowed to go in after it was all over. Larger criticisms are stated or implied: Alexander implicitly agrees with Longstreet that no 15,000 men who ever lived could successfully make such an assault, and that Lee was impatient of such talk; the attack was made in the wrong place (Cemetery Hill itself was closer to Confederate lines, could be enfiladed, the attack could be supported by artillery at short range, and no enfilading fire would threaten the attackers); even at the time, Alexander had seen "overwhelming reasons" for not making the attack. In his other version Alexander strongly criticizes the conception of the July 2 offensive as well.

The South could have won the Civil War, could have won at Gettysburg. On the human level alone, there was no inevitability. But the South had lived too long on illusion and would not see to fight. Longstreet, a critical patriot, was considered un-Southern after the War, just as critical patriots are sometimes accused of being "un-American" now—and out of the same fearful frame of mind. People perish for lack of vision.

There was no more devoted officer in the Army of Northern Virginia than Alexander, but blind, defensive devotion to Lee appeared to him to do nobody any good, and lack of honest vision had been fatal at Gettysburg. Alexander greatly respected and admired Lee; it is from him as much as from Freemantle that we get the picture of Lee riding out into the field after the attack's failure. One appreciates a mind and character like Alexander's, who could respect and admire and even love, without fearing to be honest. The battle would have gone better for the Confederates if Alexander (or Longstreet), who saw the weaknesses but still loved the cause, had had more say in things. (There was no "Lee: love him or leave him" sticker on the fanny of his horse.) As it was, Alexander had too much to say in a different respect.

There was another weakness in the planning. Longstreet was given half of Hill's Corps for the attack. Unfortunately, like the rebels in *Henry IV, Part One*, there was dissention among the dissenters. Hill and Longstreet didn't get along. The sensitive Hill, who had a tendency to get so high-strung before a battle that he became somewhat unwell, was not the person to deal with a truculent Longstreet, who was upset about yesterday and now today. So Hill's supporting troops behind Pettigrew never really got into the attack properly. That Pettigrew (actually Heth's Division of Hill's Corps) made the juncture with Pickett (of Longstreet's Corps) was phenomenal.

Longstreet was so against the assault, and so upset that it had to be made—and by him—that he couldn't bring himself to give the actual order. Longstreet was not an indecisive man. He did not shrink from responsibility. But he wrote a note to Alexander telling him that he, Alexander, must judge the effect of the artillery's fire, and when the moment was right, send Pickett forward. Alexander was dismayed. It was up to *him* to decide whether and when to launch the offensive? He showed the note to General Wright, and together the two composed a marvel:

> General: I will only be able to judge of the effect of our fire on the enemy by his return fire, as his infantry is little exposed to view and the smoke will obscure the field. If, as I infer from your note, there is any alternative to this attack, it should be carefully considered before opening our fire, for it will take all the artillery ammunition we have left to test this one, and if result is unfavorable we will have none left for another effort. And even if this is entirely successful, it can only be so at a very bloody cost.

It put, but not quite, the onus back on Longstreet tactfully yet clearly. Still, Longstreet was no slug:

> Colonel: The intention is to advance the infantry if the artillery has the
> desired effect of driving the enemy's off, or having other effect such as to
> warrant us in making the attack. When that moment arrives advise Gen.
> Pickett and of course advance such artillery as you can use in aiding the
> attack.

The game of chess was against each other. Finally, Alexander sent the note: "When our fire is at its best, I will advise Gen. Pickett to advance." Had as much acuteness been devoted to military tactics as to verbal in the Army of Northern Virginia, July 2 and 3 might have turned out differently.

So everything was more or less ready. It was the noon hour; at one o'clock two of Alexander's guns would fire in rapid succession, signaling all the rest to open. Meanwhile, soldiers along Cemetery Ridge rested in the intense, lazifying heat. The sound of fighting way over on the right at Culp's Hill, which had gone on for six hours, had ceased. For sixteen hours on the Union center and left there had been quiet—a quiet which Haskell describes as being so strange when it comes suddenly after terrible battle. For sixteen hours the fields in front lay littered with bodies; during the night, lanterns of ambulance parties bobbed and drifted out in the fields under a humid, starless sky. Cries and groans made a weak, constant chorus. Skirmishers occasionally popped away. Near the Emmitsburg Road smoke still rose from the farm buildings shelled and then burned to deprive Confederate sharpshooters of a nest. Waiting Southerners by the thousands lay in long, long rows in the trees behind the low crest of Seminary Ridge—a massive murmur of men talking.

On the off side of Cemetery Ridge General Gibbon and some of his staff, including Lieutenant Frank Haskell, formerly of the Iron Brigade, had finished a scrounged-up lunch (the first food in twenty-four hours for some) of potatoes, bread, and a little chicken, with coffee and tea, and were lying in the hot sun. Two distant artillery reports in rapid order—and in two or three seconds a terrific roar erupted from Seminary Ridge. Gibbon jumped up snatching his sword and ran toward the crest as shells screamed over and began exploding everywhere. Orderlies ran every which way; horses reared and neighed. Fragments whistled, striking caissons, horses, and men. Just yards away a bolt, an octagonal projectile fired from a Whitworth gun far away on Oak Hill, came screaming in and cut an orderly in half. Out in front of the crest the infantry clung to the ground as gunners leaped into action amid striking, thudding, splintering shot. General Webb said later it felt as though a hundred cannons were pointed directly at him. Webb and other officers walked back and forth talking to the men. Now the heaviest artillery barrage yet on the North American continent reached full voice. It was heard as far away as Pittsburgh, though the wind on the field at Gettysburg was westerly. Smoke billowed and rolled across the fields, across the crest of Cemetery Ridge. Shells exploded in the air—the peculiar neat round puff of white smoke—then the zip, whine of fragments and the screams of horses and men. Behind the ridge sixteen horses were killed around Meade's headquarters, and two holes were shot through the minuscule, two-roomed white frame structure. The Commanding General and staff, not in a rush, moved farther back.

Lieutenant Haskell's account of the bombardment and Pickett's Charge, written a few weeks afterward by a man who had been right in the midst of them, and mounted so that he could see and go to various points, could hardly be surpassed. Haskell was highly intelligent, literary, observant, and passionately involved; he had won the admiration of the Iron Brigade, not easy men to impress, and of John Gibbon, on whose staff he now served. His *The Battle of Gettysburg* is a clear, compelling gift from a man who died eleven months later at Cold Harbor. ("My God!" exclaimed John Gibbon when he was told of Haskell's death. "I have lost my best friend, and one of the best soldiers in the Army of the Potomac has fallen!")

Haskell describes "the great hoarse roar of battle" engulfing the men on Cemetery Ridge. Across the way, individual discharges of Confederate cannons could be seen but not heard in the general roar. The "thunder and lightning" were "incessant, all pervading, in the air above our heads, on the ground at our feet, remote, near, deafening, ear-piercing, astounding; and these hailstones are massy iron, charged with exploding fire." The cannoneers are no longer envied, but admired: "These grimy men, rushing, shouting, their souls in a frenzy." The projectiles "hiss, they scream, they growl, they sputter . . . ," they "shriek long and sharp."

We see the poor fellows hobbling back from the crest, or unable to do so, pale and weak, lying on the ground with the mangled stump of an arm or leg, dripping their life-blood away; or with a cheek torn open or a shoulder mashed. And many, alas! hear not the roar as they stretch upon the ground with upturned faces and open eyes, though a shell should burst at their very ears. Their ears and their bodies this instant are only mud. We saw them but a moment since there among the flame, with brawny arms and muscles of iron, wielding the rammer and pushing home the cannon's plethoric load.

We could not often see the shell before it burst; but sometimes, as we faced toward the enemy, and looked above our heads, the approach would be heralded by a prolonged hiss, which always seemed to me to be a line of something tangible, terminating in a black globe, distinct to the eye, as the sound had been to the ear. The shell would seem to stop, and hang suspended in the air an instant, and then vanish in fire and smoke and noise.

The Union lines were not much damaged despite all this, but behind Seminary Ridge the Southern boys waiting tensely for the assault, which had been carefully explained to all of them—they took losses back there. One regiment lost eighty-eight men. Not only iron killed them; heavy branches were shot from the trees along the ridge. When the order was given to get up and form, it came as a kind of relief.

Union accounts tend to put the duration of the barrage at two hours. Alexander wrote that as he had enough ammunition for one hour, he sent his message to Pickett at 1:30, and the cannonade ceased at 2:00. Whatever the duration, there came a point when Meade and Hunt had the same idea: slacken, then cease fire, not only to conserve ammunition but to fool the Confederates into thinking they had knocked out the Federal guns. At about this time also, a dozen guns were pulled back from the area around the Clump of Trees, to be replaced by fresh batteries. Alexander, across the way, saw the guns go out. He withdrew batteries to clean guns and conserve ordnance, but the Federals never did. He watched a few minutes, but no new guns came in. He wrote a note to Pickett:

For God's sake come quick. The eighteen guns have gone. Come quick or my ammunition will not let me support you properly.

Pickett received the note with Longstreet standing right there; he handed it to Longstreet, then asked, "General, shall I advance?" Longstreet could not force the words out. Pickett, confident in Lee's orders, had just written a note to his young sweetheart: he was not afraid to die, though he knew he might; it was a glorious opportunity; he was assured of its success. Flushed with anticipation, he did not know why Longstreet said nothing. The general simply lowered his head in assent. "I shall lead my division forward, Sir," Pickett said. That is how the most famous, glorious charge in American history began—innocent eagerness and a stricken nod.

In Alexander's words, Longstreet had fought his battle out alone, and obeyed his orders. The chance almost came to stop the attack. Just as Pickett started, Alexander told Longstreet that the ammunition chests were low. Longstreet, stunned, blurted that Pickett must be ordered back. But it would take too much time to replenish, Alexander pointed out; besides, there wasn't much left in the reserve train anyway. The attack went on.

This final decision was made like many—haltingly, at fits and starts, in dismay and confusion. The condition of tragedy is ignorance. In this Longstreet was the condensed picture of human life. The divisions marched on, toward and up the slope of Cemetery Ridge, against Longstreet's will, against his common sense and conscience, which made it, as Thoreau might have said, "very steep marching indeed." But James Longstreet could not wash his hands of the evil; it was his position to have to act, one way or the other, to disobey orders and attack the basis of the military organization, or acquiesce in the needless deaths and woundings of hundreds or thousands.

After the War, when he had written his embittered criticisms of Lee, enlarging his figure to the point of writing that 30,000 men couldn't have succeeded in the attack, and accusing Lee of bloodthirstiness, Longstreet was vilified in the press, in books, and in speeches by Lee's generals and veterans. He further alienated himself by joining the Republican party. He even became a Roman Catholic. He stayed away from Army of Northern Virginia reunions. About thirty years after the War, at a grand reunion, the veterans of the Army of Northern Virginia recognized a man who came in to the hall, lame and alone. Tears in their eyes, they applauded, rising to their feet. Longstreet.

The Allies' prosecution of the German officials at Nuremberg was based on the principle that evil orders should be disobeyed. Did Longstreet have the courage of his troops? Who is to say which took more courage, to disobey Lee's orders, or to do the duty his training made James Longstreet believe his duty was? What would Lee himself, who broke his oath as an officer of the United States and whose dominant idea was duty, have done? Which are the higher duties? We would perhaps have the courage to perform them if we knew clearly what they were. But we are ignorant, and our consequences come upon us unawares, well-meaning though we were. "Sin with courage," Luther said.

In the first moments it may have looked as though courage would be enough. George Pickett, Longstreet's favorite, was in the saddle, radiant with purpose, and his fine brigadiers led out their even gray lines of Virginians. They passed through the silent guns into the fields, battle flags in the sultry breeze. Who could stop such men as these?

George Pickett himself, "open, frank, and genial," gallant and adolescent, was a widower, thirty-eight years old, in love with his Sally, a teen-aged girl back in Virginia. He had had his splendid moments. In the storming of the fortress of Chapultapec during the Mexican War, it was young George Pickett who was first to climb the parapet—and, taking up the flag from the wounded James Longstreet, "was the brave American who unfurled our flag over the castle," in the words of the man who was now his corps commander. But another time, during the present war, he was seen riding in front of his men exposed to enemy fire, hugging the neck of his horse for protection—considered unthinkably bad form. While stationed in the Northwest before Secession, he performed outstanding service to the Indians. He learned their languages, translating the Lord's Prayer and several hymns, became a teacher to them, and so was called "Great Chief." This does not sound like the man who graduated at the bottom of his West Point class—whether his graduating rank was due to academics or to conduct; it does not sound like the dim bulb Longstreet's chief of staff described: when delivering orders to Pickett, Longstreet "made us give him things very fully; indeed, sometimes stay with him and make sure he did not get astray." Where did Pickett find time to curl and perfume his hair? A much remarked-at feature in the army, his

shoulder-length cascade of curls; and in a group of men who had neither time nor interest for such things, his brushed, curly, auburn
beard emanated powerfully the "scents of Araby." Minutes earlier, as
his division awaited the word and Longstreet was anticipating Alexander's note, Pickett was writing to his sweetheart—again; and *after* he
got the nodded order from his commander, Pickett penned still more!
What? While his division was moving out? Shouldn't he have been
everywhere watching, directing, inspiring? What a romantic he
was—"your soldier" as he referred to himself in those sensitive letters—his sweetheart's name upon his lips as he led his men into
death. He had, after all, noticed Longstreet's dismay; Longstreet had
now looked at him, "for several minutes," in silence before letting
him go. There were tears in Longstreet's eyes as he watched the thousands passing him; Pickett understood that his corps commander expected them to die in windrows. "Into the jaws of death" Pickett went
willingly, gallantly, his hair streaming; leaving his young love and his
joy behind, for duty, and for the Cause. He was in a way the epitome
of the mythic Southern soldier.

Was he intelligent or stupid? Was he courageous or cowardly? There
was a dispute after the charge, when one officer averred that Pickett
skulked at the Codori barn during the attack. All the other mounted
officers were either killed or wounded, and their horses shot—all but
Pickett and his staff, men and horses getting out unhit and unhurt.
Why? How? Pickett's three generals—Armistead, Garnett, Kemper—
were highly visible riding and marching toward their bullets, but nobody saw much of Pickett after his division crossed the Emmitsburg
Road. Historians generally think he was probably at the stone out-
cropping only 100 yards from the Union line, which is where a division commander should have been, directing his troops. He did send
orders throughout the attack, and Longstreet (an apologist?) says it
was Pickett himself who ordered the survivors to fall back. While stationed at Puget Sound, his sixty-eight men threatened by one thousand British in a territorial dispute, Pickett had said, "We will make a
Bunker Hill of it." But now, had Pickett lost his military sharpness?
Was his sweetheart—whom he would marry after Gettysburg—a distraction? (He had left his division that spring, against orders, to visit
his "charming Sally.") The Virginian strikes one somewhat as the

doubly adolescent middle-aged man trying to revive his youth. Pickett, before the attack probably trusting Lee's judgment, perhaps adoring or revering Lee, met Lee as the Virginia Division survivors washed back. Lee told him gently and firmly to reform his division. "I have no division!" Pickett cried. It is no bad, but rather a good, reflection on one's manhood to cry at the deaths and maiming of one's comrades—but one hears something else in Pickett's reply also. After the War, presented with the undesired opportunity to pay a brief call on Lee, Pickett said, "That old man had my division destroyed at Gettysburg." Pickett's response to Lee in front of Seminary Ridge sounds somehow different from Hood's response to Jackson at Sharpsburg: "Where is your division, General Hood?" "Dead on the field."

Lee's response to Pickett may have been essentially similar to Pickett's response to him. Pickett was the unfortunate victim of the inevitable, right at the end of the War, during the last desperate days of the siege of Petersburg. When Sheridan attacked at Five Forks, Pickett was not with his division. He was at a shad bake with some other officers—a perfectly legitimate and reasonable thing to do, unless you happen to get attacked just then. And unless the attack succeeds, and unhinges the whole army's line—stretched to the breaking point anyway—and precipitates the nightmare retreat to Appomattox. Pickett's command totally disappeared then—captured, mostly. Lee was probably nearly beside himself with rage. The Virginia Division had been his favorite before Gettysburg. Did he blame Pickett—now at Five Forks he seemed to have a reason—for what he himself had done to his Virginians? He saw Pickett walking by a campfire during that hungry, sleepless, hazy flight toward Appomattox and said, "Is that man still with the Army?"

Those people. That man.

But Pickett is paradoxical in a larger sense, greater than the contradictions of personality. How did he get his place at West Point? His uncle had moved from Virginia to Springfield, Illinois, to practice law, and young George had followed to read law under him. George came to dislike law study, but favorably impressed a friend of his uncle's, a fellow lawyer and poet; this friend was shrewd and able enough to pull the right string for George. Even during the War, Pickett would speak only respectfully of the man in the White House.

Pickett's generals were the splendid and the brave. Lewis A. Armistead, forty-six, was one of the best brigadiers in an army distinguished by its brigadiers. It was his uncle who had commanded Fort McHenry during the British attack witnessed by Francis Scott Key. (Armistead would come within a few feet of Union General Webb inside the stone wall—Webb, whose grandfather was one of the minutemen at Lexington; when Armistead was struck down there, command of his brigade passed to a grandson of Patrick Henry.) Armistead was known for his sound judgment as well as for great personal courage: both would be required at the moment of his brigade's hesitation at the stone wall.

James Kemper, thirty-nine, was a graduate of Washington College, now Washington and Lee. He was not a military man by background—no West Point; he did go to Mexico as a captain but arrived after Zachary Taylor had won his victory. He studied law and practiced in Virginia, where he had become Speaker of the House of Delegates.

Richard Garnett, though his was not the hat held high on swordpoint at the High Water Mark of the Confederacy, is the most tragic of Pickett's three. He and his twin brother were marked for their courage and compassion; in 1855 his brother had died nursing victims of yellow fever. But the General had the misfortune of commanding Jackson's old Stonewall Brigade in the unfortunate Romney campaign in 1862. Resting his tired, hungry, freezing men, he was pointedly reprimanded by Jackson, who wanted the men to be pushed on. At Kernstown, the losing battle that opened Jackson's Valley Campaign, Garnett's conduct was recognized as brave and able. Seeing himself outflanked by a preponderant Union force, he ordered his men back; his officers recognized that there was no choice. But Jackson blew up, cashiered Garnett, and brought charges. He tried but failed to keep Garnett out of further command in the Confederate service. Richard Garnett agonized for the charges against him to come to trial, but Jackson was always active elsewhere. Finally Lee put Garnett in command of a brigade (Pickett's, after Pickett had been wounded.) He served at Sharpsburg and after with distinction, but everyone knew he was oppressed by the black burden which Jackson's charges left on his honor. The Army sympathized with Garnett rather than Jackson, having seen Garnett's sterling behavior and almost excessive energy, and knowing, one imagines, that Jackson, like some other military geniuses, was a fanatic and more or less insane. A beloved eccentric to his own troops—some of them, and generally later—Stonewall was in other respects a son of a bitch. When Jackson died, Garnett showed his true nature, grieving for him and marching as a mourner in the line of officers who took the coffin to its grave. But his distinguished service could not erase the dead general's curse in Garnett's mind. His heart was oppressed by it, according to Pickett's wife, who wrote that his "sensitive mind . . . never recovered" from the injury. So now, coming off Seminary Ridge, he was riding at the head of his brigade, determined to lead his men into the face of the fire, and to expose himself conspicuously to its worst. He had been ill, and now could barely get on his horse, but he pretended to be vigorous and well. His men heard his strong voice as usual; he rode along the line with spirit. But over his own wool uniform, in the hot sun, he was wearing a heavy woolen overcoat buttoned to the chin.

General Garnett's body was never found after the battle. The overcoat he wore was blue. Perhaps he lies in the National Cemetery, one of the "Unknown" among the Union dead. Or perhaps, only a part of the ornate Confederate gray officer's uniform visible, he was buried by Federal troops in some shallow trench with the bodies of the men who always had believed in him.

Those men, who on orders and in anonymity marched across those open fields at a walk, bore the glory of the day. Pickett's Virginia Division, even on the long march from Chambersburg, had straggled less than at any other time. However historians might argue, the men felt that this was the decisive battle. For the South, for Old Virginia, for the quiet homes in North Carolina, Tennessee, Florida, Mississippi and Alabama, they were ready to die. One young Mississippian, hit by an exploding shell during the artillery bombardment, was carried to a doctor, who looked at the quivering stump of the left arm, severed at the elbow, and pronounced his opinion that the young man would survive. "Why, that isn't where I'm hurt," the soldier said. With his right hand he pulled aside the blanket covering him. The shell had torn away part of his abdomen. "I am in great agony," he said. The young man wanted to write something back home before he died; it was a short letter, covered with blood by the time it was finished, reading in part: "Remember that I am true to my country and my regret at dying is that she is not free. . . ." Lifting his last cup—a tin cup filled with opium solution—he said to the soldiers who had gathered around him: ". . . to the Southern Confederacy. . . ."

For the Southern Confederacy, then, they went forward.

As soon as they stepped out of the woods in their lines, shells and the fearsome solid shot began coming in from Cemetery Hill and Little Round Top. Whether the lines were as straight as the descriptions lead us to believe, or only relatively so, is difficult to know. General D. H. Hill, who was not at Gettysburg, said he never saw a Confederate battle line that was not "crooked as a ram's horn." Nevertheless, their discipline was superb, and the lines in order to meet as they did must have been very orderly. They certainly kept closed up as the shells tore through them.

The walk is about fifteen minutes. You might start at the Virginia Monument, in the shadow of Robert E. Lee on Traveller; you go down the path to a small paved area, then out across the fields toward the Emmitsburg Road. Starting from there, you would probably be a North Carolinian, part of Pettigrew's Division, which stretches off to your left. You are to go almost straight forward to the clump of trees. Off to your right, out of your view at the moment, are Pickett's Virginians. In front of you is a strong line of skirmishers—not a battle line but a loose formation. Your line, two ranks deep, will merge with them at the road up ahead. There are fences everywhere in the fields, some having been partly torn down during yesterday's fighting, some being taken down by the skirmishers. But you can see that others, especially along the Emmitsburg Road, are heavy post-and-rail fences that will have to be climbed. If you see this at all. Walking, you grip your clean musket. At your elbows two of your friends step determinedly. You know the fellows of the whole Company, and you are going forward together, rifles and bayonets glazed by the sun. The officers are behind you now; some have dismounted. "Keep on, men. Close up. Close up!" A shell has struck several boys on the left, and you are aware that your friend is farther from you so you verge in that direction. The line is closed again. You wonder whether the following brigade will be careful where they tread.

You are determined and strong. You will strike the enemy. In your haversack is a letter, in case you are killed, but now you are very busy. You look at the hot blue sky, the drifting smoke, the skirmishers ahead; two guns on the ridge straight before you bark streams of fire and smoke—in a second you hear two screams of shells, then a *whoosh* and explosion behind. You realize a flash and concussion have ignited beside you. The next man is 12 yards to your left. Looking back for an instant you see your friend, not badly hurt, kneeling and holding his left arm. Next to him lie several of the fellows crying out, and in the middle of them two torn bodies without legs; you don't recognize them. Men from the second rank crowd in beside you; an officer is shouting "Keep on! Close up! Close that hole! *Eyes forward, men!*" You feel a hollow nervousness for a moment, but as you walk on, the heat and exertion are what you think of, and the Yankee line you are going to strike. *Oh God, spare me to strike them!*

Officers behind you are shouting. You are aware that shot and shells are coming in from off to right and left; a few Yankee guns straight ahead are firing. Where exactly is the Yankee infantry line? Thirty yards ahead the skirmishers have stopped at the fence along the road. They can't take it down. "Let's get over that fence, boys!" "Over the fence!" You climb it as a loud rattling slams the rails—to your right men pitch backward off the fence. The Yankee gunners are loading canister now. Sounds like hailstones hitting the fence, and there is a *thug* beside you. Up ahead the Yankee infantry is lying and kneeling behind a low stone wall; over left some Yankee regiments have started firing. Straight ahead they are holding their fire. They will fire into our breasts when we get there. Let them! We will give them our steel.

You are suddenly close to the regiment's flag; it was away to the left when you started. Other flags are crowding close on both sides. Colonel Fry, right behind you now, is shouting to your right. *"What? What?"* All the Virginians are there. They have brought their line up next to ours. That must be Garnett in the blue coat, still mounted. Get down off that horse! Garnett is shouting to Fry, "I am dressing on you!"

(The men in blue, farther north where the Confederate line is not temporarily covered by that long depression in the ground, see the exposed men in gray and butternut stop, even as canister and bullets tear into them. They are falling, being knocked backward, staggering onto their knees and toppling to their faces everywhere. Still they haven't fired back, still no shouts from these silent men. What are they doing? Partly in admiration but chiefly appalled, the Yankees realize, *they're dressing their lines!*)

You have halted just below a kind of fall and rise in the ground; Yankee canister and bullets scream and hiss over you. You are ordered to dress the line. You move to touch elbows with the man next to you—someone from one of the other companies. On the right Garnett's men are trying to dress but are being pushed this way; the other brigades are crowding them. Step forward into view; how they open upon us!

Garnett is right here. He shouts, "Don't double-quick! Save your wind and ammunition for the final charge." You stare up for an instant: he is full of blood, blood from the neck down and all across the blue coat, leg dark with it—his horse is spurting blood from its chest, forelegs slick with blood. You are moving forward. You glance quickly again: the general is leaning, stooping forward; he collapses onto the horse's neck, and the horse is falling too.

"Halt, men! Ready!" At last you raise your rifle to your shoulder, aim at the smoky line of dark men at that stone fence. *"Fire!"* You squeeze the trigger and the target disappears in the kicking discharge and smoke. *"Forward, with a yell, forward!"* You raise the high hunting yell as it erupts all around you. Going forward you are crowded, pressed as much left as to the front. You are all a crowd, a mass now. Armistead's Virginians have crowded in behind. They are at the wall with you, clubbing the Yankees, thrusting in their bayonets. Over the wall? You look at Armistead. A Yankee artillery officer at his gun straight ahead has shouted, though you don't hear it, "I will give them one more shot!"

At the moment of hesitation at the wall, General Armistead recognized that the crowd must go forward or the charge would die in front of the Yankees rushing to plug the gap. In the last three minutes the charge had actually been funneled toward the clump of trees and the stone wall where Armistead now stood. On their right, Pickett's Division had been murderously raked by Stannard's Vermont Brigade, which had been positioned in some cover several hundred yards forward of the main line. As the Virginians swept past to the north—as close as 30 yards but not distracted from their objective, the clump of small scrub oaks—Stannard ordered his men to swing the line out as though on a hinge. They fired volleys into Pickett's men, making the right of that formerly long line melt away and crowd to the left.

The far left of the long lines had melted away too. Hays had done with part of his division what Stannard had done: swung out and taken the Confederates in flank with killing volleys. On the Confederate left were the two brigades so badly thinned by the First Day's battle near the Seminary. Whether or not they were intended to be mere rifle fodder, meant to absorb Union flanking fire, they became that. The survivors broke to the rear, many being taken captive.

The center—Armistead's Virginians, some North Carolinians, and some Tennesseans just north of the angle in the stone fence—was all that remained, and the mile-wide line was now a crowd pressing on a mere 500-yard front. But at the "bloody angle" it was irresistible. Here only a thin brigade line, Webb's, faced the surging mass of Confederates. It is a wonder they stood. Some were forced back, but most, incredibly, stood and fought in the clustering bayonets.

In the moment of hesitation at the wall, when the Confederates stopped to load and fire, the charge turned. South of the clump of trees Hall's Brigade had repelled Kemper's Virginians or forced them toward Armistead. General Kemper lay critically wounded. (He was taken to a Union hospital to die; survived; and later was elected Governor of the Commonwealth of Virginia.) Hall rushed his men over to help Webb. Batteries were coming, too, and more infantry.

But it might be too late for Webb. The center was pierced; the Confederates were through it. Armistead had put his black hat on his sword tip, held it up high, and shouted for his men to come on after him over the wall. "Give them the cold steel!" A crowd of Southerners rushed over the wall forcing back the Union men who remained. Alonzo Cushing's gun was in their way. His other guns being disabled, he stood by his last one; his surviving gunners had put in the last canister they had, chocking it right up to the muzzle; Cushing stood bleeding from bullet wounds, bracing against the gun itself, holding his abdomen with a hand keeping in his intestines. "I will give them one more shot!" he said, dying at the gun as it discharged.

Past mangled men the Confederates crowded toward Cushing's gun. Webb's position was filled with shouting Confederates; he turned and saw his reserve regiment in line on the crest a hundred yards or so to the rear. Running back to them, he shouted the order to charge. They didn't budge. Webb had been in command of the brigade only a few days and they didn't recognize him. Webb grabbed an officer and tried to haul him forward bodily; the man resisted. The regiment aimed and volleyed at the Confederates in the angle, but stood where they were. The frantic Webb kept his senses. He rushed back across the angle, passing behind Cushing's gun just as Lewis Armistead placed his hand on it to claim it and fell shot through by bullets from Webb's regiment. Webb reached Hall's right regiment and got it into line. A crowded battle line was forming there, made up of two brigades, Doubleday's First Corps troops having come up from farther down the line. They poured in heavy fire and advanced.

The attackers in the angle were shot down and overwhelmed. Survivors tried to run back out, but hundreds were rounded up. At the cannon in the center of the angle, as the marker on the crest now says, Armistead and Cushing lay, the blood of Virginia and Wisconsin mingling.

Just north of the angle the attack still came on for a minute or two. The fence turned uphill at the angle, then ran along the crest. Here Hays's men, only yards from Webb's, shot volley after volley into the approaching men of Pettigrew's Division, cannons along the wall tearing them with discharges of flaming canister. "Sheer murder," one Union soldier called it. Just a little farther forward than the Virginians had come to their right, the 26th North Carolina still pressed forward, to within several yards of the blazing rifles and triple charged cannons at the stone wall. These Carolinians, survivors of the battle with Meredith's Iron Brigade on the first day, pressed forward yelling grimly. As the narrow line pushed forward toward one of the Union guns, the crew finished loading; an officer yelled at the man with the lanyard, "Fire that gun! Pull it! Pull it!" In a flash of flame and smoke the astonishing Carolinians were shredded and dismembered. Flesh and blood could go no farther. This was the real high water mark, the bound of valor.

Today a rosy granite marker, newly placed and matching the one in McPherson's Woods, stands a few yards from the stone wall at the crest of Cemetery Ridge. One wonders, reading the inscription, did the gunner hesitate? Did he for a moment catch the eyes of those men just yards away, come all the way from North Carolina—did he see their faces, their determination, anger, their sudden terror as they saw him grasping their silver cord—did he see their eyes? *"Pull it! Pull it!"*

Their flags, some nights, still shimmer at the wall. The future was too small for them. We are their aftermath; the days we have made are narrow rooms for their memories. In our strained, moaning silence after battle, they are phantoms only; the long low growl and mutter of destruction are gone, the "murmur and jingle" of their advance, the "rustle of thousands of feet among the stubble" stirring up the starry dust like "spray at the prow of a vessel."

> *Who are these coming to the sacrifice?*
> *To what green altar . . .*

planting flags where no one has ever gone?

Haskell wrote, "All depths of passion are stirred, and all combatives fire, down to their deep foundations. Individuality is drowned in a sea of clamor, and timid men, breathing the breath of the multitude, are brave. . . . The frequent dead and wounded lie where they stagger and fall—there is no humanity for them now, and none can be spared to care for them. The men do not cheer or shout; they growl, and over that uneasy sea, heard with the roar of musketry, sweeps the muttered thunder of a storm of growls." That sea has ebbed across the shingles of the world, leaving us immobile on the field among the rustling trash of desperation: was it a sea of faith, or a flood of charged illusion, that made such fearsome noise, and will another come to bathe the dryness of our bones?

It is no wonder people are attracted to the High Water Mark; it is the decisive point of a civil war in all of us. The Army of Northern Virginia is the army of youth, in the sunny summer of '62, vigorous, brilliant, lucky, daring, thinking it can to anything—melting away like a dream before Cemetery Ridge, that earlier bright summer over;

it passes into memory in the face of the often-defeated, stalwart, clear-eyed army of age.

On the week of the Fourth of July people came to this lake where I write, by the thousands, to lie on the sand in windrows. Among the trees along the shore, sunbathers and sleepers lay in clumps like shot attackers; like soldiers munching hardtack after battle, picnickers sat in loud and leisurely groups, ignoring all the baking flesh around them. They came for water—though from their standing and lying just off it one might think the water came for them: warm but clear, spring-fed, crossed by a crisply finite cumulus of sails, a beautiful vision worth battling four hours of traffic to see. Its waters seem to fill gasoline-stewed tourists with something they can't drink. People come to beauty. Even the most savage executives and primitive consultants slither here on Japanese leather, on German gears and grease. The lake touches them, barely, and recedes.

17 *Dorsey Pender*

When I am condemned,
and condemn myself
utterly, I think
straightway, "But I
rely on my love for
some things." Therein I
am whole and entire.
Therein I am God-
propped.

—**Thoreau**

William Dorsey Pender was twenty-nine at Gettysburg. His letters to his wife show a transformation from youth to middle age in the twenty-nine months between his entering the Confederate service and the Gettysburg campaign. He was a very handsome man, dark-haired and -complexioned; he wore his full beard neatly trimmed short. His penetrating dark eyes were expressive; an 1863 photograph shows sensitivity, a thoughtful habit of mind, and perhaps even anxiety. He confessed that others were correct in considering him an unusually earnest young man. During the first year of the War his hairline receded to the point where, always reassuring his worried wife that her attractive husband was not really attractive, he referred to himself as "quite bald" (which he was not), looking middle-aged; and he reports that a superficial head wound left him balder than ever:

> I hope all these signs of old age will not . . . make you love me less. I cannot help it and my heart is as fresh and tender for you as if I looked only twenty.

Conscious of his short stature, he wrote to his wife: "Six feet add wonderfully in this world to a man's career." But it was his age rather than his height that prevented his becoming one of the well-known figures of the American Civil War. Dorsey Pender did go to West Point, as did many intelligent Southern young men of the middle and upper classes who wanted a profession and a career but who were not interested in law, medicine, or the clergy. However, unlike the well-known figures of the Civil War, he attended the Academy *after* the Mexican War and did not serve there with Lee, Stuart, and Longstreet.

Just twenty-seven in March of 1861, when he offered his services to the Confederacy—ahead of North Carolina's secession and ahead of most future Confederate officers—he was given a lieutenant colonelcy with the purpose of instructing the First North Carolina regiment in matters military. Another officer said Pender was "firm, very courteous," and the men "all formed a very strong attachment to him and were very sorry to part with him when they were ordered to Virginia." In Virginia the regiment impressed one observer as being the best regiment he had yet seen, and it soon distinguished itself in battle.

But Dorsey Pender stayed back home training the Third North Carolina. What if Pender, like Thomas J. Jackson, had already been a brigadier general with a brigade at First Manassas (Bull Run), instead of a young lieutenant colonel instructing recruits behind the lines? Would a hard-pressed general have pointed to him, shouting, "There stands Pender like a stone wall?" General Lee seemed to imply the possibility once.

Finally, after First Manassas, Dorsey Pender as colonel of the Third went to the Virginia army. Through the long months of inactivity— fall of 1861, winter, spring of 1862—the young husband's letters unfold a complicated, unique, yet representative story of a man and a woman of the Old South, in love and in war:

> . . . by your pen and Christian life you have shown me what I ought to be, and you have inspired such love in me as to cause me in the beginning to try to do something that would prevent our separation in the world to come. . . .
>
> I was baptized today. . . .

He had been raised by nonchurchgoing parents who, he tells his wife, probably doted on him. She and their baby son, Turner, stayed with Dorsey's parents in the autumn of 1861:

> Your patience will no doubt be tried . . . by . . . the crossness of Papa and the childishness of Mamma at home, but you must remember their love for

> me, that I have always been indulged by the former and shown by the latter what a good and affectionate mother was. . . . but none will be more anxious to do anything in the world to please you. . . . They will spoil Turner more than your father, but . . . tell them it is my direction and they will think it all right. They think there is no one like me.

The young officer had married Fanny Sheppard, sister of a West Point friend, in March 1859. But he had loved her since he had first seen her, a girl of fourteen, in the summer of 1854. In the course of his wartime letters to Fanny it becomes clear that although he always reassures her that he loves and respects her family—and she doesn't believe him—there is a problem between son- and father-in-law. At first Dorsey's references to the father are made gingerly, but by June 1863 he refers to the father-in-law's "ravings and unpleasant forebodings."

The man's influence on a young daughter must have been strong. The Hon. Augustine H. Sheppard had served in the U.S. House of Representatives longer than anyone else his age. Did he ever accept young Pender, a son of farmers, as being good enough for his daughter? ("My relatives . . . are plain people but very respectable.") The son-in-law and the father-in-law must have disagreed about the prospects and justice of Southern independence. At one point the young officer tells his wife that she should be a Democrat. It seems she always doubts the outcome of Secession, and he is always bucking her up; he is always telling her how unprincipled the Yankees are. Fanny thinks both invasions of the North are wrong.

It is not a marriage without tension. But it is the tension of a constant romance:

> Darling, did you think about yesterday being the anniversary of our marriage? Four years, how short they seem. . . . We are more violently in love than the sweethearts.

The two are not alike. She is careful with money, he is in debt. Again and again he makes a point of telling her how frugal he is being. Sometimes, it is true, the roles are exchanged, and he questions whether she really needed an expensive item of clothing. He works his small debt down but still has the uncomfortable certainty that she thinks him profligate: "You have no idea how I am eschewing to get out of debt. I intend to be as close as a miser." She wants him to list his expenses, but he "cannot."

She is prone to pessimism and a "nervous disorder" which must be periodic mild depression. He tries to look on the bright side of things; he orders a Richmond newspaper for her that "is hopeful without being foolishly sanguine." She was not robust—"delicate," as the mid-nineteenth-century woman ought to be. Lightly wounded several times during the first year of the fighting, Dorsey always shook off the effects quickly, and he was seldom sick in camp during a war that took twice as many lives by disease than in battle.

> You must keep well and not get sick to have me nursing you. I know it is pleasant to both partners, but let us try the other awhile.

Though Dorsey Pender was modest and spoke little, he was well liked everywhere, and knew it. Fanny was insecure, always seeming to need reassurance regarding her attractiveness. This he provides throughout 1861, though generally dwelling on her goodness while confessing that there are women prettier than she. Mistake! One can hardly blame her, or take his side, in the great trouble which created a turning point in Pender's life.

He may not have been all that secure himself, early in the marriage; at least he was conscious of his attractiveness to women. He had the need or desire to impress this upon his young wife all too firmly. Letters in the first few months of war are punctuated by stunning gaffes:

> Dined today with the most beautiful girl in Suffolk—and it has a great many very pretty ones. . . .

> The ladies keep my table covered with flowers and smile on me in the most bewitching manner.

He goes on to say, "Do not be jealous for none of them have the attractiveness of Mrs. W. D. Pender," and then, "I have not failed to let them know that I am married for *poor creatures I do not wish to destroy their rest."* (Teasing here. Eh, Fanny?) And soon he turns the knob farther:

> Honey I hope they have not let your figure be spoilt by not keeping your bandage sufficiently tight. [She has had their second son, Dorsey.] Anything, but do not lose your figure.

> A lady offered to make me a cap the other day; I told her if she would make a net for a lady I would take great pleasure in sending it to you, whereupon she said she was not going to make anything for my wife. . . . She has intimated once or twice that she had fallen in love with me.

> I was at a little gathering two nights ago, and had a very nice time dancing and flirting with a very nice girl. I am trying to get her to knit you a sac for the hair, but she said that she is not going to work for my wife, but will do anything for me.

That was it. In response came a prodigious, well-aimed discharge of ordnance from North Carolina:

> I have never in the whole course of my married [life] done anything deliberately that I knew would pain you. . . .
> . . . Now, I ask you candidly, in your sober senses, why you wrote me such a thing as that? Was it to gratify your vanity by making me jealous, or to make me appreciate your love still more? You are very much mistaken. I feel indignant that any woman should have dared to make such loose speeches to my husband and that he should have encouraged it by his attentions, for you must have gone pretty far for a woman to attempt such a liberty.
> . . . I never thought to hear that he, whom I loved above all the world, whom I respected and esteemed till now, would stoop to listen to such improper language—do you think the lady would have made such a remark in my presence? Then it was not proper for you to hear. I never expected to hear you admit that you had been *flirting*. . . .
> . . . I know you love me, my dear Husband. I have had too many sweet and precious proofs of it to doubt it now. You have ever been the kindest and best of husbands . . . but I can never forget that letter.

Who can doubt that Dorsey Pender could have filled the shoes of that consummate strategist, Stonewall himself? Reading his next letters, one is overwhelmed by Pender's strategic double-pronged coun-terattack—abject confession and steely reproach—but the one enveloped is Pender himself, for he is completely honest in what he says:

> If you wrote the foregoing deliberately and premeditatedly please retain this letter [he has *returned* her letter!] as evidence in the future, that you have torn my heart, that you have brought tears, bitter tears ["to" omitted in the upset] the eyes of one who has loved you and tried to honor you. Oh! Fanny my letter was cruel, but you have surpassed me. . . . I have loved life dearly, but tonight I feel that this war had no terrors to me. I at first thought that I would read part of it to David [his brother], but I could not bear that anyone should know that I had ever received such a letter from my wife.

He tells her she has accused him of being "Not only a Tyrant but a vain unprincipled wretch." In the next letter he says, "I had about made up my mind that we were henceforth to be as strangers. . . . That letter was in my mind awake and sleeping, and again and again would my grief have to be relieved by tears." Then, a few days later, the *coup de grâce:*

> Darling rest assured that as soon as your next letter was received my heart melted. I did not love you the less at any time but felt miserable at the insane notion that I might be losing you. Honey say nothing more about [it]. . . . Think no more about it.

Splendid! *He* forgives *her!* But he meant it.

His letters are different henceforth—not for the reason that having discovered her ire he simply omits to mention his flirtations. There are a couple more mild references to some woman at some dinner where he has been invited, because he is an honest man. It is not his language or his reportage that have changed: *he* has changed. The tone of everything he talks about is different from here on—not more drab, but more mature. His humor increases, but it is no longer a twenty-year-old who is speaking. And he has always been earnest:

> Honey, I try very hard to be worthy of you both in act and thought, but I am very bad in some ways.

(Naturally, her ears perked up at this, and he finds himself explaining in another letter. "Honey you asked in what I am so bad about.") He had spoken of his "ruling passions," by which he may have meant his flirting, his too much love of "the applause of men," and his tendency to be sharply frank in pointing out the shortcomings of others. It is in fact, however, the ruling will, the line of courage, in Dorsey Pender always to become better: "I am truly anxious to do right."

In nothing is this more strongly evinced than in what he writes about religion: "Oh! if I could live a Christian life." His letters are full of religious discussion; for months at a time he wrestles with baptism and confirmation. But the origin of all this is significant:

> Honey I am troubled because I fear I do not take that interest in reading the Bible as I should, and studying its truths. I read it, however, every night and try to practice by day. But darling is it against me that under all this there is a desire to please you and go where you do in the world to come. Oh! honey the idea that when we go to our final rest you will go to everlasting life and bliss and I to everlasting damnation agonizes me. Let us go together.

He was a Romantic. And she was not the kind of wife who forbids her husband even to notice the beauty of women, while at home keeping him in the frigid grip of starvation. After one of her stays with him in camp he writes:

> . . . surely if you do not want children you will have to remain away from me, and hereafter when you come to me I shall know that you want another baby.

They have two, Turner and Dorsey; she had a miscarriage in March 1861—for which he says he is "heartily glad"; in the spring of 1863 she is pregnant with their third. They had tried to prevent conception, though not by the method of abstinence:

> Ought we to complain so at what is evidently His direct will, for did we not try to oppose it? and with what effect? Let us look on the bright side of it and be cheerful.

"I did so hope when you left me that you had escaped," he wrote after she returned home, "but we poor mortals know so little of the future." He writes how at night he wishes to have her in his arms in bed, and another time: "Honey, I feel in a loving mood and if you were here I would hold you in my lap and kiss and kiss you to your hearts content."

> O you dear girl how I should like to have you with me in that big arm chair we spent so many happy moments in this last winter.

She is a jealous wife, but to a degree he likes it that way:

> If you did not fret about my absenting myself and not staying with you all day when we are together, I should feel something was going wrong. I like it, and I like the little touches of jealousy you show sometimes, but Darling you carried it a little too far to be very pleasant. . . . Bless my dear little wife if she did not abuse me a little occasionally I should think she did not love me so much as she used to. Do not try to change in those respects. I don't wish it.

He had his jealousies too. She galls him when she mentions that she and her family are still friendly with the Williams family, Unionists, which he consistently points out to her in severe disapproval—understandable, of course, considering that he is a soldier in the Confederate service. But Joe Williams had courted her:

> Honey do you ever see any husbands who are more devoted to their wives than I am. You often say I do not love you as I should, but do you see any who show more signs of affection than I do? You certainly see none who try harder to please their wives than I do. You know honey in your heart you feel that Joe Williams never was glad that you did not have him.

She also worries about former attractions:

> . . . Darling, so far as any fears you might have had about my sentiment for the lady that was Mary Summer are entirely groundless. Indeed, I tell the whole truth when I say that I never had a regret about the matter in my life, except in having allowed my vanity to have carried me so far. I never loved her. . . .
>
> . . . I never saw but two women who I would in a cool moment and in which my judgement would have allowed me to [have] married. One I never loved and the other I married. . . .

His letters often close with a prayer like the one written June 28, 1863: "Now darling, may our Good Father protect us and preserve us to each other to a good old age."

But when romance conflicts with duty, duty always wins. In March 1863 he became so "blue" after she left camp that he went to A. P. Hill, his division commander, to ask for a leave, which was approved, though with doubt as to whether the Commanding General would assent. But "I slept on it and came to the conclusion that it would not do for me to apply so soon after having a leave." He struggled with this often, and, when some movement of the army was possible, or when others couldn't get leaves, the outcome was always the same. The poor soldiers will never be able to go home while the War lasts—and he has become responsible for many of them.

At Seven Pines in June 1862, Pender takes his regiment into their first battle. President Davis has ridden the few miles from Richmond and happens to observe the battle from a place where he can see Pender's regiment. It has been ordered forward, but the regiments intended for its support do not follow. About to be cut off flank and rear by three Union regiments, Pender shouts (in the clear "ringing voice" that was always obeyed) "the only possible combination of commands that could have saved us from capture," in the words of one of his lieutenants. Redeploying his battle line at right angles to the left, Pender charges the three Union regiments, stunning them long enough for the North Carolinians to withdraw to the main line. Later, Jefferson Davis rides over to the 6th North Carolina and addresses its commander: "General Pender, I salute you."

In one action the young colonel had become a brigadier general. Dorsey told his friend Stephen D. Lee, "I could have coveted no greater honor than to be promoted by the President on the field of battle."

He was assigned a brigade of North Carolinians in A. P. Hill's Division. The man who had written, "Oh, Honey, I hope my Regt. will do well when we may get into a fight," would have ample opportunity to See the Elephant in the next months: Seven Days, Second Manassas, Antietam. But first, he must see to his brigade.

He had no illusions: "Men do not act so badly until they get to be soldiers." He was not about to hide the facts from his wife:

> My dear such a filthy unprincipled set of villains I have never seen. They have lost all honor and decency, all sense of right or respect for property. I have had to strike many a one with my sabre. The officers are nearly as bad as the men.

Nor was he a participant in the easy glory of the early days of the War: "I am sick of flags." Toward the end of June he wrote, "I am sick of soldiering and especially the fighting part." Next month:

> I am tired of glory and all its shadows for it has no substance. We work, struggle, make enemies, climb up in rank and what is the result—nothing. It is very much like gambling, money is won but soon spent and nothing left behind.

In September, before Sharpsburg, he wrote, "I am sick and tired of hearing of guns and I hope I may never see one after this war is over." He was no war lover, writing often of his wish to be home with his wife and little boys—but war sometimes had a beauty to which he was not insensible:

> I rode out in the edge of the field the enemy were forming in [during the battle of Second Manassas] and never saw such a magnificent sight in my life. As far as the eye could reach they had one continuous line of troops, with artillery it seemed to me every fifty yards. It looked fine but was not Generalship for their line was nearly perpendicular to our left and as soon as attacked were turned.

"You know I am a prudent man," he had written, but despite this and despite his dislike of war he soon developed a reputation in the army:

> The men seem to think that I am fond of fighting. They say I give them "hell" out of a fight and the Yankees the same in it.

Soon he had the most efficient brigade in Hill's Light Division.

My men say I am hard on them but that I treat them all alike. It would worry me very much if I had a reputation for injustice.

(He was not different in his approach to child rearing—as usual the following is not entirely serious:

You say Dorsey is like me. I always imagined that I could see in Turner a very good likeness of myself. He, poor little fellow, is laying up many whippings for himself. Those who laugh at him little think what it may cost him in after years.)

When Jackson's valley army was ordered to the Richmond front after the brilliant Shendandoah campaign, Hill's Division was assigned to the now-famous Stonewall, to begin a most unhappy relationship between the sensitive A. P. Hill and the procrustean Jackson. Dorsey Pender liked and admired "Little Powell" but had little use for his chief's antagonist, Jackson, "the old humbug." Conceding Jackson's effectiveness during the Manassas campaign, Pender wrote:

Lee has immortalized himself and Jackson added new laurels to his brow—not that I like to be under Jackson, for he forgets that one ever gets tired, hungry, or sleepy.

Pender had observed Jackson's incredible inaction during the Seven Days, which probably had cost Lee the decisive victories he was after. (Lee wrote that under normal circumstances "the enemy would have been destroyed.") Pender was ambitious, though he struggled to put ideas of promotion out of his mind and professed to be content with his lot, but Jackson's antipathy toward Hill prevented any of Hill's subordinates from getting Stonewall's recommendation.

Hill's recommendation Pender would have. The young brigadier had the "best drilled and disciplined Brigade in the Division, and more than all, possesses the unbounded confidence of the Division," Hill wrote. A doctor in the division called Brigadier General Pender "a very superior little man though a strict disciplinarian . . . brave as a lion," who "seemed to love danger." Lee would add his own words: "Pender is an excellent officer, attentive, industrious and brave; has been conspicuous in every battle."

At Sharpsburg, Lee's ragged army just barely fought off Union attacks until late afternoon, when Burnside's Corps finally crossed the Antietam and overwhelmed the few defenders of the Confederate right. There were no reserves left, except a division Jackson had left behind at Harper's Ferry. Looking through their field glasses, Lee and his officers saw thousands of dusty blue men advancing toward the army's rear, cutting off retreat to the Potomac. This was not mere defeat, it was destruction. Farther to the right and rear still another body of men approached along the Harper's Ferry Road. The officers could not make out these men's dusty uniforms, or the battle flags. Lee watched anxiously, and then he lowered his field glasses. It is all right; it is A. P. Hill. The Light Division struck the advancing Federals and drove them back across the Antietam, saving the Army of Northern Virginia and the Southern Confederacy for two and a half more years. One assumes Pender's Brigade struck the hardest. The arrival of the Light Division at that moment of supreme danger and tension was described with unforgettable brevity in Lee's battle report: "Then A. P. Hill came up." It left an indelible impression; both Lee's and Jackson's near-last words concerned A. P. Hill. The Light Division became thought of as the best in the army:

> You have no idea what a reputation our Division has. It surpasses Jackson's old Division both for fighting and discipline. . . . But when I tell you that this Division has lost 9,000 killed and wounded since we commenced the Richmond fight at Mechanicsville [during the Seven Days], you can see what our reputation has cost us. We started that fight with 15,000, now we have 6,000. . . . Let me cease to write about war and killing.

At last he became satisfied that his men were soldiers, although desertion continued to plague the whole army. This was especially true in the winter, when independent-minded Americans decided to go home rather than hang around camp doing nothing—at one time Lee's army had 25 percent, and the Union army nearly 40 percent AWOL, though many came back in the spring—but it was a distressing problem during the campaigns also. "This straggling is becoming the curse of the army." At one point the young brigadier writes Fanny that stragglers must be shot. This was not characteristic of Pender except in that duty was primary to him, and he had seen the results of thinned ranks: near loss of the cause and more danger for the faithful men.

The Sharpsburg campaign was itself a problem. Pender had been all for taking the war into the North, but his wife (along with her father) was not. Pender, as usual, came to agree with his wife, whom he said was "right about everything."

> . . . I have heard but one feeling expressed about it [the Maryland campaign] and that is a regret at our having gone there. Our Army has shown itself incapable of invasion and we had better stick to the defensive.

He did not lose faith in the Commanding General, however. About the Manassas campaign he had written:

> Gen. Lee has shown great Generalship and the greatest boldness. There never was such a campaign, even by Napoleon. Our men march and fight without provisions, living on green corn when nothing better can be had. But all this kills up our men. Jackson would kill up any army the way he marches and the bad management in the subsistence Dept.—Gen Lee is my man.

He recognizes Lee's tendency to want fights, but "I do not know what we should do if he were taken from us."

After Sharpsburg, Pender began to think he might be worth promoting still further. He had several times commanded other brigades in addition to his own, and found himself thinking that perhaps he was not too young to be a major general. "I would like to be a great man for your sake," he had written Fanny in May 1861. Eventually his peekaboo ambition nearly got him into bad trouble. He sent what he thought to be a tactful letter to an acquaintance in the Richmond government, asking that some suggestion of a promotion for him be made. (It was well known that political influence was a common ingredient in high promotions, North and South.) The man showed the letter to the Secretary of War, who sent it to Lee stating that such requests not through channels were against orders. Lee had little choice but to order Hill to prefer charges against his favorite subordinate. Hill sent up the charges but disapproved them, and Lee authorized Hill to withdraw them. Hill removed the transaction from Pender's file, "most kindly and delicately." Thus the brigadier was saved a court-martial that would have acquitted him but tarnished his reputation. A learner like Dorsey Pender no doubt engraved the lesson upon his mind.

Meanwhile, another battle had been fought and the army had got through another winter camp. At the battle of Fredericksburg, Pender's Brigade repulsed an assault by Gibbon's Division in the grand, wasteful Federal fiasco. Pender received another light wound—"a trifle"—but his aide and brother-in-law Jake was not as lucky. It was the second brother Fanny had lost in military service, her brother Turner having died in Kansas in 1855.

It was not an easy December. Fanny accused her husband of "want of feeling" in his not calling for her to come and join him in winter quarters, and he was affected by her "sad and despondent" tone. "Honey, the more I think of you and your letters the more sad I am. I feel like shedding tears." She is not as magnanimous as he is. ("You never forget or forgive.") She has also reproached him for not writing to her father concerning Jake's death.

> I am very sorry your father should feel hurt at my not writing. I did not have much time at first and you know—want of feeling—that I dislike sad subjects.

They have never yet quite understood each other's tone. His humor is often missed—a curse of quiet, earnest people. When their second son is born in May 1861 the father writes, "You must have little Dorsey for your favorite for I feel that none can ever be so dear to me as that incomparable boy, Turner." So starts a long back-and-forth. He is somewhat serious when he tells her, "I wrote Brother Robert that we were disappointed in the baby and had to change the name from Ruth to Dorsey." She knows there is truth in it; the admixture of humor is a delicate uncertainty. So:

> Honey you say it is not fair that I should give all my love to Turner instead of dividing it with Dorse. I have no doubt but that after I become well acquainted with the latter I shall love him as well as Turner, but Turner is such a dear boy, and the other I have had such a short acquaintance with.

She is also kidding, or so he assumes. (She does accuse him one time of not getting *her* humor.) He writes:

> You must love Dorsey as I said before, for Turner is mine. I raised him and must love him without any rival. The Mother always takes to the youngest and the father to the oldest.

This did not go down well with the newborn's mother.

> . . . or have you taken me literally when I say I love Turner and you will have to love this baby.

He reassures her later:

> There is but little if any difference in my feelings for him and Turner. He is the image of me, the seed of my body, the bearer of my name; how could I help loving him—and greater than all, the offspring of my faithful and loving wife.

Still he jokes, but more plainly:

> See how healthy my boy is and how puny yours.

Increasingly he writes this thought about his boys: "I hope with you that they may not be raised in ignorance of their father."

> I am in the keeping of God at all times and in all places. As to battles, I cannot know.

> Many is the poor heart that will be broken by this war. May God spare yours. . . .

Most letters, as the War goes on, end with a prayer ("that my life may be spared this war") and the request:

> Kiss the dear boys.

They were becoming, he says, "fat and Penderish." But he has other subjects for his humor, too. In recounting a complaint wrongly brought against him he says, "You will see when I come to run for Congress all these things will be brought against me." In thinking about applying for leave he laments that his diarrhea has quit, "so I shall have to fall back on rheumatism." There is a standing joke—again half serious—about his playing matchmaker for Fanny's sister Pamela:

> Tell Pamela I am going to write to Stephen [D. Lee] today asking him to place himself matrimonially in my hands.

Again:

> I am getting Stephen all right.

The War itself was not always occasion for seriousness. In Maryland on June 21, 1863, he writes:

> I would not be surprised if we went into Penna. so that we shall have no communication with you rebels.

But alas, he still must reassure her: He was "joking" about her having to love Dorsey best (May 1863). Perhaps because of his mixture of tones, she is also unsure of his attitude toward her sometimes: "Darling, [give] up the notion that I am always making fun of you."

They were complex people, and it was a complex relationship, further complicated during her extended visits to him. After Fredericksburg, the army built winter quarters. The brigade camp she found was one of the cleanest, healthiest, and most orderly in the Army of Northern Virginia. Sentinels saluted, and officers wore rank insignia—not common in the army. But the visit itself was not so tidy. He must have been restless, or appeared so, leaving to attend to duties at all times. And as always he said little. But how serious is he, or to what degree is he overly severe with himself?

> I often think darling that when we get together again that I will not be cross and look mad and refuse to talk as I used to do. I know you won't believe me, and I do not blame you, for I shall act as mean as ever. It is in me and I cannot help it.

They still feel the emotions of young lovers; there are tiffs and offenses as well as ecstasies. He still refers to the spring of 1861, "under the shade tree sitting on the grass, the happiest hours of my life. I shall never forget it. . . . It was complete earthly happiness."

Heavenly happiness, however, has been the constant underlying theme. He has been reading religious books all along (but Dickens's *Bleak House,* too.) At least two of the books were arguments for the Episcopal church being *the* church, but though he is impressed by the importance and cogency of the arguments, he never sounds really convinced, and does once indicate a disapproval of sectarianism. And in general, too, his religion is never a *convinced* religion in terms of theology.

Dorsey Pender reminds one of the man in the New Testament who cries, "Lord, I believe; help thou my unbelief!"

> Honey, I sincerely try to be a Christian. I have faith in Christ and hope for the best.

He debates for two years on faith and works:

> But if the hope and belief in good works is wrong, I fear I am in the wrong way. I cannot help from believing that our acts *if* done from *fear* as well as *love* will help in the world to come. For without the desire to do good and the practice of it, how are we to change? Miraculously; I fear not and hope not.

For him, being Christian is not a matter of baptism or believing only, but of practice. He would not call himself a Christian:

> Oh Darling, I so desire to be a Christian, but I know and feel that I am far from being one.

When he was finally baptized, it was on credit:

> You, darling . . . will be the success of my salvation if I ever reach it.

He agreed to be baptized as a kind of public certification on his part that he would try to live a Christian life, try to improve himself.

Self-improvement was not a matter of superficialities. He drank tod-
dies and brandy on occasion, though he hated the idea of whisky and
had "a horror of drunken soldiers." He did use profanity, though not
much, and for Fanny's sake swore off it in 1863. For him, being a
Christian was a matter of mastering his ruling passions—an idea
Dante would approve of—and having more charity, and these come
from a love of Christ *inside:* "I feel sadly the want of true religion in
my soul."

> My desire is to do everything that may gain favor with Christ and insure my
> salvation.

This is why he questions whether you can join a church before you
are perfect. Yes, he concludes before his baptism:

> I have come to the conclusion from reading Acts that I might become a
> member of the Church at once, for we cannot think that all those who
> repented and were baptized by Paul could have been as good as they should
> have been. In fact it seems to me that the act was about the commencement
> of their regeneration, for in many instances he did not perfect his work at
> once, but returned to them to complete it.

He wants to be "fixed upon" the points concerning which denomina-
tion to join, because its people will be the ones to provide "some
external help" toward his progress. So he can say:

> . . . I was baptized . . . I am not a Christian. . . .

According to the rules, he knew he did not measure up, and he
earnestly thought he should and tried to succeed in that lost cause.
But it would be incorrect to say Dorsey Pender was not a man of faith:

> Darling you must continue to be satisfied with your lot. Think how many
> are worse off than we are. O darling let us be thankful for what we have, for
> surely we are favored. Of all the trying times we have been through, no
> serious accident has ever befallen us. Instead of growing indifferent to each
> other, we grow in affection. Our children are healthy and good, and we have
> loving relatives. The Lord be praised. Honey I try to bring myself to rely on

him implicitly in all things, especially in what may befall me in this war. If I die I know He will take care of you. The leaving you is the only thing that troubles me when I contemplate such an end, but I pray that I may grow in grace until I feel that "to die will be gain." I do not write about death to trouble you, but to strengthen you, for in all cases we must submit to [His] will and if we can do it willingly how much better for us.

It may be objected that he had only a vague belief in "Providence," but that which proved so strong can hardly be called vague. Despite his baptism, then confirmation, and his feeling that he was becoming a "somewhat changed" man, he wrote before as well as after those events:

I think and feel that everything is for the best.

Be of good cheer and rest assured that He who knows of the falling of a sparrow will direct all things for the best, however hard they may be to bear.

It is he, after all, who reassures and inspires her.

His religion, and to a degree his faith, is a romantic one. The very problem he feels is part of his redemption:

My feeling for my Savior partakes more of that arising from a sense of duty, but for you it exist[s] and how it commenced and upon what principle high up I hardly know or think about.

. . . you are a part of my religion.

After one of her visits he continues to read the lessons for the day, but it is because it makes him feel more as though she were there. It is a coldhearted quibbler who could not say of them: "What love they have for one another!"

One of the amazing things about Dorsey Pender is the following:

I am reading Uncle Tom's Cabin and really you have no idea how nearly we [himself and Harriet Beecher Stowe] agree on the subject of slavery.

A soldier of the South, agreeing with *Uncle Tom's Cabin*—the extraordinariness of this hardly can be appreciated today. His views may to some degree be understood through the following incident:

> David wrote me that Ruth's husband had been sent to Richmond and sold.
> . . . I have advertised to find out where he is. I do not care so much to own
> him, but Beck [a nickname for Ruth?] is dear to me, and I hate to see her
> husband whom she seems to love, torn from her in that way. This separating
> man and wife is a most cruel thing and almost enough to make one an
> abolitionist.

It is a free man or woman who can transcend the beliefs of their time and place.

Appropriately, in the same letter he refers to his brother Robert disapprovingly, wanting to "teach him a little lesson, namely to forget sometimes that he is a business man, bringing every transaction down to cents." Elsewhere he says, "Everybody has gone crazy on the subject of money making." His concern is spent on the poor rather than on making enough to support his "loose way with money":

> If you could get up a concert in behalf of this poor Regt. it would be a good
> work for those who need it. They are mostly poor men, some of them with
> starving wives at home. Wives and children crying to them for bread and
> they unable to help them. What agony they must suffer. . . .

But could he extend his love for the poor and for the slaves into love for his enemies?

The Yankee shelling of Fredericksburg appalled Pender: "The barbarity of the thing is unheard of." One wouldn't expect a man so honest about his own side to temper his words on the Yankees. He has written to Fanny straightforwardly that the "plundering riots" in Richmond were really bread riots, has not quailed at repeatedly mentioning desertion and straggling in the army and his brigade, spared no words about the original condition of his men, has not been afraid to label the army's defeat as a defeat, and even has said, though mostly in jest, "What do you say to selling out negro property to old Abe and quitting the war?" Now, in the spring of 1863, in talking about the "conservatives" (Unionists) back home, he says, "Next to a Yankee a 'conservative' is the most loathsome sight." And on April 28:

> This spring will be our time to strike them and may we pay them for some of their devilish acts. I almost get beside myself sometimes, when I get to thinking about the way they treat our people in their lines. I could keep cool last year, but now I get very excited when the subject comes up. How shall we get even with them, unless we strove to be devils incarnate like themselves. . . .

"Can such people succeed?" he asks. "Surely a just God will punish them." Even if the South were wrong politically and morally, it would not justify the acts that the Yankees have been guilty of.

Of course, some of this is meant to convince Fanny of a cause she has always doubted. He tells her of the piety in the Army of Northern Virginia, assures her of the importance of the women of the South, and identifies the chief reason for fighting: "our children with the help of God will be free." She must not doubt the success of the Cause, and she should never despair. "They cannot conquer us."

He will get a chance to "strike" the Yankees (a word Lee uses) in early May. The new Union commander, Hooker, has assembled a huge army—which of course Pender underplays in his reassuring letters. In fact, while reading his letters one would hardly think there is a war on—which is exactly his purpose. Many other subjects are discussed. Continue your music lessons, he urges Fanny; "read and improve your mind for the benefit of your children in their future education."

> I want to educate my children if nothing else.

"And above all I want to see them fully imbued with reverence for things holy." He discusses her plans for where to spend the hot summer, tells her of packages (once a heavy box of sugar) he has sent her, requests items of clothing. He bought and sent her a sewing machine.

As he confesses, he is very proud of that purchase. He asks about it in every letter, hoping it is saving her effort and also providing her an interest. Then it becomes clear that the machine has never reached her. Somewhere it has got lost! (Their lives are like all of ours.) He writes to the manufacturer and manages to locate it, and finally all is well.

He talks often about getting out of the service after the War and buying a farm. After over a year of such thoughts, he finally decides he would be too isolated out in the country. Despite his quiet nature, he is a social person, accustomed to the company of the army. In any case, right now he has his duties.

Duty is a controlling idea for him, whether to the army and the South, to his wife, to his children, or to God:

> If Turner shall ever get over his puny looks as his father has and learn to try as hard to do his duty as I have, he will not give us a great deal of trouble, for I have tried always to do my duty in whatever position I have found myself.

> God bless you and the children and let them know that their father has tried to do his duty both to God and his country. . . .

> I try to do my duty to God and my government and am desirous of harming or injuring no man.

Duty is not always clear; the necessity of deciding for the old Union or the new Confederacy was a case in point—and even more difficult is the conflict between wife and command:

> If I can go see you without any neglect of duty, I will.

> My dear wife, God knows that if there is one human being in this world that I desire to make happy and at the same time do my duty, it is you.

The deepest issues, to paraphrase Faulkner, concern "the human heart in conflict with itself."

As Hooker's 130,000 troops threatened Fredericksburg and then crossed the Rappahannock, Pender's immediate duty was clear. Part of Jackson's flanking column on May 2, Hill's Division attacked the unprovided Federal right flank in the forest twilight.

That night Stonewall Jackson was shot reconnoitering in front of his now disorganized lines. Dorsey Pender was one of the officers who encountered the General as he was being brought back: "Ah, General, I am sorry to see that you have been wounded!" Pender, thinking of the condition of the army in the dark, then said, "The lines here are so much broken that I fear we will have to fall back." But Jackson would not hear of stopping to reorganize. The man who in the cold and snow of Fredericksburg proposed that the troops strip down to their undershirts for identification and make a night attack barked his last order, to Dorsey Pender: "You must hold your ground, General Pender, you must hold your ground, sir!"

In the next day's attack on the now strengthened Federal line, Pender at one point grabbed a regimental color and carried it himself at the head of his men, right into the Yankee trenches. Accused by his wife of having a "cold, unfeeling nature" and confessing that he does not much express his emotions, Dorsey Pender expressed his soul in valor. After the brilliant, if lucky, victory at Chancellorsville, Pender reported that his men fought "with unsurpassed courage and determination. I never knew them to act universally so well. I noticed no skulking, and they never showed any hesitation in following their colors." Those men, now ready for the supreme test, were soon on their way to Gettysburg.

And now the promotion came. Stonewall Jackson was gone; the army was reorganized and A. P. Hill was moved from division to corps command. The new commander of the former Light Division was Major General William Dorsey Pender, at twenty-nine the youngest officer of that rank. There were two outstanding major generals with two clearly superior divisions among the army's nine—Hood and Pender. Though probably incorrectly, the army believed that Lee had said "General Pender was the only officer in the army that could completely fill the place of 'Stonewall' Jackson."

Dorsey Pender kept up his letter writing as the army moved north from Fredericksburg, though his words carry the deeper tones of a man with heavier duties: "Responsibility is a load that is anything but pleasant." One of his former brigadier colleagues is now cool toward him; the problem with desertion and straggling continues—and worst of all there has been the "sad" affair of the cavalry fight at Brandy Station, in which "our loss was very serious," though Stuart "retrieved the surprise" by driving off the Federal cavalry.

I suppose it is all right that Stuart should get all the blame, for when anything handsome is done he gets all the credit. A bad rule either way.

Spoken like an experienced general officer.

Someone he knew has been killed in the cavalry battle, and the loss is understood by the Penders:

Poor Sol Williams and just married. I pity his desolate young widow.

But in general he is positive and optimistic, telling Fanny (correctly) that Hooker's short-term men have gone home and the Army of the Potomac is down to 90,000 men, not many more than the Army of Northern Virginia has. "In Gen. Lee's army we shall whip [them], I feel confident." But he is a prudent man, as he has said, always looking out "for contingencies as much as in man lies":

If Gen. Lee should not be completely victorious at the first brush, recollect that more than a third of his army will probably be absent at the time.

Lee, however, was trying to get as many troops as he could bring together for this campaign. Pickett's Division is called up from near the coast, and Hoke's Brigade is (unsuccessfully) sent for. Pender says he suspects they are bound for Pennsylvania; though he is not quite sure of that much, he can at least "see far enough to look into Md."

Before leaving Virginia, he writes to Fanny of something odd:

I had a funny dream the other night. I thought I had been married to a young lady without ever seeing or hearing of her before. I was very bashful and had a hard time to keep jealousy from arising in the first of my two wives. . . . She was nothing like as pretty as you.

The two of them took dreams seriously. Earlier in the War, Pender reported a soldier's dream, in which the dreamer forecast peace that month and his own death the next day at a certain hour. "The latter part of the dream was fulfilled," Pender wrote, and he wondered whether the other part would materialize also. Fanny has written about a dream last March, in which she was riding in a hearse. Trying to cheer her, Dorsey casually writes, "I thought dreams were interpreted by contraries; that hearses indicated a wedding or something of that sort." And he moves right on to talk about the army's having fresh shad to eat this spring. But she is not easily reassured. She believes her dreams are telling her there should not be an invasion of the North.

He continually addresses her fears:

> I think our prospects here are very fine. Gen. Lee has completely outgeneralled Hooker thus far and then our numbers are more equal than they have been. . . . The General says he wants to meet him as soon as possible and crush him.

> Our army is in splendid condition and everyone seems hopeful and cheerful. Cheer up my dear little girl. . . .

He reports that one of his colonels is "the greatest old granny" and has "had the impudence this morning to ask me to recommend him for promotion which I did not promise to do, nor shall I." But amid the encouragement and amusing irritations is the same, but now more somber, request: "May we meet again is my constant prayer."

On June 24 he writes, "Tomorrow I do what I know will cause you grief, and that is to cross the Potomac." He reassures her that "Gen. Lee has issued [an] order which altho' prevents plundering, at the same [time] makes arrangements for the bountiful supplying of our people"—a distinction, she must have observed, more neat in the wording than in the practice. They are ordered to pay for authorized seizures of civilian property in Confederate money:

> Until we crossed the Md. line our men behaved as well as troops could, but here [Fayetteville, Pa., June 28] it will be hard to restrain them, for they have an idea that they are to indulge in unlicensed plunder. They have done

nothing like the Yankees do in our country. They take poultry and hogs but in most cases pay our money for it. . . . The people are frightened to death and will do anything we intimate to them. . . . We pay about 200 percent.

Here is the opportunity Pender said he was waiting for. In April, before Chancellorsville, he had written of the Yankees:

They have gone systematically to work to starve us out and destroy all we have, to make the country a desert. I say let us play at the same game if we get the chance.

Well, here is the chance. And this is what he writes:

I am tired of invasions for altho' they [the Northerners] have made us suffer all that people can suffer, I cannot get my resentment to that point to make me feel indifferent to what you see here. . . . I never saw people so badly scared.

That may not be perfect love for enemies, but it would be fatuous to ask for more than this under the circumstances. Nearly two years ago he had written disgustedly of the unconvincing example a chaplain had set—outspoken Christian, of course, with all the credentials.

The southern Pennsylvania farmers are not appealing to Dorsey Pender, however. His description reads like an excursion through contemporary America: "Their dwelling houses are large and comfortable . . . but such coarse louts that live in them."

This is a most magnificent country to look at, but the most miserable people. I have yet to see a nice looking lady. They are coarse and dirty, and the number of dirty looking children is perfectly astonishing. A great many of the women go barefooted and but a small fraction wear stockings. I hope we may never have such people.

As to matters military, his confidence is at its height: "I wish we could meet Hooker and have the matter settled at once."

I never saw troops march as ours do; they will go 15 or 20 miles a day without leaving a straggler and hoop and yell on all occasions.

Three days later he would send them at the Iron Brigade, Battery B, and the rest of the Union First Corps on McPherson's and Seminary ridges. With the remnants of Heth's Division, Pender's Division formed that magnificent concave half-mile line, and taking terrible casualties drove the outnumbered Federals back from the woods and ridge, across the fields to their last stand at the Seminary. As the Federal right flank north of town crumbled and streamed to the rear, Pender's men charged the flaming muzzles of the First Corps survivors, and at the end of the afternoon of July 1 had possession of Seminary Ridge.

Dorsey Pender was too busy to write a letter that night. The next day, the afternoon of July 2, as the echelon attack along the Emmitsburg Road moved toward Pender's waiting division, the other woman—"nothing like as pretty" as Fanny—the one Fanny had been jealous of all along—took her man, as God, who directs "all things from above and for our good," suffered Dorsey Pender to be mortally wounded by a shell fragment on Seminary Ridge.

The wound had not seemed serious, but back in Staunton, Virginia, where General Pender had been transported, the healing artery in his punctured leg broke. In response to a chaplain's question about his soul, Pender said quietly, "Tell my wife that I do not fear to die. I can confidently resign my soul to God, trusting in the atonement of Jesus Christ. My only regret is to leave her and our two children. I have always tried to do my duty in every sphere in which Providence has placed me." A surgeon tried to repair the artery, failed, and then undertook the fatal amputation.

General Hill called Pender the best major general he had ever known, and said, "No man fell during the bloody battle of Gettysburg more regretted than he, nor around whose youthful brow were clustered brighter rays of glory."

Robert E. Lee talked about the battle at his headquarters some time afterward. How could they have lost? Lee could have stated many reasons: improper concert of action, absence of the cavalry, Ewell's failures, Longstreet's slowness, the ordering of Pickett's Charge, the fight of the Union army. These were all factors that could have been overcome, Lee evidently thought, because the only thing he said was, ". . . we would have succeeded had General Pender lived."

Oh hast thou forgotten how soon we must sever?
Oh! has thou forgotten this day we must part?
It may be for years and it may be forever—

Mrs. William Dorsey Pender, six months pregnant, went to her bedroom when she was told. She stayed for three days, and when she came out, according to witnesses, her hair was white.

She lived up to her husband's trust and expectations, as he had tried to live up to hers. She refused all outside support. She raised her boys—three of them now—herself, supporting them herself by opening a school—how he would have liked that—and by working as postmistress. She never remarried. For fifty-nine years, until her death in 1922, she never was able to talk about her husband.

His dear wife is buried next to him in the churchyard of Calvary Parish in North Carolina.

The inscription on the stained-glass window of the church, in memory of the general, applies to them both. It is his favorite verse, from St. Paul:

I have fought a good fight—I have kept the faith.

18 Conclusion

Nothing human except ignorance could have produced this war. Ignorance is not a lack of knowledge but the map of our condition, the tragic field we are concentrated in. Lack of understanding is the territory of an illness, a consumption that can't be cured by feeding it the facts. Curses can't be assuaged by information. Their germs and principalities don't fight according to the book. Good and evil, dark and light, the human mind itself, are fruits of some divided root, the pattern and articulation of some deep struggle in the heart. Narrow-eyed shadows pace the crest of Cemetery Ridge, mumbling multitudes approach; they clash across gray depth and distance; we turn on our beds and cry out in the night, battling with sticks and stones. Civil war is our perennial human theme.

Perhaps all of us are veterans of battles long forgotten. We have only dreams, our mysterious loves, our reverence for beauty, and the long faint call of duty to tell us what those ghostly advances and retreats were that have given us our faces and our fates. Like the virtue that enables it, duty is its own reward. Each duty is a vessel in which to carry forward courage, until the wall is breached, and courage flowers into glory.

There's nothing between us and eternity but our bodies. I think we all suspect an eternity, otherwise we would not be so afraid of time. We know that whatever is wrong is terribly wrong, and its consequences are too vast to face. What we want are lives that will wear well. What we make are lives that will wear out. There are no slaves in Valhalla;

each of us must do our own work, and a jewel among gifts is the grace of an eternity to do it in.

As courage is the primary virtue, cowardice is the primary vice. But fear is our ruling passion—our primary passion; it stands behind all the others that endanger us.

A person who is afraid, really afraid, is capable of anything, and will do it to anyone, including and perhaps especially, those closest— wives, husbands, and children. These are the easiest and softest targets—and when a person is afraid it is exactly such a target he or she wants. Ethics, reason, practicality are alike taken under the rule and into the service of this passion. Hunger, lust, all the drives give way to abject fear. Only love seems to be resistant, because it is willing to forget the basis of fear: self-preservation. Thus courage is born.

A running soldier cannot be stopped. In a Civil War infantry engagement there was a line of officers, and sometimes a special detachment of men, called "file-closers." The officers would stand a couple of paces behind the firing line and constantly talk to the men: "Steady, boys." "Give 'em hell, boys!" "Aim low." "Load your musket." When holes were shot through the line, these officers would encourage the men to close up, to stay in formation. Men under pressure would have two natural tendencies—and discipline in battle is meant to negate the natural tendencies, which are based on self-preservation. One tendency is to bunch up, breaking the line's integrity. The bolder men tend to advance a step or two while firing; the less bold tend to edge in behind such men in clumps, partly protected by the body of the leader. The other tendency is to drift backward; unchecked, this could result in actually leaving the line for the rear. These tendencies are rational, and can be neutralized by discipline, reason, threats, and all the other motivators of people in battle. It is in itself insane to stand in a line out in the open and trade bullets with a well-armed enemy; a gerbil would know better. Human beings can be induced to do it for a number of reasons, in addition to killer instinct or death wish: shame at being seen as cowardly, for instance, a culturally induced phenomenon more effective, obviously, at some times and places than at others; hatred of the enemy; discipline inculcated by intense training; fear of punishment—the old British navy comes to mind; ideology—applicable to the volunteers of 1861; devotion to comrades; stupidity; mass psychological influences; sense of duty. But sometimes soldiers cannot be reached by any of these.

Occasionally a man runs from the line, eyes wide and unfocused, and no amount of exhortation, cajoling, threats, or profanity can stop him. The officer may hit him full force with the flat of his sword—but he could also slice off a hand and have the same noneffect. The soldier is in what was called "shell-shock" in World War I. In World War II it was called "battle fatigue." A man may have been steady, even valorous, in all previous battles, and might be so again. But unreasoning fear takes control; the only instinct is to get away, either by running or by falling into a catatonic world. File closers knew by experience that such men could not be turned, though no doubt many were struck, beaten, even shot in exasperation. It was known during World War II that *all* soldiers eventually reach that state, if subjected to continuous battle. The nineteenth-century ideas of courage, character, and conscious will gave way to the facts of modern war. Under the stress of constant combat, the soldier breaks down if he survives long enough. Death or shock: there is no third alternative for anyone—assuming no end to combat. Some will hold out longer than others: those are the ones we are interested in.

In modern war this reality is provided for by tours of duty. In the Civil War there was no such provision. Shock was considered a failure of character. There was no sustained combat of twentieth-century proportions until Grant's offensive in 1864. Though it was not Verdun or the Somme, fighting was fairly constant, and casualties horrific, from the Wilderness to Petersburg. The armies coped in two major ways: on the macro level, they went into siege. On the individual level, the soldiers became "battle wise," and would not pose in battle lines to get shot. Gettysburg was about the last of the old standup battles. At Spotsylvania the two sides at the Bloody Angle went to ground, keeping up constant fire for more than twelve hours within yards or feet of each other, but the attrition did not match one hour at Antietam or in the Wheatfield. Men took cover and stayed there. When Grant ordered his troops to attack frontally at Cold Harbor, they eventually refused. It can be said that the 1861 volunteers fought more valiantly than the draftees of 1864, which is probably true, but the veteran volunteers of 1864 (re-enlistees) had also learned that stand-up charges were murder, as well as indecisive. No more of this bullshit.

Until 1864 the soldiers fought only one, two, or three days at a time, only several times a year. The greatest intensity occurred in the summer of 1862, when Jackson's men fought a series of small battles in the Valley in June, took part somewhat in the Seven Days in July, were heavily engaged at Brawner's Farm and Manassas in late August, and went to Sharpsburg in mid-September. Otherwise the men spent months in camp, in drill and boredom. In 1863 there were five days of heavy combat. It was attitudes—primarily of Grant and Lee—rather than technology or tactics that changed the American Civil War from a Napoleonic war through 1863 into a somewhat twentieth-century war in 1864–65. Until Grant, nobody but Lee was willing to fight it out on one line all summer.

But what contemporary Americans find amazing is not the long-term fighting of 1864 but the stand-up fighting and attacks, epitomized by Pickett's Charge. Realistic movies depicting lines of men blazing away at 50 yards, and attacking shoulder-to-shoulder, or better, elbow-to-elbow, surprise and awe audiences who are not familiar with Civil War tactics. How could they do it? The question, really, is, Could I have done it?

That was the essential question for Civil War soldiers too. What will I do in battle? Will I run when I "see the elephant"? They rightly interpreted courage as being the key to character. And under their circumstances—one or two hours of shocking combat at a time—the traditional measure of it had some feasibility. Today, when war is different, there are different ways of testing our mettle. But the elephant is still out there.

Or rather, he's in the kitchen.

We would like courage to be easy, but it's only the tawdry substitutes that are easy. When Webb's regiments put their national flags at the stone wall in front of Lee's men on July 3, and stuck to them, it was not easy. Today the largest American flag is at K-Mart. At Gettysburg that flag in the smoke, torn by bullets and held up by grimy, bleeding men, must have been one of the most beautiful sights on earth. The other day in the supermarket I saw an individual wearing a

T shirt, a U.S. flag printed on it stretched across his beer belly, above it the words: "If you want to burn a flag burn this one"—and under it, "ASSHOLE." I don't think Pickett's men would have bothered to charge such breastworks.

Like fourteenth-century Europe, which was also obsessed, though more openly, by death, we have a good deal to be afraid of. As in the days of the bubonic plague, we have black death looming over us. Either our weapons will annihilate the world, or our industry will. (We might ask, Would a nuclear bomb find many of us alive enough to kill?)

Those crippled by a fear hasten the very thing they fear. A man in battle who becomes catatonic or disoriented is an especially easy target, and if his unit's discipline is harsh he will be shot or court-martialed. Likewise an all-consuming fear of death: we are the ones consumed; we will come to our death not having lived. The ones who stand to the work die no sooner, and have a better chance of surviving—and feel, in the end, that they have lived. They outlive their monuments. But do we live a better life than a Toyota does?

Life in America is in some ways a nightmare made visible. What a troubled sleep we sleep. As Thoreau says, "the nearest approach to what we are is in dreams." The New American Dream has become a cruel reality, like the appropriate tortures in Dante's *Inferno*, as palpable as plastic. The dark demons of our beds approach with heavy steps—and we have left our formations, dropped our weapons, and are beyond all appeals to honor. We are about to be overwhelmed.

The frantic nature of our occupations and amusements show that we don't believe in what we are doing.

The sustainer of humankind—which lives, as a whole, a tragic and unhappy existence, hounded by death and trying to limp away from it on aging legs—has been love that becomes action, that is, faith. In America the dominant religion has not been a faith but a drug; while the enemy advances, we are stoned. Literalism and legalism have mixed well with our material fantasy; it is a mixture brought on by circumstances, and as circumstances change, which they will, only the nasty side will remain. Fundamentalists are sinister. Most American "evangelicals" are fundamentalists who shop at Marshall Field's.

I may be a patriot who did not survive the Civil War, but I have nothing against something new in religion.

Something very new and untried. Our massive popular religion, characterized by self-righteous, sectarian, willful ignorance, is based on exactly the wrong thing: fear. As such, it will readily join hands with any other movement so based. That is the evil of contemporary "patriotism": it is based upon fear—helpless fear for the future of this country—a well-founded fear; but our reaction is that of battle fatigue. It is desperate rather than hopeful. Patriotism today, like fundamentalism, can turn pathetic and nasty, rather than, as Gibbon's men and those Virginians would have said, "manly and true."

Afraid fundamentally of death, how can we be unselfish? Compassion, justice—all the virtues assume the unselfishness only courage can impart. Religion, then, should be difficult to reconcile with our economy of selfishness; instead of its ally, it should be its enemy. If you pay the devil to beat the devil, the devil always wins.

We should instead try something entirely new, something that has not been tried before—something so mad and valorous that it would confound fundamentalists and liberals alike, arouse envious scorn from them and all pagans, and do us not one whit of material advantage: something like Christianity. The faith, not the religion.

One could characterize Dorsey Pender's faith by three things: his performance of duty, his love for his wife, and his trust in God's providence. This is not to say that one faith is as good as another. I don't say ours is as good.

His faith never did him any good in the world, just as his soldiers' battle at Gettysburg didn't do them any good in the world of cause, effect, and desire. He didn't get the one thing he wanted: "May God protect us from all danger" and "preserve us for each other to a good old age." But his wishes were not masters of his faith, even his strongest wishes. God turned out to be more mysterious than Dorsey Pender knew. But he had had his intimations. Always a prudent man, the general had not left himself unprovided. Perhaps one thing faith is, is confidence in God's mysteries.

At strange, profound times, locked in the mysteries of some deep and surprising battle, taken out of ourselves in the stunning stare of beauty, we almost see God. We feel the reins of time's chariot in our

hands; we are not afraid. Meanwhile, we play out the mean and cring-
ing lives we live, doing illimitable damage. The battle has passed; let
the war rage on.

General Lee looked back to Chancellorsville in explaining to himself his failure at Gettysburg. Indeed there was a sense in which Chancellorsville contributed to the loss in Pennsylvania, though quite
opposite to what Lee was thinking, that is, Jackson's death. In
the minds of Lee and much of his army, Chancellorsville reinforced
the wrong lesson. Chancellorsville looked like a great victory for the
South, but really it was an unnecessary loss for the Union. The Army
of Northern Virginia won that battle only because Joseph Hooker lost
it, because, as he said, "I lost confidence in Joe Hooker." Jackson's
flank attack demoralized—but did not destroy or even fatally disorder—the weakest corps in the Army of the Potomac, the Eleventh.
Just arriving from Fredericksburg was the best corps in the army, and
second largest—Reynolds's First Corps. E. P. Alexander wrote that
Hooker's retreat saved Lee's men from a horrendous defeat, a frontal
assault against a prepared position. But the order had been given; Lee
had decided to throw his whole army against the new Union line and
was "saved," not by strategy, or by his best executive officer, or by
audacity, but by fate or luck—perhaps bad luck after all.

Which division commander made the most ghastly mistake at Gettysburg? Rodes. Rodes, who had done so well in that all-out attack at
Chancellorsville. So coming down from Oak Hill toward Paul's and
Baxter's concealed men behind that stone wall the First Day, Rodes
tried to duplicate the rushing, spirited assault. The slaughter of Iverson's Brigade was exceeded only by Garnett's loss, and that was no
division commander's fault.

Perhaps Hill and Archer and Davis suffered from the same fault on
the First Day. But the big problem was with Lee; he didn't need more
lessons on how an attack would make huge numbers of Yankees run;
he didn't need to learn that his men, "if properly led, can do anything."

Another lesson from Chancellorsville was that there is no point in
brilliant victories if the Union army can walk away, stoke itself up
again in safety, then come back when it's ready. Lee wanted to do two

things after May 1863. One was to win a victory where it would not be possible for the Army of the Potomac to pull away and recover: win in the North, where a victory would mean the capture of Washington or some other city.

The other thing was to destroy the Army of the Potomac, not merely smack it one. I think Lee's otherwise absurd deployment of his army at Gettysburg was made in hopes of achieving a Cannae, a double envelopment. Don't hit them on one flank only, as at Chancellorsville; cup both flanks and scoop 'em up. Never have to mess with those people again. (I sometimes wonder whether Lee's phrase for the enemy—"those people"—was, instead of a magnanimous euphemism, a disdainful epithet, expressing something close to abhorrence or revulsion.)

Surely even the audacious Lee would not have spread his line twice as far as the Union line unless it was for some such reason. He may have had contempt for Union numbers and density, but surely he would not have so overestimated his own officers' and staff's ability to communicate and coordinate—without a compelling reason to take such a risk. Long risks he knew he must take. In this case it was to grasp the supreme prize.

An element in his thinking must have been Stuart's absence. Not making optimal use of the cavalry he had (Jenkins's Brigade), Lee felt himself to be in the dark, and if he had no eyes he would use his hands—both hands, like William the Conqueror, grip those people, box their ears, and then, if they were still standing, belt 'em between the eyes.

The decisions were calculated, but not cool. The Third Day shows this. Lee wouldn't have done that if he hadn't been—as Eisenhower or Montgomery said when they toured the battlefield together—mad as hell at that guy over there and just wanted to hit him. What you see when you look at some of the pictures of Lee—especially the one in Richmond in April 1865 with Walter Taylor—is a man who's mad as hell. Not a kindly grampa. No saint. A man who's mad as hell.

He did have a frightening temper, though his Southern manners compelled him to rein it in most of the time in social situations. But he was monumentally irritated at Gettysburg. "Where is Stuart?" "Has anyone heard from my cavalry?" Throw in diarrhea. (I don't think he was the impaired heart patient portrayed in a recent good novel about Gettysburg, however.) Throw in his irritation with Longstreet. And, most important, throw in his dislike of Yankees and his belief that his men could whip twice or more their numbers of them (as Chancellorsville seemed to prove), and you get attacks on the strong natural positions of the Yankees, culminating in Pickett's Charge.

They hadn't told him how bad off Heth's Division was. (Its general was still suffering from having been konked July 1.) That division should be in good trim; all it did was plow through the Yankees in the great victory Wednesday. In fact, it had been ground up by the First Corps. If Lee had received an accurate report of the First Day's damage to Heth's Division, would he have been converted? Would he have learned not to order headlong frontal assaults?

Nah. At most he would have thrown in Pender's or Anderson's Division instead. What he learned, he learned by watching Pickett's Charge—watching it fray and melt and disintegrate before the Yankee guns and infantry. Then, *then*, he became the great general he was in the summer of 1864. But even then, how he itched for the offensive. Champaign taste on a beer budget.

Lee was the worst brilliant general in American history, something like Napoleon. The South could have won the War, as Alan Nolan observes; no battle was lost for lack of supplies, munitions, men. Livermore shows that the manpower ratio was really only about 2:3 overall. (As he factored for enlistment terms, however, should Livermore have factored for ages of Confederate versus Union draftees? Seventeen- and forty-five-year-olds should not be as effective as twenty-year-olds. Or was this balanced by noncombat use of slaves?) Follow Kutusov's strategy against Napoleon; follow Lee's hero Washington's strategy against the British. But no. The two worst battles in American history, Antietam—the bloodiest single day's battle—and Gettysburg, were fought by Lee needlessly and unwisely. Together, those two battles finished off the South. The officers and men couldn't be replaced, nor the propitious times.

Robert E. Lee had indeed saved the South in the summer of 1862, but Sharpsburg should never have been fought. After McClellan foolishly failed to attack and wipe out Lee's fragment army on September 16, Lee should have got out. Outnumbered two to one, troops barefoot, footsore, hungry, ragged, tired after a nearly continual summer campaign, unsure of what they were doing in Maryland—backs to a river, relying upon one very exposed ford—and McClellan in possession of orders showing exactly what Lee had and where. Lee may have known McClellan, but he didn't know physics. What was the best he could have hoped for?

McClellan fought only 53,000 of his men; still, they were successful in nearly every attack, to the verge of breaking Lee's line decisively. The Army of Northern Virginia was most heroic, and most lucky, that day. What could be learned from that useless battle?

When the Yankees made their frontal assaults that winter at Fredericksburg, Lee answered the question of why he would attack at Gettysburg. It was not only pride, though it was that; nor was it only pride with anger. Lee, like many great soldiers, was a war lover. "It is well that war is so terrible, else we should grow too fond of it," he said as the long lines of Union blue came toward his wolfish cannons on Marye's Heights—a logically screwy statement. It is not what it appears to be, a wise lament on the attractiveness of battle. It's a nineteenth-century genteel, educated aristocrat's way of saying, *"Hot damn!"*

But one large caution should be made regarding criticism of Robert E. Lee. What would we think of a modern general who took Lee or Grant as their examples? We would admire that student of history. And what would we say of a general who studied closely one of the greatest generals of them all? For this is what Lee did. Lee, who graduated first in his class at West Point, was one of the best students in American military history. Whom did he study? Of the perhaps four greatest commanders known to history, he did not primarily study Alexander, Hannibal, or Ghengis Khan—but rather the equal of them who was almost contemporary with Lee, who was fighting some of the great battles of history during Lee's early childhood—the man whose weapons and armies resembled most closely what Lee would have to work with. It made sense for Lee to learn thoroughly the strategy and tactics—though not the character—of the world's greatest winner and loser—that "very great, very bad man," Napoleon Bonaparte. It is not to fault Lee to realize that he was following the example of the general who, in his own time, had revolutionized

strategy and tactics, and who had fought under circumstances sometimes similar to Lee's: pressed on several frontiers by "overwhelming
numbers and resources."

Insufficient attention has been paid to the raw material of Lee's
military education: Napoleon's battles. Why did Lee show such apparent avidity for the offensive? It was the first principle of Napoleon.
And it had been borne out by Lee's own experience during 1862–63.
On the Peninsula and at Chancellorsville, Lee's offensives against
greatly superior forces had saved the Confederacy. At Sharpsburg, Lee
had stood on the defensive and was almost destroyed. Lee had
learned, he thought, that he must either whip them or they would
whip him. A complex interaction among character, personality, education, and experience moved within Robert E. Lee.

Before Gettysburg, Lee had successfully followed Napoleon's strategic and tactical principles. Where practicable, there was Napoleon's
favored strategic-tactical combination, *manoeuvre sur les derrières*
(movement upon the rear): take and keep the initiative, thereby
throwing the enemy off balance; continue the psychological intimida-
tion by fast, unexpected movements and threats to the enemy's line of
communications; then employ the circling tactic upon the enemy at a
location of one's own choice. This tactic began with a series of pinning attacks which encouraged the enemy to establish and reinforce
his main, straight line of battle; but an undetected large detachment
would make an encircling march and fall upon the rear of one of the
enemy's flanks. The enemy would then bend his line to face the startling new threat and commit his reserves to that wing. At this point
Napoleon would throw his own reserve right at the point where the
enemy had bent his line. All good Civil War generals knew about this.
McClellan, in his grandly torpid way, had tried it at Antietam; and, I
think, Lee had something like this in mind for Longstreet and Hill's
offensive on the Second Day at Gettysburg. But Lee had also studied
his Hannibal, and the idea of a double envelopment predominated on
the Second Day. However, when neither flank attack, much less coordination, proved successful, Lee planned yet another kind of Napoleonic battle for the Third Day: Waterloo.

It should be interjected that Napoleon used a different strategic
method when threatened by more than one army. The "strategy of

the central position," in modified form, provided Lee with a pattern for coping with the Federals' multiple armies and contingents. Using cavalry to gather exact information as to the enemy contingents' positions, Napoleon would move to a carefully calculated point between the enemy bodies, then strike one while holding the other with a small force; then turn on the other enemy with a reunited force. It was a matter of economy. In Napoleon's words: "The art of generalship consists in, when actually inferior in numbers to the enemy [overall], being superior to him on the battlefield." Part of the brilliance—and luck—of Chancellorsville was that Lee successfully combined both the "strategy of the central position" and the *manoeuvre sur les derrières*. The two largest Union corps were temporarily held at Fredericksburg by one Confederate division; the rest of Lee's army marched to Chancellorsville to face Hooker's main body. Pinning Hooker with McLaws's Division, Lee again split his force, sending most of it under Jackson around to the Union rear. When the demoralized Hooker retreated, Lee turned with his whole army back to the Union contingent at Fredericksburg. Civil War books often note, with an intake of breath, that Lee "divided his force in the face of the enemy." Napoleon did it all the time.

When the flank and fulcrum movements failed at Gettysburg, Lee resorted to Napoleon's battle at Waterloo. This was not foolish. Napoleon had lost at Waterloo because a second army, Bluecher's, came to Wellington's relief; but there was no second Union army coming. Indeed, when one looks at Lee's thinking at Gettysburg in general, a strongly Napoleonic pattern emerges, with a strange confirmation supplied by Meade: he knew Lee was following Napoleon; that in part explains Meade's intuition the night of July 2 that next day Lee would hit his center with a frontal assault.

He might have even guessed that Lee would first barrage him with massed artillery and then try to advance some guns during the infantry attack itself. These were Napoleonic tactics. So was massed cavalry, though Lee had only light horse, not Napoleon's breastplated *cuirassiers;* Meade could oppose his own massed cavalry. Waterloo was spread across two days at Gettysburg: after two failed flank attacks, the culmination would come at the center—not Napoleon's Imperial Guard, but the Confederate counterpart: Lee's own Virginians.

(One might even see the counterparts of Wellington and Napoleon in Meade and Lee at Gettysburg: Wellington and Meade riding to various points all along the lines; Napoleon and Lee doing the initial work, then on principle leaving the actual battle to subordinates at the points of attack. The hands-off role is natural for offensive battle, however, where plans have been drawn; the active role is natural for defensive battle, which is reactive and requires continual decision making and direction.)

The evening attacks by Marshall Ney and the Guard nearly broke the stalwart English lines at Waterloo, but the Redcoats held all day, if barely, until the Prussians arrived to turn the French flank. Lee knew that Wellington's tactics had been successful in every battle the Duke had fought against Napoleon's subordinates, and finally against Napoleon himself. He had studied the Iron Duke's reverse slope formations. French attacks would wash up an elevation that Wellington had chosen, capturing the artillery on the crest and sending the British skirmishers flying. Panting, flushed with what they thought was victory, the French would pour over the crest only to confront the long, thin red line of British infantry, waiting silent as death.

But Lee had learned this lesson too well. He thought Meade was playing Wellington to his Napoleon. He thought there was a long blue line waiting on the reverse slope of Cemetery Ridge. That is why the Confederate artillery bombardment was ineffective: it was too smart. And finally, it was a little arrogant. Surely the Yankees would want to have plenty of men along that ridge. (And just as surely, Pickett's disciplined advance would be as intimidating as an attack made by the tall Guards, with their high plumes and shimmering helmets.)

But if Lee's military character was a flawed household of prejudices, emotions, beliefs, training, and experience, Lee must also be credited with being one of the best economists of all time. "Strategy is the art of making use of time and space," Napoleon said. Lee gave the Confederacy nearly three years of life past the point where it should have died. And he did it with skill and the content of his character—parts of which were pride and audacity, the very things that the ironic art of history making must call flaws.

Robert E. Lee is one of us. And more so. Larger, more able, but cursed as we are cursed, weak as we are weak, noble to a degree despite this. As a general he ranks with the brilliant lovers of war—Napoleon, Patton, Stonewall Jackson; but not with Washington, in whom wisdom was in fact the better part of strategy. Temperamentally, Lee was in part a curious mixture of fundamentalist Christian and hot dog. Vain and impatient by nature, he curbed his tendencies valiantly according to Christian virtues—but missed some big ones, including "truth in the inward parts."

His correspondence is strangely disharmonious, euphemistic, removed from common reality. I refer to his letters. The letters of Hawthorne, Whitman, Lincoln are direct, and they sound, even to us in this century, like normal talk. Lee's farewell order (General Order No. 9) at Appomattox, written by an aide, is a good imitation by a man closely familiar with Lee:

> After four years of arduous service marked by unsurpassed courage and fortitude, the Army of Northern Virginia has been compelled to yield to overwhelming numbers and resources.

This is in its way lovely, rhythmic, and memorable. (Not having seen or heard it for twenty years, I still remember it.)

> I need not tell the brave survivors of so many hard fought battles who have remained steadfast to the last, that I have consented to this result from no distrust of them.
>
> But feeling that valor and devotion could accomplish nothing that would compensate for the loss that must have attended the continuance of the contest, I have determined to avoid the useless sacrifice of those whose past services have endeared them to their countrymen.

Those words are typical Lee. Polished, removed, euphonious, genteel, educated, aristocratic, and somewhat Pentagonese. Not that it would be entirely preferable, but one could imagine Grant writing, "I surrendered not because I lost faith in you but because I didn't want you to die for nothing." Lee's prose, like his strategy and tactics—and postwar statements—attempts to avoid reality. There is an element of the heroic in this, as well as of the neurotic or pathologic. Lee, like other geniuses in any field, changed or nearly changed reality to suit his view or his wishes. He is as such an epic representation of human life: the attempt to defeat circumstances. The failure was noble.

What was Lee, then? Not a tragic hero, not a tragic figure at all, but a charismatic, gifted soldier. Onto charismatic figures we put our wishes, and we dress them according to our dreams. They stand in front of our quiet desperation, and the last thing we will let them be is what they are.

The man that Lee made, that we have made of him, is a phantom, more devouring than someone who sends his soldiers into the maws of cannons. General Lee was indeed a man to be afraid of, but we have made him our slave—poetic justice, it may be, but the very worst we could do to him; perhaps now he is a tragic hero after all. He did not deserve this. But we have all become slaves to our Hollywood fantasies, and the Great Emancipator is dead.

Courage sees things for what they are. We have yet to distinguish dreams from fantasies, and ourselves from the advertised commercial world. When we do this, it will be with the courage of the best at Gettysburg. I am convinced that life is meant to rouse in us this courage.

One learns much about the Battle of Gettysburg by reading such things as Gregory Coco's work on the hospitals *(A Vast Sea of Misery)* and the dead *(Wasted Valor)*. Similarly it was Whitman, who worked in the hospitals, and Lincoln, who dreamed of its dead, who knew most about the War. Such dreams may be our nearest approach to what the battle was. History is the penumbra of the soul. In the delirium and sleep afterward, some understanding of the battle comes.

Suppose you knew nothing of the battle and found yourself on the field July 5 or 6. What had happened? Your first effort would not be to look around and solve the puzzle, but to get out of there.

Before the visual horrors registered, you might be overcome physically. The smell fills your head and becomes a slippery growth in your stomach. One veteran wrote of throwing himself face to the ground and vomiting himself empty. Many were made quite ill by the odor alone.

Before the stretcher-bearers and ambulances finished their work picking up the perhaps ten thousand wounded actually lying on the field, you would have heard the constant moans and screams, the unceasing pleas for water whispered, sobbed, screamed, begged—a nightmarish and pathetic cacophony everywhere rising across the fields and at your feet. You would have seen men with every conceivable bullet and artillery wound, mouths bubbling blood, shot lungs and throats foaming and whistling, blood-soaked shattered limbs.

And the dead. In all positions—some restful, some in frozen, open-eyed terror or rage, some twisted with agony. In some of the fields you could have walked in any direction just stepping on the mutilated dead. Hundreds of Southerners were buried on the Rose Farm. The dead were bloated, sometimes moving before your eyes as gasses inside them shifted. Their faces were blackened by the hot sun; perhaps their fishlike mouths were ringed with gunpowder from the cartridges they had bitten open before being stricken. Their eyes bulged. Some seemed twice the size they should be.

That was not all: the dead were dismembered, lacerated, some naked in their death agonies having torn off their clothing, some shoeless and with pockets and haversacks turned inside-out, some with sides or abdomens shot away and organs spilled and rotten, crawling with maggots. (Green bottle flies were everywhere in the millions, covering dead and living.) Visitors reported hands and arms in tree limbs, boots lying with feet and legs still in them, heads on the fields and among the rocks: artillery was hideous in its effects. One female nurse described the headless trunk of a man sitting against a tree, arms shot off, the torn clothing of the drained body flapping in the breeze. Shell concussions flattened bodies against rocks, into shapeless horrors. All these were you and me, hit by bullets (21 inches of human body mass was needed to stop a bullet at 150 yards, a doctor calculated), by iron shell fragments, by solid shot. Clubbed muskets and bayonets. Heat, thirst, delirium. After a few days, buzzards.

Hospitals everywhere behind the battle lines and in town: farmhouses, barns, public buildings, schools, churches, stores, houses. Some of these buildings still have bloodstains on the floors. Hundreds lay on boards placed over pews in churches; men were put on floors, tables; they covered all the space in Gettysburg side by side, with only a few nurses and doctors for every several hundred wounded. A woman who nursed Confederates at the main building of Pennsylvania College said that each morning a dozen or more corpses lay out-side the door for burial.

Doctors operated and sawed, sleeves rolled up, covered all over with blood, hundreds of men waiting for each of them. Some stood for thirty-six hours at a time, held up like Moses by others; at least one doctor became hysterical. There was little support staff, no under-standing of germ theory, and the big, soft Minié bullet smashed bones, leaving nothing much to reconstruct: outside windows of tem-porary hospitals and piled in front of the big tents lay arms, hands, legs, feet. Union doctors had chloroform and ether; when Southern doctors ran short they resorted to "Confederate chloroform"— whisky. Men lay for hours, then days, on hard floors and balconies, with little or no straw under them, as long as six days without food— waiting for such treatment as could be given.

Back on the fields burial groups, some men with handkerchiefs tied uselessly across their faces, dug graves and marked them for the Union casualties. Soldiers talked loudly—deafened by two or three days of battle—doing the horrifying, disgusting, sad, numbing work. Lee's dead men had no one but the Yankees to bury them. (That is why most of the photographed dead at Gettysburg are Southern— their bodies were still there when the photographers arrived.) Several days after Lee retreated, the remaining bodies were turned into shal-low trenches, dirt hastily shoveled back over them. Visitors reported that hands, feet, even faces protruded from the soil—and that at night the decomposing bodies so near the surface gave a phosphorescent glow across the ground.

Southern prisoners were ordered to help with burials, but the work was done in revulsive haste. Sometimes penciled lettering on a shin-gle or piece of bark said "54 Rebs."; sometimes someone would write a name and company on a board half-buried or on a cartridge-box flap. But in a short time all such markings would be gone. There are probably still Southern bodies in the Valley of Death and elsewhere at Gettysburg. Gregory Coco reports findings of bones as recently as 1977, and figures that a thousand Confederate graves still remain un-discovered in Adams County.

The fields were covered with ramrods, rifles, bayonets, clothing, and every item a soldier might have carried: toothbrushes, Bibles, books, photographs, cards, letters, paper, pens. The trees were pocked with bullets; during the next thirty years many trees in McPherson's Woods died from lead poisoning.

Dead horses lay everywhere, about five thousand. Crops were trampled, fruit trees were shattered, fences had been torn apart and burned, barns were partly disassembled; carpets, walls, mattresses, blankets, sofas, tables, yards, and parcels of earth everywhere were soaked with human blood. In the Northern states, and in towns and villages of the South, people stood and read the lists.

At the end of anger are grief, horror, revulsion, pity. As you stand in the dizzying stench and gasp your disbelief, you wonder what these creatures fought for. Were the issues as important as whatever set the red ants on the black in *Walden*, and had there been heroics? What was it all for? The aftermath of battle, and the fighting itself, are clean divorced from the causes of the war; things went on under their own power. It could have been Oates attacked on Seminary Ridge by Cutler's Brigade as easily as the Alabamians charging Little Round Top. "O my people, they which lead thee cause thee to err!" What is all this waste and guilt, this sorrow and despair, the suffering and ghastly death—*for?* What is the meaning of the battle?

At the new cemetery 3,512 bodies were buried. Nearly everything else has disappeared, but the bodies are still there, still holding the field against loss of memory. The North lost 3,155 killed, according to Livermore, the South 3,903; 18,735 Southerners were wounded, 14,529 Northerners. Busey and Martin calculate 3,149 and 4,559; 12,355 plus an unknown number, and 14,501. The Southerners left thousands of their wounded (though reporting only about 700)— spared the horror of Lee's seventeen-mile train of bleeding men on his retreat—to be paroled or to die in Northern prisons. Ten thousand North and South were captured by the other side, or went unaccounted for.

Suppose sometime during the battle one act of humanity, clear and arresting, had startled both armies, and the men on both sides had stopped. Would that not have been a moment of sanity in a sea of insane convulsion? Men by thousands settle their muskets to the ground and look as if awakened; gunners drop their hands and rammers clatter to the ground, no artillery fires; has someone cried, *"What are you doing?"* The generals, and any of the men still fighting or trying to fight in that silence, would look like raving maniacs. Wouldn't they be? But if everyone fights, battle is sanity?

However, no such reveille sounded, and the battle built to its maddened, incredible climax on July 3. And then, not sanity but a kind of battle wisdom, as Meade did the best and only thing: nothing, except allow Lee's defeat to ripen. Now the witnesses shake off their transfixed silence—Haskell has written, "the impassioned soul is all eyes"—and the grieving raise their wail. When all we see is waste and carnage, the shot-dead and the battlefield litter, what evidence exists for sanity or hope?

In Washington, New York, and Richmond—all across North and South—the politicians, businessmen, lawyers, everyone who profited got away scot-free and left the widow at her door. The Gilded Age would follow. Electoral swindles, city political machines, racism, and violence would ride the sleep of Gettysburg like dragons in the nineteenth century; and now the violence of horses has drained to this callous parade of inadequacy 130 years later.

When somebody asked him why there was no monument to him at Gettysburg, Daniel Sickles said, The whole damn place is my monument. In a way he was right. Sickles was a politician.

Thousands of men found themselves, one moment healthy and normal, the next—or a few days later—without a leg, without a jaw, no right arm, freaks for life now. *Never* able again to plow or write or talk. And thousands more dead. *Why?* Whitman had it right: because of the politicians.

So it is in the world and always has been. We think the world is under some kind of human control, but it isn't. We speak of notifying "the authorities," but there aren't any authorities. The people who run the world are people like you and me. Right before the Civil War the politicians, who should have solved the *political* problems, caused mortal ones. *Massa damnata.* Politicians are not always patriots. Dorsey Pender thought patriotism and honesty are connected.

Patriotism tends to call forth the deep virtues we see in Dorsey Pender—honor, sense of duty, courage, honesty. But in recent years a supposedly superpatriotic President was not capable of such virtues, only a cheesy sentimentality which the country accepted in place of patriotism. Now self-proclaimed patriots marry the flag to obscenities on their T shirts—"louts" is Pender's decent term. They have not done the country any good.

After 1865, without much pause, America has been sold down the river by corporate greed and political cowardice. Today we are a colonial country, still scrambling after manufactured evils we can't even produce by ourselves any more—losing at our own wicked game. All this at the expense not mainly of power or economic well-being, but of justice.

What is American patriotism? Patriots both North and South fought at Gettysburg for freedom. The battle, the War were ways of figuring out—all other ways failing as too subtle or too much trouble—what freedom is, particularly American freedom. Pender's idea and to an extent Lincoln's and Lee's, was that there is no freedom without justice. *No freedom for me if the ones I touch are not free.* The Great Emancipator is dead; now "it is for us, the living," to look into the eyes of the poor.

Courage! Patriots "dream of things that never were," a waking dream that rolls up its sleeves and plants its tattered flag. At stake are things more sacred than we know. The battle spreads across the stars.

> Oh my God, I cry by day,
> but you do not answer;
> and by night, but find no rest.

So the wounded on the field. (It is the prayer quoted on the Cross.) Joshua Chamberlain was miraculously spared, but why not

> Adams, Aaron
> Beadle, Charles M.
> Billings, Charles W.
> Walker, Orrin
> Wentworth, John
> Wyer, Oscar
> York, George H.

and all the others? Why did Lincoln die?

He tried to answer these questions on the nineteenth of November, 1863, at the dedication of the National Cemetery:

> . . . this nation shall have a new birth of freedom; and . . . government of the people, by the people, for the people, shall not perish from the earth.

The speech was made to motivate the people of the North to go on fighting, more than to explain the conflict. The heights ascended at Lincoln's Second Inaugural were not scaled on Cemetery Hill. What comfort did the Gettysburg Address give to Mrs. Pender, or to the families of four thousand Southern dead?—they fought for the same thing, freedom and republican government. But not equality, not justice.

The Second Inaugural Address, March 4, 1865, written from a longer, deeper view, at last settles on a mystery and leaves aside all politics and human purposes. There is a larger economy:

> . . . The Almighty has his own purposes. . . . Fondly do we hope—fervently do we pray—that this mighty scourge of war may speedily pass away. Yet, if God wills that it continue, until all the wealth piled by the bond-man's two hundred and fifty years of unrequited toil shall be sunk, and until every drop of blood drawn with the lash, shall be paid by another drawn with the sword, as was said three thousand years ago, so still it must be said "the judgments of the Lord, are true and righteous altogether."

The ship of liberty—even the world of politics itself—floats like a chip upon the moral sea, which answers not to human pilots but to a distant moon and sun.

Is this, then, why wishes were not granted? Was each dead Southern boy and each hobbling chair-sitter the flotsam of this moral sea, as inexorable in its heave and crush as a North Atlantic swell? If God is personal, we want Him to intervene for us, to scatter the timbers of other ships; but what His intervention is, what *for us* means, is just as much a mystery as the sea, to us who don't even know ourselves. The last freedom we are willing to grant is the freedom of God. "Men are not flattered by being shown that there has been a difference of purpose between the Almighty and them," Lincoln wrote on March 15, 1865. "To deny it, however, in this case, is to deny that there is a God governing the world."

So be it, then. There is a system, a pattern, a "moody, tearful night" ordained somewhere among the dales of Arcady. One it saves today; another it bends low before the musket's shock; but who is blessed when tomorrow comes or time wears through its shallow bowl of stars, who can say but Him whose judgments are true and righteous altogether?

Gettysburg is the seat of Adams County; it lies within the moral bounds of cause and pain which human flesh inherits, and what is Adam's shall be rendered unto Adam. But what is God's is God's.

> *'Beauty is truth, truth beauty,'—that is all*
> *Ye know on earth, and all ye need to know.*

Gregory Coco has found a description of the Confederate advance toward Gettysburg on July 1 which depicts the newness, actuality, depth, and eternal mystery of that battle and the War:

> . . . we noticed up the road, coming over the nearest hill, great masses of troops and clouds of dust . . . the first wave swelled into successive waves, gray masses with the glint of steel as the sun struck the gun barrels, filling the highway, spreading out into the fields, and still coming on and on, wave after wave, billow after billow.

Still they come, across pale spring meadows, under autumn red in the cool air, through silent, wheeling stars. "Close up, men," say the officers, riding their jeweled blue horses.

> *Never was there a time when I did not exist, nor you, nor all these kings; nor in the future shall any of us cease to be.*

In the valley of the shadow of death along Plum Run, as in other parts of Adams County, the bodies still lie, shells of the dead.

He leadeth me in the paths of righteousness
*   for his name's sake.*
He maketh me to lie down in green pastures:
he leadeth me beside the still waters.
He restoreth my soul. . . .

NOTE ON SOURCES

General background sources for this book are Edwin B. Coddington, *The Gettysburg Campaign* (Dayton, OH: Morningside, 1968); Harry Pfanz, *Gettysburg: The Second Day* (Chapel Hill: University of North Carolina Press, 1987); and Alan T. Nolan, *The Iron Brigade* (New York: Macmillan, 1961). An introduction to Gettysburg with a Southern shading is Glenn Tucker, *High Tide at Gettysburg* (Dayton, OH: Morningside, 1973). William A. Frassanito, *Gettysburg: A Journey in Time* (New York: Scribner's, 1975) is a fascinating camera-lens view of the battlefield.

This book might not have reached some of its conclusions without the work of Gregory A. Coco *(Wasted Valor: The Confederate Dead at Gettysburg* [Gettysburg: Thomas Publications, 1990]; *A Vast Sea of Misery* [Gettysburg: Thomas Publications, 1988]) and John W. Busey and David G. Martin *(Regimental Strengths and Losses at Gettysburg* [Hightstown, NJ: Longstreet House, 1986]). The world little notes the labors of many diligent people who nobly advance our understanding of such important events as Gettysburg, but one trusts that somewhere where it counts, their efforts will be long remembered.

All Henry David Thoreau quotations are from *Walden (Walden and Civil Disobedience* [New York: Norton, 1966]), except the initial quotation, which is from Thoreau's journal, August 9, 1841 *(The Journal of H. D. Thoreau*, Vol. 1 [New York: Dover, 1962], p. 85).

The figures for Civil War losses (ch. 1) are from Thomas L. Livermore, *Numbers and Losses in the Civil War in America 1861–65* (Dayton, OH: Morningside, 1986). The Gulf War figure is adjusted slightly upward from the 115 given in *Facts on File* (Vol. 51, No. 2624, March 7, 1991). Gen. Norman Schwartzkopf (ch. 1) is quoted in the *Chicago Tribune* (June 11, 1991). Vietnam casualty figures, somewhat like Civil War figures, are difficult to determine exactly. Allan Reed Millet *(The War the Wouldn't End* [Bloomington: Indiana Univesity Press, 1978], p. 54) reports 45,933 from hostile action, adding 10,298 non hostile (a figure itself worthy of attention); Gen. William Westmoreland *(A Soldier Reports* [Garden City, NY: Doubleday, 1976], p. 299) gives 46,397 killed in action. In *The Vietnam Wars 1945–1990* (New York: HarperCollins, 1991), p. 324, Marilyn B. Young reports that "at least sixty thousand" Vietnam veterans have committed suicide.

The four Walt Whitman statements at the end of ch. 2 are from *Walt Whitman's Civil War*, edited by Walter Lowenfels (New York: Da Capo, 1960), pp. 287, 285, 6, 7, 286, respectively.

For Frassanito's correction of the misconceptions referred to in chs. 3 and 12, see Frassanito, pp. 222–229. The information from Griffith in ch. 3 is in Paddy Griffith, *Battle Tactics of the Civil War* (New Haven: Yale University Press, 1987), chs. 3, 6.

The lyrics from "Lorena," "Somebody's Darling," "Just Before the Battle, Mother," "All Quiet Along the Potomac," "Weeping Sad and Lonely (When this

Cruel War is Over)," and "The Faded Coat of Blue (The Nameless Grave)" are quoted from *Songs of the Civil War* , ed. Irwin Silber (New York: Columbia University Press, 1960), pp. 134, 145, 151, 128, 124, 162, respectively. The lyrics referring to "Jeffdavise" (ch. 4) are from "I Can Whip the Scoundrel" (Silber, p. 179). "Sometimes I Feel Like a Motherless Child" is in *Negro Spirituals*, edited by H. T. Burleigh (New York: G. Ricordi and Co., 1917). "Kathleen Mavourueen" is in *Choice Irish Songs*, Vol. I (White-Smith Music Publishing Co., 1892).

General Lee's statement at Fredericksburg (ch. 4) is quoted in Douglas Southall Freeman, *R. E. Lee*, Vol. II (New York: Scribner's, 1934), p. 462. Lee's General Orders Numbers 72 and 73 are in *War of the Rebellion: Official Records of the Union and Confederate Armies*, Series I, Vol. 27 (Washington: Government Printing Office, 1889), pp. 912–913, 942–943. (Number 73 is also available in Clifford Dowdey, *The Wartime Papers of Robert E. Lee* [New York: Da Capo, 1961], pp. 533–534.) Other books of interest pertaining to General Lee are Alan T. Nolan, *Lee Considered* (Chapel Hill: University of North Carolina Press, 1991); Thomas L. Connelly, *The Marble Man* (New York: Knopf, 1977); Charles Bracelen Flood, *Lee: The Last Years* (Boston: Houghton Mifflin, 1981); the reminiscences by his son, Robert E. Lee *(Recollections and Letters of General Lee* [Wilmington, NC: Broadfoot, 1988]), his nephew, Fitzhugh Lee *(General Lee* [Greenwich, CT: Fawcett, 1961]), and his chief staff officer, Walter Taylor *(General Lee 1861-1865* [Dayton, OH: Morningside, 1975] and *Four Years with General Lee* [New York: Bonanza, 1962]); and of course the irreplaceable though uncritical work of D. S. Freeman. For the relative roles of mainline and literalist denominations in American society, see Garry Wills, *Under God: Religion and American Politics* (New York: Simon and Schuster, 1990), p. 19.

The Bible quotation (Ezekiel 7:2b, 4b) in ch. 5 is from the New Revised Standard Version (New York: Oxford University Press, 1989); the Twenty-Third Psalm, however, is quoted from the King James (Authorized) Version. The quotation preceding the lines from Psalm 23 at the conclusion of ch. 18 is from the *Bhagavad Gita (Bhagavad-Gita As It Is*, A. C. Bhaktivedanta Swami Prabhupada [New York: Baktivedanta Book Trust, 1968], p. 22). Lines from John Keats's "Ode on a Grecian Urn" are quoted from *Literature of the Western World*, Vol II, Third Edition, edited by Hurt and Wilkie (New York: Macmillan, 1992), pp. 862–864.

Iverson's report is in *Official Records*, Series I, Vol. 27, pp. 578–581.

Losses reported in ch. 7 are from Busey and Martin, pp. 239, 307, 299–301; those reported in ch. 11 are from Busey and Martin, pp. 280, 248.

The quotation pertaining to the wounded horses (ch. 10) is from Pfanz, p. 335; Pfanz's statement regarding the battle and planning is in Pfanz, p. 302.

For arguments favoring Chamberlain's point of view regarding the battle for Little Round Top see Alice Rains Trulock, *In the Hands of Providence: Joshua L. Chamberlain and the American Civil War*. An acquaintance of Chamberlain's showed James Trulock a pistol which the General said had been surrendered to him by Lt. Colonel Bulger.

In ch. 16, the messages sent between Gen. Longstreet and Col. Alexander are in E. P. Alexander, *Fighting for the Confederacy* (Chapel Hill: University of North Carolina Press), pp. 254–255. His note to Pickett is in Alexander, p. 259—briefer than the one usually quoted: "Come quick or I can't support you." The other version (which I quote) is in E. P. Alexander, *Military Memoirs of a Confederate* (Dayton, OH: Morningside, 1977), p. 423. Conclusions drawn from Alexander rely on his later book.

The Col. Haskell quotations in ch. 16 are from Frank A. Haskell, *The Battle of Gettysburg* (Boston: Houghton Mifflin, 1969), pp. 86, 88, 111.

For the wounded Confederate before Pickett's Charge (ch. 16), see Tucker, p. 353. The gallant soldier's name was Jere S. Gage, Co. A, 11th Mississippi.

For a book that takes issue with Tucker and others regarding General Garnett's health and the blue coat, see Busey and Harrison's *Nothing But Glory*.

The Papers of William Dorsey Pender are at the University of North Carolina, Chapel Hill. They have been edited by William W. Hassler *(The General to His Lady* [Chapel Hill: University of North Carolina Press, 1962]). All my quotations from the general's letters are from Hassler's invaluable book.

The book on General Reynolds to which I refer is *Toward Gettysburg: A Biography of General John F. Reynolds* (Gaithersburg, MD: Olde Soldier Books, 1958).

In addition to Alan Nolan's history of the Iron Brigade, the work of Alan Gaff (*Brave Men's Tears* and *If This Is War*), and Lance J. Herdegen and William J. K. Beaudot (*In the Bloody Railroad Cut at Gettysburg*) are to be recommended. Lance Herdegen read parts of this manuscript relating to the Iron Brigade, which means that if there are any mistakes here regarding the First Brigade, First Division, First Corps, Army of the Potomac, they are his fault. Both Mr. Herdegen and Mr. Beaudot provided valuable information on ballistics.

I have used David G. Chandler, *The Campaigns of Napoleon* (New York: Macmillan, 1966) for my discussion of Bonaparte's strategy and tactics. I thank Bruce A. Evans for bringing this volume to my attention.

Lee's farewell order can be found in Dowdey, pp. 934–935. A footnote on the persistence of General Lee's influence might mention Karen Lee Craig, the copy editor for this project, one of whose ancestors fought under Robert E. Lee and began the custom of including "Lee" in the name of each descendant. (The coincidence might be noted as well, whatever it means.)

Lynelle Gramm made the map which appears at the front, reconciling many printed sources with my own memories, the latter often being expressed only *after* locations had been painstakingly drawn.

For travel funds I thank the Aldeen Fund and those who administer it.

The quotation from Psalm 22 (ch. 18) is from the NRSV. The names which follow are in John W. Busey, *These Honored Dead: The Union Casualties at Gettysburg* (Hightstown, NJ: Longstreet House, 1988.)

The Lincoln quotations in ch. 18 are from *The Collected Works of Abraham Lincoln*, edited by Roy P. Basler (New Brunswick, NJ: Rutgers University Press, 1953), Vol. VII, p. 21, Vol. VIII, p. 333.

INDEX

Alexander, E. P., 116, 126, 127, 199, 247;
ammunition supply, 197; characteristics,
191; criticism of Lee, 191–192;
exchange of messages with Longstreet,
193–194; memoirs, 191; message to
Pickett, 196; on Lee at Chancellorsville,
244
"All Quiet Along the Potomac Tonight," 55
Anderson, George T. "Tige," 151
Antietam, battle of, 7, 20, 37, 42, 78, 124,
149, 201, 218, 219, 240, 241, 248; A. P.
Hill's arrival, 221; "artillery hell," 126;
battlefield size, 115; Hood's division's
losses, 200; Iron Brigade in Cornfield,
72; needlessly fought, 246
Arcturus, 94, 155
Armistead, Lewis A., 199, 201, 205–207
Army of Northern Virginia, 3, 68, 181, 192,
194, 225, 233; Appomattox (Gen. Order
No. 9), 251; at Antietam, 247; foot
soldiers, 20; inferiority of cavalry, 189;
lack of effective artillery chief, 191;
Longstreet at reunion, 197; losses First
Day, 86–87; piety of, 230; position at
Gettysburg, 18; summer of 1862, 208;
saved at Sharpsburg, 221; victory at
Chancellorsville, 244; worst-run battle,
116, 180
—CORPS:
First (Longstreet's), 68, 87, 117, 132, 133,
145, 191, 193
Second (Ewell's), 3, 8, 16, 68, 77, 189,
191, 236
Third (Hill's), 21, 26, 68, 77, 132, 145,
186, 193
—DIVISIONS:
Anderson's (Richard), 96, 132, 133, 145,
246
Early's, 16, 66, 183
Heth's, 15, 16, 26, 77, 78, 84, 87, 193,
236, 246; Pettigrew's, 203, 207
Hood's, 72, 116, 128, 132, 138, 143, 146,
200; Robertson's, 84
McLaws's, 128, 143, 145, 249
Pender's, 15, 77, 78, 87, 96, 236, 246
Pickett's, 143, 233. See also Pickett's
Charge
Rodes's, 15, 42, 77, 84, 86, 87, 91

—BRIGADES:
Armistead's, 28, 205, 206
Avery's: 6th North Carolina, 218
Barkdale's, 120, 121, 129, 132, 143
Benning's: 15th Georgia, 150
Brockenbrough's, 77
Davis's, 62, 66, 67, 70, 71, 74, 75, 77, 102
Garnett's, 28, 86, 205, 244
Hampton's, 28
Kemper's, 28, 206
Kershaw's, 115, 128, 129, 132, 142, 146,
149, 151
Law's, 20, 72, 116, 167; 15th Alabama,
135, 136, 139, 140
Lee's [Fitzhugh] (Cavalry), 28
Pettigrew's, 66, 67, 77, 189; 26th North
Carolina, 1, 78, 83, 87, 161, 179, 207
Robertson's, 149, 173; 1st Texas, 150
Semmes's, 151
Stuart's: 1st North Carolina, 211; 3rd
North Carolina, 211
Wofford's, 151
—REGIMENTS:
Fifteenth Alabama, 135, 136, 139, 140
Fifteenth Georgia, 150
First North Carolina, 211
Third North Carolina, 211
Sixth North Carolina, 218
Twenty-sixth North Carolina, 1, 78, 83,
87, 161, 179, 207
First Texas, 150
Army of the Potomac, 2, 7, 23, 26, 54, 63,
67, 86, 124, 125, 134, 195, 233, 245;
artillery, 21; artillery's troop percentage,
43; best battle, 180; character of, 181,
189; Lee's failure at Gettysburg, 24,
188; movement toward Gettysburg, 20,
68; position at Gettysburg, 18; "shock
troops," 72; size of units, 21; surprise of
Confederates at arrival, 73; weakest and
best corps, 244
—CORPS:
First, 15, 16, 21, 26, 63, 67, 68, 70, 115,
236, 246; army's best corps, 244;
Cemetery Ridge position, 187, 207;
defense of Seminary Ridge, 77–79, 81,
84–87; night of July 2, 180
Second, 5, 19, 68, 78, 102, 125, 128, 149,
150, 187, 190, 191

Third, 19, 21, 63, 68, 78, 86, 116–117, 120, 128, 136, 142, 149
Fifth, 68, 128, 144
Sixth, 69
Eleventh, 16, 63, 68, 77, 81, 84, 87, 183, 244
Twelfth, 68, 180
—DIVISIONS:
Birney's, 128
Buford's (Cavalry), 26, 62, 63, 67, 136
Caldwell's, 149, 151
Crawford's, 151, 152, 173
Gibbon's, 223, 243
Hays's, 187, 188, 206, 207
Humphreys's, 128, 130, 133–134; 11th New Jersey, 133
Robertson's, 84
Rowley's, 84
Wadsworth's, 70, 180
—BRIGADES:
Cross's, 149, 150, 151; 5th New Hampshire, 150
Custer's (Cavalry), 28; 7th Michigan, 28
Cutler's, 16, 42, 51, 62, 70, 71, 74, 75, 78, 79, 84, 87, 255; 84th New York, 158 (14th Brooklyn, 62); 95th New York, 75, 158; 56th Pennsylvania, 62
Graham's, 128
Hall's, 187, 206, 207
Harrow's: 1st Minnesota, 170
Kelly's (Irish), 151
Meredith's (Iron Brigade): 19th Indiana, 4, 7, 71, 73, 78, 79, 86; 24th Michigan, 38, 71, 73, 78, 79, 83, 86, 87, 146, 161; 2nd Wisconsin, 4, 5, 7, 71, 73, 78, 79, 86, 138, 161; 6th Wisconsin, 4, 7, 62, 70, 71, 74, 78, 83, 84, 85, 86, 158, 159; 7th Wisconsin, 4, 7, 71, 73, 77, 78, 79, 86, 161
Stannard's, 205
Vincent's, 116; 20th Maine, 139; 83rd Pennsylvania, 174
Ward's, 128
Webb's, 187, 206, 207, 241
Zook's, 151
—REGIMENTS:
Nineteenth Indiana, 4, 7, 71, 73, 78, 79, 86
Twentieth Maine, 139
Seventh Michigan, 28
Twenty-fourth Michigan, 38, 71, 73, 78, 79, 83, 86, 87, 146, 161
First Minnesota, 170

Fifth New Hampshire, 150
Eleventh New Jersey, 133
Eighty-fourth New York, 158 (Fourteenth Brooklyn, 62)
Ninety-fifth New York, 75, 158
Fifty-sixth Pennsylvania, 62
Eighty-third Pennsylvania, 174
Second Wisconsin, 4, 5, 7, 78, 79, 86, 138, 161
Sixth Wisconsin, 4, 7, 62, 70, 71, 74, 78, 83, 84, 85, 86, 158, 159
Seventh Wisconsin, 4, 7, 71, 73, 77, 78, 79, 86, 161
—ARTILLERY:
Battery B, Fourth U.S., 77, 236; under Gibbon's command, 4; at Brawner Farm, 5; approaching Gettysburg, 70; on Chambersburg Pike, 84–85
Bigelow's Battery, 127–131, 133
Cushing's Battery, 61, 206
Hall's Second Maine Battery, 70, 77
Fifth Maine Battery, 84, 85
Sixth Maine Battery, 131
McGilvery's First Volunteer Brigade, 128, 129, 130, 131
Phillips's Battery, 127, 128, 129
Ashby, Turner, 26
Augustine, 120

Barksdale, William, 129, 143
Beaudot, William, 44
Bible, 32, 44, 122, 123, 139, 140, 157, 216
Bigelow, John, 128–131, 139
Birney, David B., 128, 132
Black Hat Brigade, 6, 7, 51. See also Iron Brigade
Bloody Angle (Spotsylvania), 206, 240
Bluecher, 215, 249
Brahminists, 89, 109, 135
Brandy Station, battle of, 25, 233
Brawner Farm, battle of, 3, 6–9, 12, 20, 41, 42, 71, 139
Buford, John, 25–27, 67, 68, 69, 70, 77, 125, 182
Bush, George, 52

Candy, Charles, 181
Cannae, battle of, 245
Catton, Bruce, 49, 139
Cemetery Hill, 16, 18, 76, 82, 96, 139, 181, 182, 203, 258; Alexander's objective, 192; defense by 11th Corps artillery, 183; defensive line First Day, 85

Cemetery Ridge, 16, 18, 61, 86, 118, 128, 144, 150, 151, 181, 182, 197, 238, 250; batteries on, 3rd Day, 190–191; Confederate barrage, 194–196; fallback position, 117, 130, 132, 133; features of, 186–187; importance of, 67; N.C. high-water mark, 208; Sickles's position on, 128; Woolson statue, 170
Chamberlain, Joshua, 125, 181, 257; at Little Round Top, 135–138; controversy with Oates, 135, 138; spared by sniper, 139
Chambersburg Road, 69
Chancellorsville, battle of, 19, 42, 63, 68, 124, 149, 183, 232, 235, 244–246, 248, 249
Chartres, 175
Children of Pride, The, 65
Christ Lutheran Church, Gettysburg, 97
Christianity, 59, 63, 113, 184, 185, 243
Churchill, Sir Winston, 39
Coco, Gregory, 31, 252, 254, 259
Coddington, Edwin, 81, 117, 119, 142, 166, 183
Cold Harbor, battle of, 195, 240
Computers, 13, 14
Copse of Trees, 86, 87
Cornfield (Antietam), 72
Cross, Edward E., 149–150, 152–155
Culp, Wesley, 58, 111, 179
Culp's Hill, 18, 82, 177–179, 185; Confederate night attack, 181; fighting on July 3, 194; Iron Brigade defends, 86; origin of name, 111
Cushing, Alonzo H., 206
Custer, George A., 26–28
Cutler, Lysander, 70, 181

Dana, Charles A., 125
Davis, Jefferson, 218
Davis, Joseph R., 244
Dawes, Rufus R., 181
Desert Storm, 118, 165
De Trobriand, Philip, 128, 149, 151
Devil's Den, 18, 19, 38, 52, 54, 86, 115, 117, 118, 128, 146, 149, 167, 173, 174, 181
Doubleday, Abner, 63, 73, 74, 85
Duke, Archibald, 120–122
Duke, J. W., 121, 122, 123
Duty, 122, 123, 140, 218, 238, 240; Lee, 107, 108; Longstreet, 198; patriotism, 256; Pender, 222, 228, 231, 236, 243;

Pickett, 199; relationship to future, 22, 89, 107, 108

Early, Jubal A., 143
East Cavalry Field, 27
Economics of Glory, 8, 32. See also Theologiae gloriae
Economics of the Cross, 15. See also Theologiae crucis
Emerson, Ralph Waldo, 49
Erickson, Christopher, 128, 131
Evangelicalism, 31, 112, 184
Ewell, Richard S., 8, 19, 139, 236; does not attack Cemetery Hill, 16; inefficient use of artillery, 191; loses leg, 8; shortcomings, 180

"Faded Coat of Blue, The," 261
Farnsworth, Elon, 26, 27
Faulkner, William, 231
Fighting for the Confederacy, 191
File-closers, 182, 239
Five Forks, 200
Forrest, Nathan Bedford, 26
Frassanito, William, 38
Fredericksburg, battle of, 37, 41, 124, 149, 223, 225, 229, 231, 232, 244, 247, 249
Freeman, Douglas S., 127, 129, 143
Freemantle, Arthur, 16, 192
Frost, Robert, 46, 49
Fundamentalists, 57, 112, 251

Gaff, Alan, 44
Galilean, 86, 112
Garnett, Richard, 199, 201, 202, 204, 205, 244
General Order No. 9, 65, 251
General Orders No. 72, 64
General Orders No. 73, 63, 64
Germans, 59, 69, 88, 183
Gettys, James, 69, 104, 177
Gettysburg Address, 258
Gettysburg Lutheran Theological Seminary, 1, 34, 35, 69, 82, 86, 87, 90, 96, 97, 158, 206; break-in, 2; chapel, 112–114; Confederate burials, 31, 33; cupola use, 69; defense by US First Corps, 15, 76, 80, 81, 84–85; history, 88; professors, 32
Gibbon, John, 4–6, 8, 181, 194, 195
Gibbon's Brigade: at Brawner Farm, 4–7; renamed Iron Brigade, 7
Goebbels, Joseph, 47

Gospels, 65
Grant, Ulysses S., 8, 11, 13, 29, 162, 181, 189, 240, 241, 247, 251, 258
Greene, George S., 139, 180, 181
Griffith, Paddy, 41, 42, 44

Hall, Norman J., 206
Hampton, Wade, 26, 28
Hancock, Winfield S., 125, 181; artillery-fire test of discipline, 127; Col. Cross, 150; handling of artillery on July 3, 43, 190, 191; on Cemetery Hill, 16, 85
"Harbor, The" (poem), 110
Haskell, Frank A., 166, 194, 195, 208, 256
Hawthorne, Nathaniel, 43, 251
Hays, Alexander, 181, 206
Hazlett, Charles, 139, 174
Herdegen, Lance, 44, 75
Heth, Henry, 66, 67, 79
Hewitt, Katherine, 73, 74, 162
Hill, A. P., 19, 218, 248; approves Heth's advance, 66; attitude 1st day, 244; clears Pender's file, 222–223; difficulties with Jackson, 220; difficulties with Longstreet, 193; estimate of Pender, 236; Hill's Light Division at Sharpsburg, 221; inefficient use of artillery, 191, 192; personal characteristics, 193; promoted to corps command, 232; receives report of Federal presence, 67; recommends Pender for promotion, 220
Hill, D. H., 203
Hill's (A. P.) Division, 218, 219, 220; at Brawner Farm, 4; at Chancellorsville, 232; at Sharpsburg, 221
"Home Sweet Home," 50
Hood, John B., 21, 116, 139, 145, 200, 232
Hooker, Joseph, 20, 42, 63, 72, 125, 230, 231, 233, 235, 244, 249
Howard, O. O., 63, 68
Humphreys, Andrew A., 181; characteristics, 125; ordered to withdraw, 128; prior to War, 124; retreat of division, 132–134
Hunt, Henry A., 190, 191, 196

"I Can Whip the Scoundrel," 50
"Invalid Corps, The," 50
Irish Brigade, 151
Iron Brigade, 1, 8, 15, 16, 38, 44, 53, 62, 67, 70, 81, 82, 88, 112, 160, 162, 170, 183, 194, 195, 207, 236; battle of Brawner Farm, 3–7, 12; battles for McPherson's Woods, 70–80; casualties,

86–87, 138, 161; named at Turner's Gap, 72; stand at Seminary, 84–85
Iverson's Pits, 81, 90

Jackson, Thomas J. ("Stonewall"), 139, 183, 200, 211, 214, 221; antipathy toward Hill, 220; Brawner Farm, 3–6; cashiers Garnett, 201; Chancellorsville, 244, 249; death, 19; 1862 campaigns, 241; Garnett at funeral, 202; last order, 232; losses at Brawner Farm, 7–8; war lover, 251
Jesus of Nazareth, 32. *See also* Galilean
Jones, Lawrence, 113
Jones's Brigade (John M.), at Sharpsburg, 72
Jung, Carl, 57
"Just Before the Battle, Mother," 49

Kane, Thomas L., 181
Kelly, Patrick, 131, 151
Kemper, James L., 199, 201, 206
Kepler, Johannes, 109, 110
Kershaw, Joseph B., 142, 145, 146, 147
Kilpatrick, Judson, 26, 27
Kraus, John, 129

Lee, Henry, 164
Lee, Robert E., 7, 13, 17, 18, 19, 20, 21, 23, 24, 26, 31, 33, 40, 49, 66, 67, 68, 72, 78, 82, 86, 94, 105, 111, 116, 124, 139, 142, 173, 180, 181, 197, 198, 201, 203, 221, 222, 230, 232, 233, 234, 241, 255, 256, 257; attitudes, 25, 54, 63, 162–166, 244; Chancellorsville, 42, 244; criticism of, 191–193; duty, 107; estimation of Pender, 211, 220, 236; feelings toward Pickett, 200; First Day's battle, 16; General Order No. 9, 65, 251; General Orders No. 72, 64; General Orders No. 73, 63–64; Peninsula campaign, 3, 42; personality and characteristics, 163, 245, 247, 251, 252; planning for Third Day, 187–192; preparation for Second Day, 117, 143–145; pride, 189; religious beliefs, 64, 65; strategy and tactics at Gettysburg, 245–251; Stuart's absence, 25; the War's economy, 8, 10
Light Division, 219, 221, 232
Light Horse Harry Lee (Henry Lee), 164
Lincoln, Abraham, 35, 36, 104, 105, 119, 164, 183–184, 251, 252, 257; appearance and personality, 60;

Gettysburg Address, 258; guilt of the North, 11, 22; "I Can Whip the Scoundrel" (song), 50; "moral universe," 22–23, 108; Second Inaugural Address, 22, 61, 108, 258; slavery, 24; slaves' contribution to war effort, 72; *theologiae crucis*, 48; war's "arithmetic," 8; will of God, 259

Little Round Top, 18, 41, 70, 77, 99, 117, 128, 140, 142, 143, 144, 146, 173, 174, 181, 182, 255; artillery fire during Pickett's Charge, 191, 203; battle for, 135–139; dominant position, 115–116; importance recognized by Reynolds, 67; O'Rorke memorial, 175; uncovered by Sickles, 118; use of bayonet at, 42

Longbow, 101–103

Longstreet, James, 16, 19, 21, 68, 87, 116, 118, 121, 126, 132, 133, 142, 151, 180, 186, 189, 191, 198, 211, 236, 246, 248; after the War, 197; at Appomattox, 27; at Second Manassas, 3, 4; relationship with McLaws, 143, 144; reluctance concerning Pickett's Charge, 192–194, 199; Second Day's preparations, 117, 144–146

"Lorena," 46, 47

Luther, Martin, 8, 32, 75, 112, 157, 185, 198

Malvern Hill, 20, 163

Massa Damnata, 120, 256

McClellan, George B., 124, 246, 247, 248; Lee's lost orders, 72; Peninsula campaign, 3, 4

McGilvery, Freeman, 127–131, 139, 191

McLaws, Lafayette, 128, 145, 249

McPherson's Barn, 69, 71, 160

McPherson's Ridge, 27, 62, 67, 69–71, 181

McPherson's Woods, 15, 51, 53, 54, 112, 139, 160, 208; afternoon battle, 78–79; Archer's advance, 71; description, 69; Iron Brigade's attack, 71, 73; results of battles, 86; tactical value, 69; trees poisoned, 255

Meade, George G., 16, 40, 118, 124, 142, 189; achievement, 166; advance toward Gettysburg, 20, 63, 68; artillery barrage, 196; Gettysburg's importance, 67–68; Lee's estimate of, 21; Wellington and Napoleon, 249–250; wisdom, 256

Mears, Woods, 121–123

Medjugorje, 57, 153

Meredith, Solomon, 70

Mexican War, 29, 30, 124, 198, 211

Military Memoirs of a Confederate, 191

Morrow, Henry A., 79, 80, 84

Napoleon Bonaparte, 87, 163, 222, 251; at Waterloo, 248–250; Lee compared to, 246, 247; tactics, 6, 41, 42, 190, 241

Napoleon (cannon), 43, 54, 70

Nolan, Alan, 44, 246

Oak Hill, 77, 91, 195, 244

Oates, William C., 135–138, 255

"Ode on a Grecian Urn," 112

Official Records of the War of Rebellion, 44

"Oh, I'm a Good Old Rebel," 50

O'Rorke, Patrick, 175

Ovid, 111, 124

Patton, George, 51, 251

Peace Light Memorial, 157, 158

Peach Orchard, 18, 19, 86, 120, 122, 124, 139, 144, 149, 159, 172, 181; artillery battle, 126–127; Kershaw's attack, 146; McGilvery's stand, 129–132; Park Service, 171; Sickles's controversy, 115–118

Pender, Fanny Sheppard, 212–215, 221–223, 225, 227, 229, 230, 233, 236

Pender, William Dorsey, 1, 15, 21, 96; attitude toward Northern people, 229–230, 235; baptism, 211; Chancellorsville, 232; children, 211, 216, 220, 223, 224, 231; Division's attack on Union First Corps, 77–78, 84; Division's losses, 87; dreams, 233–234; duty, 231; first commission, C.S.A., 211; humor, 213–214, 224, 225; invasions of the North, 222, 225, 234–235; Lee's estimate of Pender, 220, 236; marital difficulties, 214–215, 217; opinions on Jackson, 220; opinions on Lee, 222; Pender's Brigade, 219; personal characteristics, 210, 213; promotion to Brigadier General, 218; promotion to Major General, 232; relationship with Fanny Sheppard Pender, 211, 212, 217, 225–226; religious faith, 216, 226–229, 236, 237; Sharpsburg (Antietam), 221; spared a court-martial, 222–223; *Uncle Tom's Cabin*, 228–229; wounded at Fredericksburg, 223

Pendleton, William N., 191

Petersburg, 200, 240
Pfanz, Harry W., 115, 121, 126, 132
Phillips, Charles A., 129
Pickett, George E., 193, 194, 196;
    Appomattox, 200; asks for order to
    advance, 197; authority in Pickett's
    Charge, 186; critic of Lee, 192; during
    Mexican War, 198; Five Forks, 200;
    named "Great Chief," 198; personal
    characteristics, 198–199, 200; reaction
    after failure of Pickett's Charge, 200;
    relationship with Abraham Lincoln,
    200; relationship with Lee after
    Gettysburg, 200; relationship with
    Longstreet, 198, 199; stationed at Puget
    Sound, 199; whereabouts during
    Pickett's Charge, 199; wounded, 201;
    writes to Sally, 197, 199
Pickett's Charge, 19, 27, 42, 70, 96, 102,
    115, 116, 140, 161, 164, 165, 166, 170,
    236, 241, 246; artillery bombardment,
    190–196; defeat, 205–207; infantry
    advance, 203–205; Lee's intentions,
    188; losses in, 28, 66, 87; name, 186
Plum Run, 130, 152, 173, 259
Providence, 116, 120, 154, 161, 228, 236,
    243

Quayle, Dan, 52

Railroad Cut, 51, 70, 76, 91, 92, 139, 159;
    Davis enters, 74; Dawes's attack, 75,
    83–84, 158; Heth's report, 67; Iron
    Brigade marker, 86
Reagan, Ronald, 67, 76, 98
Reed, Charles, 131, 132, 137
Reynolds, John F., 77, 95, 125, 139, 169;
    arrival, 62–63; chooses battlefield, 16,
    27, 67, 68; confers with Buford, 69,
    182; death, 73, 162; directs deployment,
    70; engagement, 73; fiancée (Katherine
    Hewitt), 73–74, 162; monument in
    woods, 74; strategy, 117
Robertson, Jerome B., 149, 173
Rodes, Robert Emmett, 83
Rose Farm, 58, 115, 128, 142, 146, 148, 253
Rose's Woods, 146
Rosengarten, Joseph G., 69
Round Top, 58, 59

Schwartzkopf, Norman, 15
Second Inaugural Address, 22, 61, 108, 258

Seminary. See Gettysburg Lutheran
    Theological Seminary
Semmes, Paul J., 151
Sentimentality, 46–48, 50, 257
Seven Pines, battle of, 218
Shakespeare, William, 29, 157
Sharpsburg, battle of, 200, 201, 219,
    221, 222, 241, 246, 248. See also
    Antietam
Sheads' Wine, 82, 83
Sheppard, Augustine H., 212
Sheridan, Philip, 26, 200
Sherman, William T., 27, 64
Sickles, Daniel, 86, 128, 132, 142, 144, 149;
    controversy, 115–120; fighter, 68;
    "monument," 256
Simpson, Ernest, 122–124
Slavery, 11, 12, 21, 22, 34–36, 65, 96, 139,
    140, 159, 164, 228
Socrates, 178
"Somebody's Darling," 165
"Sometimes I Feel Like a Motherless Child,"
    47
Songs: "The Faded Coat of Blue," 261;
    "Home Sweet Home," 50; "I Can Whip
    the Scoundrel," 50; "The Invalid
    Corps," 50; "Just Before the Battle,
    Mother," 49; "Lorena," 46, 47; "Oh,
    I'm a Good Old Rebel," 50;
    "Somebody's Darling," 165;
    "Sometimes I Feel Like a Motherless
    Child," 47; "When This Cruel War Is
    Over," 132
Sophocles, 123, 151
South Mountain, 7, 72, 175, 182, 191
Spangler's Spring, 180
Spotsylvania, battle of, 240
Stannard, George J., 206
Stephens Knoll, 86
Strategy of the Central Position, 249
Stuart, J. E. B., 26, 211; absence, 24, 65,
    245; arrival, 25; Brandy Station, 25,
    233; described, 24, 162; expedition, 25

Theologiae crucis, 48
Theologiae gloriae, 8, 32, 48
Thomas, Lewis, 30
Thoreau, Henry, 43, 49, 60, 158, 166, 175,
    197, 242
Todd, Mary, 104
Trostle Barn, 127, 159
Turner's Gap, 72
Twain, Mark, 27, 60

Uncle Tom's Cabin, 228, 229

Valley of Death, 173–175, 254
Vast Sea of Misery, A, 252
Veil, Charles, 73, 162
Vietnam War, 12, 30, 47, 75, 76, 97, 147
Vincent, Strong, 109, 118, 139, 175
Vincent's Spur, 140, 174
Virginia Monument, 116, 162, 163, 165, 203

Wade, Virginia (Jenny or Ginnie), 58, 111
Wadsworth, James S., 70, 71, 181
Walden, 118, 184, 255
Washington, George, 173
Wasted Valor, 31, 252
Waterloo, battle of, 248–250
Webb, Alexander S., 181, 195, 201, 207
Webster, H. D. L., 36

Wellington, 1st Duke of (Arthur Wellesley), 249, 250
Wheatfield, 18, 19, 86, 116, 128, 130, 144, 147, 240; battle, 150–152; Crawford's counterattack, 173; Cross, 149–150; Kershaw's attack, 146
"When This Cruel War Is Over," 132
Whitman, Walt, 252, 256; character of Americans, 36–37, 106; letters of, 251; on cause of the War, 36, 37, 108–109; on Lincoln's appearance, 60; service in hospitals, 35; "the real war," 49
Wilder, Thornton, 120
Wofford, William T., 151
Woolson, Albert, 170, 171
Wright, Ambrose R., 193

Zook, Samuel K., 151

KENT GRAMM lives in Lake Geneva, Wisconsin, and is the author of a novel, *Clare*.